'*The Complete Volunteer Management Hand...* volunteer managers. Through its clear and prac... will be supported, creating an even greater imp... **Jenny Betteridge, Strategic Lead Volunteering, Spo...**

'Having worked for more than 30 years in the volunteer management space, I highly recommend this book. It provides a comprehensive and clearly written pathway for the running of any successful program. Most importantly, it recognises the complexities of volunteer leadership in the 21st century and deals with issues far beyond the usual suspects of recognition, reward and recruitment.' **Andy Fryar, Better Impact Pty Ltd, Australia**

'This is a hugely comprehensive book that I would recommend not only to people involved in managing volunteers, but also to public sector leaders and policy makers so they can consider the benefits of volunteers to their services. This book reminds us that volunteers offer more than their time and skills, the gift they are offering is personal contact, human experience and the simple intent to make someone else's day better – and that goes a long way to making life better for all involved. To maximise the value of volunteering requires good quality management, and this handbook sets the bar rightly high.' **Paddy Hanrahan, Managing Director, HelpForce**

'This book is a really practical starting point for people looking to involve volunteers. It covers the range of issues likely to come up in a readable, approachable way.' **Denise Hayward, Chief Executive Officer, Volunteer Now**

'A valuable source of information for anyone seeking to empower and support volunteers through effective management, enablement and support. The book is well researched, clearly presented and easy to navigate quickly.' **Rebecca Kennelly, Director of Volunteering for Royal Voluntary Service**

'A no-nonsense guide to involving people who give their time. This book goes beyond the basics by including chapters on specific challenges. It offers both practical pointers and research-based perspectives on the topic for those who want to explore a little more.' **Ruth Leonard, Chair of Association of Volunteer Managers and Head of Volunteering Development, Macmillan Cancer Support**

'There is a Greek proverb that says, "a civilisation flourishes when people plant trees under which they will never sit". If you need a roadmap and guide on your journey in helping people plant those metaphorical trees through donating their time and talents to your cause – then this is the book you need to read. It's packed full of expert advice and handy hints and tips to help you get your volunteer management right for your organisation and perhaps most importantly your volunteers.'
Alan Murray, Head of Volunteering and Employee Engagement, RSPB

In association with:

University of
Kent

The Complete
Volunteer Management
Handbook

4th edition

Rob Jackson, Mike Locke,
Dr Eddy Hogg and Rick Lynch

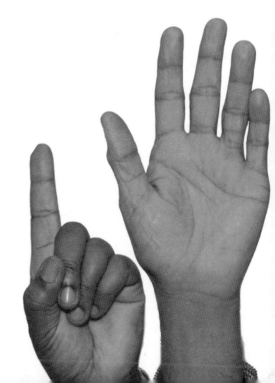

dsc
directory of social change

Published by the Directory of Social Change (Registered Charity no. 800517 in England and Wales)
Head office: Resource for London, 352 Holloway Rd, London N7 6PA
Northern office: Suite 103, 1 Old Hall Street, Liverpool L3 9HG

Tel: 020 7697 4200

Visit www.dsc.org.uk to find out more about our books, subscription funding websites and training events. You can also sign up for e-newsletters so that you're always the first to hear about what's new.

The publisher welcomes suggestions and comments that will help to inform and improve future versions of this and all of our titles. Please give us your feedback by emailing publications@dsc.org.uk.

It should be understood that this publication is intended for guidance only and is not a substitute for professional advice. No responsibility for loss occasioned as a result of any person acting or refraining from acting can be accepted by the authors or publisher.

First published as *Essential Volunteer Management* 1994
Second edition 1998
Third edition 2012
Reprinted 2015
Fourth edition 2019

ISBN 978 1 78482 056 5 (print edition)
ISBN 978 1 78482 057 2 (digital edition)

British Library Cataloguing in Publication Data
A catalogue record for this book is available from the British Library

Cover and text design by Kate Griffith
Typeset by Marlinzo Services, Frome
Print edition produced by Page Bros, Norwich

MIX
Paper from responsible sources
FSC
www.fsc.org   FSC® C023114

This book is dedicated to Susan J. Ellis, founder and President of Energize Inc., Philadelphia, USA.

For more than forty years Susan provided leadership and inspiration to leaders of volunteer engagement around the world.

Susan's impact on volunteer management was huge. Without her, volunteer management wouldn't be what it is today.

Susan J. Ellis

18 March 1948 to 24 February 2019

Contents

About the authors

ROB JACKSON

Rob is an international speaker, trainer and consultant in volunteer leadership and management with over 25 years' experience. He founded Rob Jackson Consulting Ltd in 2011 and has since worked with an extensive list of clients around the world. Previously, Rob was Director of Innovation and Impact at Volunteering England, Head of Fundraising Strategy and Volunteering Development Manager at RNIB, and Regional Volunteering Development Manager at Barnardo's.

In 1997, Rob founded UKVPMs, the UK's first internet networking resource dedicated to British Volunteer Programme Managers, now the largest group of its kind in the world. He remains an active volunteer, both as moderator of the group, and as a member of the editorial team for e-Volunteerism.com, an international journal on volunteering issues.

Rob is co-author of *The Complete Volunteer Management Handbook* – 3rd edition (DSC, 2012), *From the Top Down* – UK Edition (energize Inc., 2015), and writes regularly for *Third Sector* magazine and his own blog.

MIKE LOCKE

Mike Locke is Honorary Research Fellow with the Centre for Philanthropy, University of Kent, and has worked as a volunteer, researcher and writer, teacher and consultant with voluntary organisations since getting involved in community organisations in the North Kensington area of London in the 1970s. At University of East London he developed teaching and research on voluntary organisations and volunteering, and was joint founder of the Institute for Volunteering Research with Volunteering England. At Volunteering England and the National Council for Voluntary Organisations (NCVO), he led on policy and management for volunteering. His research has focused largely on policy analyses and evaluations concerning voluntary and community organisations and has produced numerous research reports, articles and conference papers.

Mike has been engaged as a trustee and committee member for numerous organisations, notably as Vice Chair of Volunteer Centre Kensington & Chelsea and as Chair of the Greater London region of Riding for the Disabled Association.

DR EDDY HOGG

Dr Eddy Hogg is Lecturer in Social Policy at the University of Kent. His research looks at volunteering, charitable giving and public attitudes to the voluntary sector. Recently he has worked on research looking at volunteering across the life course, on volunteering and charitable giving in schools, on youth volunteering, on the value of charity involvement in supporting young people, on attitudes towards charity regulation in England and Wales and, on charity engagement with the Fundraising Regulator. He teaches a range of courses at undergraduate and postgraduate levels on the voluntary sector and volunteering.

Eddy speaks regularly at events for volunteer managers, sharing research findings and exploring how these can translate into volunteer management practice. These include events organised by the NCVO, the Association of Volunteer Managers and the Sports Volunteering Research Network.

RICK LYNCH

Rick is a Seattle-based management consultant and Principal Consultant of Lynch Associates with a variety of clients in the US, Canada, the UK, Ireland, Australia, Singapore, Portugal, Russia and Brazil. Each year Rick speaks at approximately 100 workshops, conventions and conferences across the world.

He is co-author of *The Complete Volunteer Management Handbook*, first published in the UK in 1994 by DSC as *Essential Volunteer Management*, and *Keeping Volunteers*.

About the Directory of Social Change

The Directory of Social Change (DSC) has a vision of an independent voluntary sector at the heart of social change. We believe that the activities of independent charities, voluntary organisations and community groups are fundamental to achieve social change. We exist to support these organisations in achieving their goals.

We do this by:

- providing practical tools that organisations and activists need, including online and printed publications, training courses, and conferences on a huge range of topics;
- acting as a 'concerned citizen' in public policy debates, often on behalf of smaller charities, voluntary organisations and community groups;
- leading campaigns and stimulating debate on key policy issues that affect those groups;
- carrying out research and providing information to influence policymakers, as well as offering bespoke research for the voluntary sector.

DSC is the leading provider of information and training for the voluntary sector and publishes an extensive range of guides and handbooks covering subjects such as fundraising, management, communication, finance and law. Our subscription website, Funds Online (www.fundsonline.org.uk), contains a wealth of information on funding from grant-making charities, companies and government sources. We run more than 300 training courses each year, including bespoke in-house training provided at the client's location. DSC conferences and fairs, which take place throughout the year, also provide training on a wide range of topics and offer welcome opportunities for networking.

For details of all our activities, and to order publications and book courses, go to www.dsc.org.uk, call 020 7697 4200 or email cs@dsc.org.uk.

Foreword from the University of Kent

Volunteers play a crucial role in a wide range of organisations, from health care to sport and from care for the elderly to education. How these volunteers are managed is fundamental to this role, as volunteers must feel that their time has been well organised and that they are equipped to make a difference. At the University of Kent, we are proud that our research is used in practical ways, such as this book, to contribute to the establishing and sharing of best practice. It is central to our role as academics that we address not just theoretical questions but also practical solutions; through the partnership of academic knowledge and practitioner experience, this book does that for the vital task of volunteer management.

Professor Karen Cox, Vice-Chancellor, University of Kent

Foreword

Volunteering is integral to the way British society functions, and there is no doubt that volunteering is a huge benefit both to the individuals who partake of it and to the wider community. There are few people who have not been touched by volunteering at some time in their lives, whether as a giver or receiver. They may not have even realised they were volunteering with a capital 'V', or indeed, on the other side of the coin, that they benefitted from the help of volunteers.

People choose to volunteer for a variety of reasons, in a large part because they know that they are helping others, but also because they gain valuable experience and enjoyment from the process. As a retired athlete I well and truly understand the importance that volunteering had on my own sporting career. The majority of my coaches were volunteers. In addition to the attention they gave to individual athletes within the clubs like myself, they also gave up significant amounts of time to attend coaching courses and further develop their own skills. I have fond and grateful memories of those who were there in the wind, rain and sometimes sunshine who believed in me and the other athletes with whom I trained. They sought to bring out the best in me.

In an evolving society where there is competition for people's time there are many routes to becoming a volunteer. My first job on graduating was to support a group of volunteers in a sports programme. What I learnt from that role undoubtedly helped develop my own skills, challenged me constantly, and that know-how I use every single day.

Individuals need to be inspired with volunteer opportunities that connect with them. It is also important that their contribution is recognised, valued and supported. To do that well, requires aptitude, thoughtfulness and an understanding of what and why people want to contribute. They are a set of attributes that can only be acquired through hard work and dedicated personal development.

This book provides extensive guidance on effective volunteer management, matching people to the right roles and creating an effective volunteering strategy. It is a valuable resource for everyone who works in this hugely significant aspect of our lives.

Cary Thompson

Baroness Grey-Thompson, DBE, DL

Acknowledgements

The publishers and authors would like to thanks the following individuals and organisations who have given so freely of their time and experience in order to provide or give permission for text, examples, case studies and advice.

Jenny Betteridge, Denise Hayward and Ruth Leonard, for looking over the manuscript at an early stage and making insightful comments.

Professor Karen Cox, Vice-Chancellor, University of Kent and Baroness Grey-Thompson for sparing their valuable time to contribute forewords.

Chapter 1: An introduction to volunteer involvement

Indiana University Press for permission to quote from Marc A. Musick and John Wilson, *Volunteers: A social profile*, 2007, p. 50.

NCVO for permission to reproduce the quality experience wheel from their *Time Well Spent* report.

Chapter 2: Planning for high-impact volunteer involvement

East Anglia's Children's Hospices, Football Beyond Borders and Samaritans for permission to quote from mission statements on their websites.

Chapter 3: Embedding volunteer involvement

Blue Cross for a case study.

The Institute for Volunteering Research for permission to quote from Angela Ellis Paine and Justin Davis Smith, *Exhibiting Support: Developing volunteering in museums* (also chapter 5)

Chapter 5: Recruiting volunteers

British Red Cross for top tips on writing a convincing volunteer message.

Chapter 8: Managing and empowering volunteers

Jossey-Bass for permission to quote from James Kouzes and Barry Posner, *The Leadership Challenge*.

Chapter 13: Building and maintaining relationships with volunteers

United Parcel Service Foundation for permission to quote from *Managing Volunteers: A report from United Parcel Service*.

Chapter 14: Building staff and volunteer engagement

Energize Inc. for permission to quote from the blog post *Start early: Teaching students about volunteering, not simply doing it*.

Preface to the fourth edition

This book, now in its fourth edition, is a practical guide to the profession of volunteer management. There are thousands of books on various aspects of managing paid staff, but managing volunteers is fundamentally different from managing paid people. Although there are some similarities, these areas differ dramatically in other respects. People who try to manage volunteers as though they are the same as paid staff will not do well in retaining or getting the most out of their volunteers in today's world.

Volunteer management is a very young profession, but it is a profession nonetheless. This book explores the major functions of the manager of volunteers, the person with overall responsibility for volunteer engagement in an organisation, and all those who manage volunteers in an organisation. Although it has a focus on how that role is practised in the UK, the principles apply to other countries as well, and previous editions of this book have been translated into four languages.

The first edition of this book was based on *Volunteer Management*, published in the USA by Steve McCurley and Rick Lynch. Although Steve has regrettably retired, much of the content of this book is based on his unique and, frankly, brilliant insights into the nature of volunteer engagement. Without his contributions, the profession would be vastly less effective.

The book begins with an overview of the profession. It then has chapters exploring various skills that managers of volunteers need in order to play their role effectively: skills in planning, role design, recruitment, screening and interviewing, training, supervision, motivation, consultation and evaluation.

Each chapter can be used as a stand-alone document, guiding the manager of volunteers on specific aspects of the role. There is, however, a logic to the arrangement of the chapters. Planning leads to role design, which leads to recruitment, which leads to interviewing and placement, which leads to training, which leads to supervisory and motivational concerns.

The chapter on planning (chapter 2) introduces the concept of strategic volunteer management. For too long, non-profit organisations have had a scarcity mentality. They are always lamenting their inadequate funding, chafing at the limits of their financial resources. By involving volunteers in non-traditional, mission-critical roles, as described in this book, non-profits can overcome their financial constraints.

There are a variety of trends, discussed in this book, that have been in play for quite some time but have now reached a point where they can no longer be ignored. For a long time, we have managed volunteers as though they were paid employees, often confining them to useful, ancillary functions. This 'human resources model' still works with people who volunteer as an alternative to working for pay. But most people today volunteer as an alternative to other uses of their leisure time. Engaging them and keeping them engaged requires a different approach.

The main thing to keep in mind is that volunteering is voluntary, which means people will give you their time to do what they *want* to do. Employees will do lots of things they don't want to do, but volunteers increasingly will not.

The chapter on role design (chapter 4) introduces the reader to the concept of designing roles for volunteers that are as appealing as other uses of their leisure time. We need to make sure the volunteer is doing something that they want to do. Part of that is about matching a volunteer's motivations to the work that needs to be done, but part of it is also about designing the role so that it has some of the same motivational characteristics as leisure-time activities. The volunteer's role should not feel like a job, in the traditional sense.

The principle of making sure volunteers are doing something they want to do also underlies a key difference in recruitment. When we recruit people to work in a paid position, we may try to convince them that we are the right organisation for them to join. When it comes to volunteers, recruiting is about showing people that they can do something they already want to do.

Non-profit organisations exist to solve community problems or meet community needs. In every community, there are people of goodwill who care deeply about those problems or needs, but often feel helpless to do anything about them. Recruiting is about letting those people know that there are opportunities to help solve those problems or meet those needs.

Nowhere is the difference between managing paid and volunteer staff more evident than in the function of interviewing and screening. When we interview people for a paid position, we appropriately focus on finding someone who most closely matches the skills, knowledge and attitudes we need; we try to find the right person for the job. When we interview volunteers, our primary focus is on finding the right job for the person. The chapter on interviewing and screening (chapter 6) points out that this 'right job' may be one we hadn't previously imagined anyone doing.

The principle of making sure volunteers are doing what they want to do also applies to supervision. While new volunteers appreciate being told what to do, that approach tends to breed resentment over time. In the chapters on management, we lay out a strategy whereby the volunteer's manager or supervisor can allow volunteers to control their own actions while ensuring that the volunteer does the right thing (see chapters 8–13).

The thing that makes volunteer management tricky is that what a volunteer wants to do may change over time. Part of the task of the manager of volunteers is to keep in regular contact with volunteers and see whether they would be more satisfied by doing something other than their current role.

In the UK, managers of volunteers have become quite sophisticated in their volunteer engagement strategies in recent years. In larger organisations where volunteers are supervised by other staff, that knowledge must be shared with those staff. This implies a new role for the manager of volunteers, one in which they act as a coach and an internal consultant to other staff to help them do a good job of applying the principles contained in this book.

This changing role of the manager of volunteers is one of the topics covered in the chapter on building staff and volunteer engagement (chapter 14). This chapter addresses the concerns staff might have about volunteers having significant responsibility and offers a strategy for allaying those concerns. The chapter contains several practical tips for getting staff on board.

Volunteers do not work for money, but they do receive a 'motivational pay cheque'. They are rewarded by satisfaction of their motivational needs. This theme, which runs throughout the book, is expanded upon in the chapters on supervision and retention (particularly chapter 13).

When paid people are managed in demotivating ways, they will still come to work, at least until they find other employment. Volunteers, increasingly, will not. In the chapter on building and maintaining relationships with volunteers (chapter 13), we offer practical advice on creating a volunteer experience that builds the volunteer's self-esteem and may even make their volunteer role the best part of their life.

This book also contains a chapter on measuring volunteer impact (chapter 15). Traditionally, when non-profits have been asked to put a financial value on their volunteer programme, the response has simply been to multiply the number of volunteer hours spent by how much it would cost to pay a person. In this chapter, we present a method for measuring the value of the difference volunteers make in adding value to an organisation.

The fact that this book is in its fourth edition is a testament to its continued relevance and value to managers of volunteers. The addition of two new authors (both leading academics working on volunteering and non-profits), alongside a leading expert in volunteer management practice, means that this is the most complete and up-to-date version of the world's best-selling book on volunteer engagement, and it will continue to be a go-to resource for leaders and managers working with volunteers for years to come.

Rick Lynch
September 2019

1 An introduction to volunteer involvement

This is a book about volunteering, volunteer management and how organisations can make the most of the time and talents of volunteers. In it you will find advice, evidence and examples of practices from the UK and beyond. This advice, supported by experience, statistics and examples of best practice, will help anyone who manages volunteers, or has strategic responsibility for managing them, to make the case for volunteering within their own organisation and to establish the need to put adequate resources into the engagement of volunteers.

This chapter will first establish our approach in writing this book, what we are aiming to do, and how we approach volunteering and volunteer management. Next it gives a brief overview of volunteering in the UK, including trends and changes in volunteer engagement and management. We review the language and terminology used around volunteering and managing volunteers, and we consider reasons for volunteering and how the volunteering population is changing.

1.1 OUR APPROACH: VOLUNTEER MANAGEMENT IN THE 2020s

This book is written mainly from the perspective of a formal volunteer programme within an organised structure. Those of you in less formal structures, and those of you in much smaller organisations, will quickly note that many of the recommendations are probably more intensive than you either need or can implement. This is intentional – the idea is that it is easier for you to discard items that are beyond your needs than to have to invent them on your own.

Our goal is that anyone who has responsibility for volunteers in their organisation should be able to pick up this book and learn the essentials needed for successful volunteer involvement. Some may choose to read the book from cover to cover while others may want to dip in and out as needed. It is our aim that, regardless of how you use this book, it will become your go-to source on all things related to engaging volunteers and ensuring that they can be as effective as possible for your organisation.

Before we begin to explore volunteer management and the key topics that those who manage volunteers should consider, it is first necessary to be clear what it is that we are talking about.

What is volunteering?

If we are to talk about volunteering and volunteer management, we need to start by defining what is meant when we talk about 'volunteers'. This may seem obvious, especially to those of you who are managing volunteering in an organisation. However, it is an area that can lead us into knotty debates, which, if unresolved, may distract us from tackling the problems that face us.

Consider these examples. A person who, without financial compensation, cares for patients under the supervision of a manager of volunteers in a hospice is obviously a volunteer. But what if the person carries out the same activities for a neighbour, unconnected to a hospice? What if the neighbour is the person's mother? What if the person undertakes these activities at the hospice in order to keep receiving their state benefits or allowances?

While it may seem that quibbling about the definition is simply an intellectual exercise, the definition that is chosen affects statistics about how many people volunteer and has an impact on how these people might need to be managed. Many people who do voluntary work don't consider themselves to be volunteers (sports coaches, for example) and may not answer 'yes' when asked whether they volunteer. Therefore, different positions on such definitions may also affect how people are treated by managers and through policy, and whether members of the public are prepared to put themselves forward to do the work.

There is no universal definition of volunteering. The UK legal system does not provide an overall definition of volunteering, but some legislation and regulations define volunteering – in slightly different ways – for their specific purposes. Following a comprehensive review of both academic literature and policy documents, Eddy Hogg provided a broad definition of volunteering as 'any act that involves giving time and effort, for no financial payment, of free will, to provide for those beyond one's own close family'.[1]

This definition is inclusive of both formal volunteering – undertaken with an organisation – and informal volunteering – undertaken without an organisational structure. Therefore, for the purposes of this book, we need to add a further element to our definition of volunteering: that it takes place through an organisation where it needs to be, to various extents, managed.

It should also be noted that numerous attempts have been made to find an acceptable alternative to the word 'volunteer', without success. In the UK and the USA, at the time of writing, the notion of 'service' is in vogue as an alternative to 'volunteering'. The notion and associated language of 'social action' have also become popular among policymakers and some organisations that seek to encourage and support youth volunteering.

As you may have gathered, volunteering is not neat and tidy, and so no definition can ever be truly definitive. Understanding which tasks constitute volunteering and which do not is not particularly necessary in day-to-day practice.

Where does formal volunteering take place?

Volunteering takes place across all sectors of the economy. According to research undertaken by the National Council for Voluntary Organisations and published in 2019, 67% of formal volunteering occurs in organisations that operate in the voluntary sector, with 17% occurring in the public sector and 10% occurring in the private sector. Additionally, almost 7% of volunteers do not know which sector their volunteering occurs in.[2] Therefore, while traditional ideas of volunteering consider it an activity undertaken in voluntary organisations, this is far from the case.

The sector where most volunteering takes place has a number of different names – voluntary sector, non-profit sector, charitable sector, third sector, civil society and so on – and there are differences in what constitutes the sector from one term to the next. This book, for the most part, avoids references to any particular designation and, as such, simply uses 'organisation' as a broad umbrella term for volunteer-involving organisations across the public, private and voluntary sectors.

Is volunteering 'work'?

Whilst typically we refer to 'involving volunteer' and having them 'fill roles' and 'perform tasks', people sometimes mention volunteers doing 'work' and being given volunteer 'jobs'. We know that some people feel uncomfortable with the use of these terms because they can be identified with paid employment, but this isn't true for everyone.

We are aware of, and sympathetic to, arguments that referring to volunteering as work may undermine its unique character. However, in day-today work with volunteers, a range of short-hand terms are used and borrowed from other fields. Volunteering should be distinct from paid work but that doesn't preclude what volunteers do sometimes being called work.

This book may, therefore, refer to 'volunteer work' and 'volunteer jobs' because these terms are occasionally used. However, if like many people that is not your preference, you can use any term in your organisation with which you feel comfortable. Most of the time we will refer to what volunteers do as a 'position', 'role', 'task', 'assignment' and 'responsibility'. Along with 'work' or 'job', all of these terms may simply be taken as referring to what the volunteer does.

A brief word on legal issues

Generally speaking, the same laws that apply to your paid staff and beneficiaries also apply to your volunteers – you should provide them with the same level of health and safety protection and should look after their personal data according to the guidelines set out in the GDPR (General Data Protection Regulation) legislation.

However, there is one key difference that you need to maintain – volunteers are not employees and do not have the employment rights a paid employee has. If your volunteers do perceive themselves to be employees, this could land your organisation in difficulty if they seek to use employment legislation to establish a legal case against your organisation. Clearly this is a worst-case scenario, but, as with any worst-case scenario, it is worth taking precautions against it.

We suggest you take the following precautions to avoid any confusion about whether volunteers have employment rights:

- Try to keep volunteering agreements and other documents you provide volunteers with as informal as possible. Do not simply use the same documents you would use with paid staff. Do not use the word 'contract' either in writing or in conversation.
- Make sure that expenses payments are only made for out-of-pocket expenses which are genuinely accrued. Do not pay a flat fee of expenses – this could be interpreted as a wage.
- Only offer training that is relevant to the volunteer role that someone is undertaking. Additional training could be seen as a perk or reward of volunteering, which could be perceived as payment in kind.
- Discuss what volunteers do in terms of an expectation, rather than an obligation. Stipulating a core number of hours or formal processes for taking leave are likely to appear contractual and could land your organisation in hot water.

All of these are broadly best practice in volunteer management anyway, rather than arduous additional tasks to keep you the right side of employment law. Nonetheless, it is worth keeping them in mind at all times and ensuring that all paid staff are aware of them.

What do we call those who manage volunteers?

There is wide debate about who is best placed to manage volunteers, and this is reflected in the name we give to those who manage volunteers. The seemingly simple term 'volunteer manager' would seem to imply that managing volunteers is that person's primary, or indeed only, role. This is rare! More often, management of volunteers is one part of someone's wider set of responsibilities.

Use of the term 'volunteer manager' can also result in it being assumed that the person themselves is a volunteer, which may or may not be the case.

'Manager of volunteers' is the term we use in this book for those who have responsibility within an organisation for managing volunteer efforts. The term indicates an individual who takes responsibility for the involvement of volunteers, but also recognises that this might not be their only or even their main responsibility.

In larger organisations, managers of volunteers may also be known by other titles. Their role may additionally focus more on strategic oversight of volunteer involvement rather than day-to-day management of individual volunteers, and they may be members of a senior management team. In this book we use the term 'director of volunteering' to make this distinction. Likewise, we occasionally refer to a 'supervisor' or 'line manager' or 'team leader' as someone who works directly with a volunteer on a task or project but is not the manager of volunteers. This person could be a paid staff member or a volunteer.

It should be noted, while we are defining language, that we refer to beneficiaries throughout this book. By that we mean your organisation's beneficiaries or service-users or, for a sports organisation, your athletes and spectators. Whether your organisation is a charity, or in a different space in wider civil society and public services, then in your mind you will naturally replace beneficiaries with your preferred terminology.

1.2 AN OVERVIEW OF VOLUNTEERS AND VOLUNTEERING

Volunteering is a very popular activity across the world. However, data-collection methods vary and we do not have detailed, reliable and comparable data on volunteering across countries. In general, the data we draw from in this book comes from the Community Life Survey for England and Wales, the most comprehensive study in the UK and one which has been running in various forms for almost two decades.[3] This data shows that, in 2018–19, 22% of adults in England and Wales engaged in formal volunteering at least once a month and 36% did so at least once a year. The rates are higher for informal volunteering, outside an organisation, which 26% of adults engaged in monthly and 52% did at least once a year.

Who volunteers?

Different groups of the population volunteer in different ways and to different extents. Differences can be observed according to age, gender, level of education and religious attendance.

Looking at age, the proportion of people volunteering goes up and down across the life course. Again drawing on Community Life Survey data from 2018–19, we find that engagement in formal volunteering varies between different age groups. Of young people aged 16 to 24, 35% engaged in formal volunteering at least once in 2018–19. This falls for 25–34 year-olds to 29%, the lowest of any age group, before rising to 40% of 35–49 year-olds – the highest rate of any age group. For 50–64 year-olds, the rate of formal volunteering falls slightly to 36%, before rising to 39% for 65–74 year-olds. Participation in formal volunteering tails off for over 75s, with 31% of this age group volunteering in 2018–19, the second lowest of any age group.

These differences reflect the fact that different age groups have different situations and responsibilities, which facilitate or constrain volunteering. Being at school or university, having primary-school-aged children and retirement all create opportunities for people to be asked to volunteer, while ill health in particular can be a barrier to engagement.

Moving on to gender, the Community Life Survey shows a small difference between men and women for formal volunteering, with 34% of men and 37% of women engaging in formal volunteering once a year or more.[4]

Education levels have a significant association with whether people undertake regular, formal volunteering, according to the 2016–17 Community Life Survey data. Among people with a degree, 36% engage in formal volunteering at least once a month, compared to 30% of those with higher education below degree level, 29% of those with A Levels as their highest qualification, 22% of those with GCSE grades A–C as their highest qualification, 21% of those with GCSE grades D–E as their highest qualification and 13% of those with no formal qualifications. Therefore, someone with a degree is nearly three times more likely to do formal volunteering in an organisation than someone with no qualifications.[5]

The relationship between religion and volunteering is complex. The 2007 *Helping Out* report observes that those who consider themselves to be religious but do not actively attend religious services are no more likely to volunteer than the population as a whole.[6] However, those who do attend services are more likely to volunteer than those who do not, with Community Life Survey data from 2016–17 showing that 35% of those who actively practise a religion engage in formal volunteering at least once a month, compared to 24% of those who do not. A similar gap can be found for those who do formal volunteering at least once a year, with 49% of those who actively practise religion engaging in this compared to 38% of those who do not.[7]

Diversity

In looking at who volunteers, it is useful to take a few moments to consider diversity in volunteering. This remains a key issue for managers of volunteers who want to engage what are often perceived to be under-represented groups in volunteering. Whether that means younger people, disabled people, BAME (black, Asian and minority ethnic) communities, people of lower socio-economic groups or other groups, the goal is often the same: to increase the reach and relevance of the organisation and avoid the majority of volunteers being white, middle class and older.

Such goals are laudable. Organisations should broaden the diversity of their volunteer teams and tackle any practical barriers to the engagement of a wide pool of volunteers, as we discuss in chapter 5. Barriers include a wide range of things, including expenses (so that people aren't financially disadvantaged through giving their time) and adaptations to premises or ways of working (to remove physical barriers to some people getting involved).

However, there is a danger that, in striving to diversify, we may inadvertently disregard the great volunteer work that these supposedly under-represented people already do.

Consider disabled people as an example. These individuals are generally under-represented in formal, mainstream volunteering. The associated assumption made all too often is that people with disabilities therefore do not volunteer. In our experience this assumption is wrong. They do. A lot. They are involved in advocacy, self-help support networks, campaigns for disability rights and lots more. What they do flies under the radar of many people because it doesn't sit comfortably with the mainstream concept of volunteering.

In this example there is a kind of discrimination at work, one that is far more subtle, far more common and far more insidious than not providing ramps into a building or only making opportunities available at times that suit certain types of people. Instead, what managers of volunteers may be inadvertently doing, is downplaying the existing volunteering these so-called under-represented groups do, not viewing it as valid unless it is done on the organisation's terms.

Diversity in volunteer involvement is a goal any manager of volunteers should strive for, but we should all first take a moment to reflect on whether there might be less obvious barriers created by our personal and/or institutional beliefs about volunteering. These are perhaps the barriers we need to challenge first, particularly around getting organisational and staff buy-in for volunteering, as explored in the following chapters.

Who does what?

The most common volunteer activities in England and Wales, according to the report *Time Well Spent*, involved activities related to events and fundraising, with 45% of volunteers engaging in activities around an event in the last year and 29% engaging directly in raising or handling money. Helping with administrative or clerical work is also a common volunteer role, with 36% of volunteers doing so.[8]

Other forms of volunteering are less common but nonetheless are undertaken by a significant number of volunteers. According to *Time Well Spent*, the following activities were undertaken by volunteers:

- 32% of volunteers got other people involved in a group, club or organisation;
- 32% of volunteers represented a group, club or organisation at meetings or events;
- 27% of volunteers led a club, group or organisation, were a trustee or were a committee member;
- 26% of volunteers gave advice, information or counselling to people;
- 25% of volunteers provided other practical help;
- 21% of volunteers campaigned on behalf of a group, club or organisation;
- 20% of volunteers befriended or mentored people;
- 19% of volunteers handled money in a role such as treasurer;
- 17% of volunteers provided transport or driving;
- 12% of volunteers visited people in need.

There are a range of differences between who does what in terms of all of the characteristics considered above – age, gender, level of education, ethnicity and religion. The best analysis of these is in the 2007 survey *Helping Out: A National Survey of Volunteering and Charitable Giving*.[9]

How does the UK compare internationally?

Each year the Charities Aid Foundation produces its World Giving Index, which explores whether people help their neighbours, donate money and, usefully for us, volunteer, across 139 countries.[10] In this data, the UK is treated as one entity (rather than data being given for England and Wales). While the data collected should be treated with caution – volunteering has very different cultural meanings in different countries – it nonetheless provides an interesting comparison.

The measure of volunteering asks people whether they have volunteered through an organisation in the past month, and the top ten countries in 2018 were as follows:

1. Indonesia: 53%
2. Liberia: 47%
3. Kenya: 45%

4. Sri Lanka: 45%
5. New Zealand: 40%
6. Australia: 40%
7. Ireland: 40%
8. USA: 39%
9. Singapore: 39%
10. Mauritius: 38%

The UK came 23rd on the list, with 23% of people having volunteered in the past month,[11] similar to the figure of 22% found in the 2018–19 Community Life Survey.[12]

Where to find out more

If you would like to focus only on statistics involving England and Wales, the most comprehensive source remains the 2007 survey *Helping Out.*[13] More recent but less wide-ranging information is available in the government's aforementioned Community Life Survey,[14] data and results from which are published annually.

1.3 REASONS FOR VOLUNTEERING

Trying to understand why people volunteer has been the subject of a huge amount of research, both by academics and by managers of volunteers. To date this has yielded, based on a search using Google Scholar, nearly 4,000 academic journal articles, yet no definitive answer. In the academic research, two schools of thought prevail: psychological approaches and sociological approaches. This section considers both briefly, before asking how useful it is for us to know why people want to volunteer.

Psychological approaches

Approaches to explaining why people volunteer which stem from the academic discipline of psychology are based on the assumption that a desire to engage in volunteer activities likely results from enduring predispositions to engage in certain types of activity. This approach argues that people will be motivated to act when they perceive that a voluntary activity will answer a particular need of theirs. Different people undertaking the same volunteering task may be satisfying different needs by doing so, and people with the same needs may chose different ways to satisfy them.

Perhaps the most widely used psychological way of understanding why people volunteer is E. Gil Clary and Mark Snyder's 'functional approach'.[15] This approach seeks to link motivation (the need) to behaviour (the volunteer) and apply this connection to volunteering. The approach identifies six categories of motivation that can be addressed through volunteering:

- **Values:** volunteering affords people the chance to express values around altruism or concern for others. For example, someone who is concerned about the plight of refugees might volunteer with a refugee support organisation.
- **Understanding:** people volunteer to have new learning experiences, develop or practise skills that might otherwise be unused, or increase their knowledge. For example, a retired bank manager might volunteer as a carpenter for a local country park.
- **Career:** volunteering serves to provide skills and experience that help people to further their careers. For example, a young person might volunteer at a wildlife conservation charity to enhance their CV and help them get a paid job.
- **Social:** volunteering affords the opportunity to be with friends; it is about the social rewards of volunteering. For example, a student might volunteer with their ultimate frisbee society because their friends are already involved. But social rewards can also be negative – people may volunteer to avoid the social disapproval that may come from not being involved. For example, a student might volunteer with their ultimate frisbee society because they fear they will be seen as boring if they do not.
- **Protective:** people can volunteer to escape negative feelings and protect their sense of themselves as a good person. For example, a well-off pensioner might volunteer to work with young people in order to assuage feelings of guilt about being more fortunate than others.
- **Enhancement:** volunteering for enhancement is about personal development and growth, and self-esteem. This may sound similar to the protective function, but Clary and Snyder suggest this is in fact an opposing category. They suggest that research indicates that negative and positive effects are separate dimensions, not just two ends of one scale, and helping others can provide positive effects rather than just lessening negative ones. Therefore, while the protective function is focused on eliminating negative feelings, enhancement is about how people grow and develop. Lots of volunteering should bring these feelings, so we will not single out one example!

This approach to understanding volunteer motivations has the advantage of being clear – six neatly defined categories from which most volunteers can find one or more that reflects their reasons for volunteering. However, life is rarely so simple – motivations may change over time, for example – and that is where the sociological approaches come into their own.

Sociological approaches

Among sociologists who research why people volunteer, there is a sense of scepticism about the idea that there is a finite number of 'underlying needs' that explain volunteer involvement. This is perhaps best summed up by Marc A. Musick and John Wilson, who argue that:

> Even highly motivated people are unlikely to volunteer unless they are asked, and people with little motivation might agree to do so if they are constantly badgered by friends to give some of their time.[16]

Experience tells us that this is often the case. As such, it is useful to explore the wider social context in which decisions to start, continue and stop volunteering are made.

Based on analysis of the British Household Panel Survey from 1991 to 2007, Daiga Kamerade found that, over that period, just 11% of people volunteered in every year and only 13% did not volunteer at all.[17] The vast majority (76%) of people moved in and out of volunteering over this period. Given this, it would seem hard to argue from a psychological point of view that there is a certain type of person who volunteers and therefore, by definition, a certain type of person who does not. If 87% of the population of England and Wales volunteer at some point over a couple of decades, it seems reasonable to conclude that nearly all of us are potential volunteers. This is good news!

That being the case, how might sociology explain why people come to start volunteering? The Pathways Through Participation research project developed a model which argues that volunteering begins when four elements are present:[18]

- **Motivation:** motivation, as identified by psychological analyses of volunteering, can help to explain why people want to volunteer, but it nonetheless usually takes a trigger for them to get started.
- **Trigger:** a trigger can be anything from seeing a news story to, most commonly, being asked by someone to do something.
- **Resources:** to volunteer, people need a number of resources. Money is one of these resources – time spent volunteering is time not spent in paid work, and it is often the case that volunteering requires certain clothes, transport and other small but potentially prohibitive incidental expenses. But perhaps an even more important resource that people need is the confidence to believe they can make a difference. Without this, they are unlikely to devote their time and effort to volunteering.
- **Opportunity:** this is where organisations come in, providing opportunities for people to respond to triggers in a supported way where they can see that their work is making a difference.

Does it matter why people volunteer?

The psychological and sociological approaches are not necessarily in opposition to one another, and there are often overlaps between the main reasons they give for people volunteering, as found in survey data such as the Community Life Survey[19] and *Helping Out.*[20] Therefore, understanding both is useful in understanding why people want to volunteer. However, it is worth questioning how useful it is to know why people want to engage.

Perhaps more useful is to know *how* people engage, and here the picture becomes clearer. The 2007 *Helping Out* survey found that word of mouth – being asked by a family member, friend or acquaintance – was by far the most common route into volunteering, with 66% of volunteers reporting that they had become involved in that way.[21] A further 20% of volunteers had got involved having previously used the services of the organisation they now volunteered for. Additionally, 15% of volunteers had seen a leaflet or poster, while 7% had become involved after attending a local event and the same percentage had heard of volunteering opportunities through their employer. Often there is no single route into volunteering – for example, someone may be asked by a friend having previously used the services of an organisation.

These routes into volunteering should give great hope to managers of volunteers. While psychological approaches suggest that someone either has the right psychological make-up to want to volunteer or they do not, and while sociological approaches suggest that there are times in life when people will engage and times when they will not, what this data on routes into volunteering shows is that a good ask is a great way to get people involved.

1.4   CHANGING PATTERNS AND TRENDS IN VOLUNTEERING

While the proportion of the British population who volunteer has remained remarkably consistent over the past few decades, the ways in which people engage have changed. Alterations in lifestyle and the transformative impact of new technologies have affected the nature of volunteering. It is important not to overstate the impact of these changes – in many ways, volunteering is the same as it ever was. However, in other important ways volunteering has changed, as this section explores.

Demographic changes and changes in lifestyles and family composition have all had impacts on the ways in which people engage in volunteering. Two changes in British society are particularly relevant to volunteering: the ageing population and increased female participation in the paid workforce.

Ageing population

The population in the UK and many other Western nations is ageing rapidly. According to data from the Office for National Statistics, a baby born in the UK in 2005 can expect to live to 76.5 if they are a boy and 80.9 if they are a girl. In just twelve years there is a noticeable improvement so that a baby born in 2017 can expect to live to 79.2 if they are a boy and 82.9 if they are a girl. For those reaching the age of 65 in 2017, a man has an average further 18.6 years of life remaining and a woman 20.9 years.[22] This may seem like excellent news for organisations that depend on volunteers – we saw earlier in this chapter that older people are one of the age groups most likely to volunteer. However, older people are also facing increasing pressures – paid work beyond what would have been a standard retirement age, caring commitments for elderly parents and/or grandchildren – and they may also want to travel and enjoy some leisure time after a long working life. Their later life will not be the same as that of their parents and so they will not necessarily choose to volunteer in the same ways, if at all.

In the UK, the Commission on the Voluntary Sector & Ageing, which reported in 2015, highlighted the value that older volunteers bring for all organisations whose work involves volunteers.[23] The commission suggested that, with volunteering competing against other responsibilities and choices in older people's lives, organisations need to ensure that volunteering opportunities can be flexible, can use skills and can give people opportunities to learn new skills in later life.

Increased female participation in paid work

Over the past few decades, there has been a trend in the UK and in many other Western countries towards greater female participation in paid work. The Office for National Statistics reports that female participation in paid work rose from 63% in 1996 to 71% in 2018. The paid employment rate of mothers in England increased even further during this period, from 62% in 1996 to 74% in 2018.[24] A factor associated with this trend has been economic pressures on families through insecure employment, wage rates falling behind costs of living, a greater number of women wanting to have careers in paid work and the social acceptance of that desire.

This may have an impact on volunteering. Research from the USA shows that stay-at-home mothers are more likely to volunteer than mothers who work in part-time paid employment, who in turn are more likely to volunteer than mothers who work full time.[25] Nonetheless, the study also found that women with school-aged children were more likely to volunteer than women of the same age without children, even if they were in full-time employment.

The main impact that these changes, and other societal factors, have had on volunteering is demand for more flexible types of volunteering.

1.5   CHANGING MODELS OF VOLUNTEER MANAGEMENT

Volunteer management became a profession during the late 1960s and early 1970s, when long-term volunteering was the prevalent type of opportunity. Changes in lifestyles and patterns of paid employment mean that this is now a much less significant type of volunteering. To understand how volunteer management needs to change, we must look at how the volunteers in those earlier decades differed from today's volunteers.

A fundamental difference is that, at the time the volunteer management profession was being formalised, a significant proportion of volunteers rarely did paid work. Instead, they volunteered as an alternative to employment. As volunteer management techniques developed, they mirrored many employment practices, such as the use of written job descriptions and interviews to determine a volunteer's suitability for a job. People who volunteered as an alternative to work found that these practices gave their efforts a bit more status, and they responded positively.

Today's volunteers, by contrast, do not usually volunteer as an alternative to work. They often have paid jobs and volunteer in their leisure time, which is why some refer to the concept of volunteer work as 'serious leisure'. While the traditional practices will still work with today's volunteers, and while it is still possible to find long-term volunteers, it requires much more effort and sophistication to make these practices work.

Effective volunteer engagement means involving volunteers as partners in accomplishing the organisation's mission. How this is done can vary. In some organisations the manager of volunteers is a part- or full-time employee, completely dedicated to working with volunteers. In others, the manager of volunteers may be a part- or full-time employee who has responsibility for volunteering tagged onto other priorities. In still others, the manager of volunteers may themselves be a volunteer.

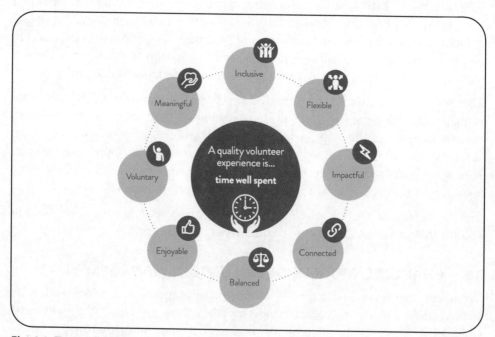

Fig. 1.1 Time well spent

A report by the National Council for Voluntary Organisations (NCVO) published in 2019 lays out really clearly how good volunteer management can ensure a positive volunteer experience.[26] Figure 1.1 lays out the eight key features of a quality volunteer experience:

- volunteering should be inclusive, welcoming and accessible to all;
- it should be as flexible as possible to allow people to fit it around their circumstances;
- it should enable people to have a positive impact on causes that are important to them;
- it should give people a sense of connection with others, a cause, an organisation and/or their local area;
- it should be balanced to ensure that volunteers are not overburdened;
- it should be enjoyable! People are giving up their free time and so volunteering should make them feel good about what they are doing;
- it should be genuinely voluntary, and;
- it should be meaningful, giving people a sense that they have achieved something that resonates with their interests and beliefs.

To achieve this, we believe that the organisations which involve volunteers most effectively do so as part of a concerted and co-ordinated effort. This requires a manager; someone to find people who want to help and match them with the needs of the organisation. This person plans and co-ordinates all the activities of volunteer management, seeks to embed volunteering across the organisation and is supported by colleagues at all levels to deliver a great experience to the volunteers.

This does not always mean that the manager of volunteers directly supervises the volunteers, although they may do so in some settings. Instead, volunteers may work under the direct supervision of other paid staff, with the manager of volunteers playing a supportive role. This has parallels with HR, where it is rare for managers to line-manage all paid staff, instead providing support to managers throughout the organisation.

If volunteering is to have the optimum impact on an organisation's mission, then the managers of volunteers should be involved in the development of new projects and new directions right from the start. They can play an important role helping upper management to identify the skills and expertise that will ensure projects succeed, and they should work with the relevant teams to design volunteer roles to meet those needs.

Increasingly, then, the modern manager of volunteers needs to focus their attention on securing top management support for volunteer efforts and helping individual staff to do a good job of managing and retaining the volunteers they work with.

1.6 **PRACTICAL POINTERS**

- Volunteering is an activity which is undertaken by people of all ages, from all walks of life. While there are some groups of people who volunteer more than others, and people of different ages, genders, ethnicities, religions and social classes are more likely to do different types of volunteering, the fundamental message is that everyone is a potential volunteer.

- There is a huge amount of research into why people volunteer, with little agreement on the answers. What we do know is that people respond to being asked, and that even people who have never considered volunteering often take part when they are approached and are able to undertake the role they are invited to do.

- Changes have occurred – and are still occurring – in society that are affecting the nature of volunteering. These include the ageing population, alterations in family composition and changes in the make-up of the paid workforce. Managers of volunteers need to recognise how these changes will affect those whom they manage. However, it is also important not to overstate their impact. Volunteering will change and evolve in the coming years just as it always has – not overnight, but slowly and surely.

2 Planning for high-impact volunteer involvement

This chapter outlines how your volunteers can help you to deliver effectively on your organisation's vision and mission. We show how you can set SMART (specific, measurable, achievable, relevant, time-bound) objectives for volunteer involvement. By starting planning at this fundamental stage, you will ensure that volunteers are serving the best interests of your organisation and are delivering maximum impact.

Voluntary organisations exist to solve problems or meet needs in communities or the wider world. Often, the way that voluntary organisations can make a serious difference is through the involvement of volunteers who work on the problem (or need) in significant ways. The main work of the organisation may be carried out by paid staff, but the problems are often far greater in magnitude than the financial resources your organisation has available. When volunteers are involved in this way, staff will regard volunteers as a core part of the organisation's ability to make a difference. This does not happen easily, however. It often involves a change in the way the organisation looks at itself and how it looks at volunteers. It requires a clear vision of how the organisation plans and operates.

2.1 IDENTIFYING YOUR MISSION

Effective planning begins with the vision and mission of your organisation. We know that the most commonly given reason for volunteering is to improve things and to help people (when surveyed, 53% of volunteers in England and Wales gave this reason) while the second most common reason is because the volunteer perceives the cause as being important to them (41% of volunteers).[1] As a result, the mission of your organisation is central both to attracting volunteers and to deciding what they will help your organisation to achieve.

Your vision is the ultimate goal of your organisation. It is your dream, and that of your volunteers. Your mission crystallises this and outlines how you will get there: it is a statement of the purpose of the organisation in terms of how it can achieve its ultimate goal. For some organisations, the mission will be a one-off outcome that can be delivered and, once achieved, the organisation will no longer need to exist. For others, the mission will be something more ongoing which can be achieved and re-achieved for evermore.

The most useful mission statements are those which are phrased in terms of meeting a need or solving a problem, and which offer a clear (even if not easy) solution. It may not be particularly exciting to prepare and serve hot meals; however, if your vision is to help put an end to loneliness and hunger among older people, then your mission should outline how volunteers preparing and serving hot meals can help to achieve this.

It is important to be able to communicate your vision and mission to prospective and current volunteers, to make it clear what their efforts can and do achieve. While it may be tempting to seek volunteers by advertising that 'we need volunteers', this is unlikely to attract much interest. Instead, make it clear what the organisation exists to do and how people can help it achieve that.

Some examples of clear mission statements are:

> Football Beyond Borders uses the power of football as an educational tool to inspire young people to achieve their goals and make their voices heard.
>
> Football Beyond Borders

> We support families and care for children and young people with life-threatening conditions across Cambridgeshire, Essex, Norfolk and Suffolk.
>
> East Anglia's Children's Hospices

> We offer a safe place for you to talk any time you like, in your own way – about whatever's getting to you. Samaritans

Your mission statement should be developed with the involvement of the people who will be attempting to carry it out, including volunteers. This will ensure that they feel a sense of ownership of the mission.

Your mission statement should galvanise your volunteers and paid staff, and be a source from which their daily activities draw meaning. It should be a living declaration of what your organisation is trying to accomplish. It should be a statement of the difference your organisation intends to make in the world.

2.2   CONSIDERING YOUR VOLUNTEERS IN STRATEGIC PLANNING

Your organisation's mission statement should be the foundation of your strategic planning. This involves three basic steps:

- identifying obstacles to accomplishing the mission;
- developing a strategy to overcome these obstacles;
- setting achievable and measurable goals to implement the strategy.

An effective plan should take into consideration the resources available to you in the wider community that could help to achieve your mission. As well as being a potential source of people who might be willing to volunteer to support you in delivering your mission, the community will offer you lots of opportunities to help you overcome obstacles and achieve your goals. Local media, community groups, schools, businesses and many other individuals, groups and organisations can offer a range of benefits to you.

Most organisations will lack the financial resources to hire enough paid staff to accomplish all of their strategic goals. One reaction to this problem is to prioritise those goals and pursue the most important or the most feasible. This limits the organisation's mission to that which it can afford financially. However, a more aspirational, motivating and effective approach is to look at how volunteering could help to accomplish the organisation's goals and help you to access the wider resources available in the community. Volunteers can therefore be a critical and integral part of your organisation's success – they can add value over and above the work of paid staff.

Volunteers can be involved in roles across your organisation, making use of their diverse skills. It is likely that nearly every role or task that your organisation needs to be undertaken *could* be fulfilled by a volunteer. That is not to say that they *should* be undertaken by a volunteer – volunteers rarely have the appetite to undertake tasks where they feel they are being asked to replace paid staff, and replacing paid staff with volunteers raises profound ethical questions. It is up to your organisation to consider how roles are allocated to paid staff and volunteers.

This notwithstanding, your strategic planning should consider all of the roles and tasks you need to be undertaken and who is best placed to undertake them, whether paid staff, volunteers or a combination of the two. The next step is to think about how to attract and support volunteers to be a part of delivering your mission.

2.3 MAKING VOLUNTEERING INTEGRAL

In organisations where volunteers are most effective, the role of volunteers is widely understood and appreciated. The role of volunteers and the contribution they make should be an integral part of the mission of your organisation.

It is important to have a carefully formulated sense of the role of volunteers in the future that the organisation is trying to create, so that all within the organisation have a common purpose and a sense of excitement. Part of this is the sense of change that will be brought about through the accomplishment of the organisation's mission. The other part is more internally focused. It is a vivid sense of what the organisation will look like, how it will operate and how it will

...rded in the future. And this vision should provide a positive role for ...eers to play in activities critical to your mission.

Your plan to make volunteering integral to your organisation should focus on your mission. Creating an effective plan to make volunteering integral involves answering the following questions:

- Who can help us to implement our strategies?
- What do we want them to do?
- How can we support them in doing it?

A systematic way to do this is to list the resources (both actual and potential) that your organisation has, or could call on, to help in moving towards achieving your mission.

A statement outlining how volunteers can help your organisation to deliver its mission may involve setting an ambitious and stretching set of goals. At first, these goals may seem daunting. But, as volunteers and paid staff make small steps towards the realisation of these goals, the sense of purpose and excitement will grow.

There are many different elements that could form part of your organisation's plan for making volunteers integral to delivering your mission. Consider the following examples:

> Football Beyond Borders is an organisation built by the passion and energy of volunteers. Without volunteers we would be unable to provide the one-to-one support and mentoring that young people receive on our programmes.
>
> Football Beyond Borders

> Our hugely valuable team of over 1,300 volunteers are at the heart of East Anglia's Children's Hospices. Our volunteers help us reach more families than we could possibly achieve without their support, and we are very grateful for the gift of their time.
>
> East Anglia's Children's Hospices

> You can make an amazing difference at Samaritans helping to support people around the UK and Ireland when they need someone to talk to or they are going through a difficult time in their life. We welcome and value every volunteer, from all walks of life.
>
> Samaritans

These factors interact to create a perception among everyone in your organisation that volunteers have a significant purpose to play in delivering your mission. In doing so, they demonstrate how volunteers enable an organisation to achieve much more of its mission than if it only relied on paid staff.

It is essential during planning that volunteers are not seen as an add-on to the essential work of the organisation but as an integral part of its efforts to achieve its mission. Effectively involving volunteers gives an organisation access to all the skills, experience and passion in the community. Your plan to make volunteers integral to your organisation both leads the efforts of those involved and encourages them to contribute their utmost to achieving your mission. As a manager of volunteers, you will be responsible for helping those in the organisation to develop and deliver the plan.

It may also be appropriate to involve your volunteers in co-developing their own roles to ensure that they fully buy into the aims of the organisation and have helped to shape the plan for how to deliver those aims. This approach also ensures that volunteers are given the best possible opportunity to undertake roles which meet their own needs while also meeting those of the organisation.

2.4   SETTING OBJECTIVES FOR VOLUNTEER INVOLVEMENT

The ultimate goal of involving volunteers is to help your organisation's beneficiaries, and therefore the planning that you do needs to be based on knowing their needs and putting them at the forefront of your planning process. This is another area where volunteers can be invaluable – as members of the community, they may be best attuned to what is needed to make your organisation most effective in meeting community needs.

As a manager of volunteers, hopefully you already advocate support for the organisational value of involving volunteers. But making the benefits of volunteer involvement a reality requires clear planning. When making plans, it is important to ensure that they are clear and practical. One widely used means of achieving this is to ensure that the objectives you set are SMART:

- **Specific:** your objectives in involving volunteers should specify what it is you want to achieve and how you intend to work with volunteers to achieve it. This is what sets your objectives apart from your mission – while the mission is your organisation's overall ambition, the objectives for your volunteer involvement should be clearly defined with a specified plan of how to achieve them.
- **Measurable:** engaging volunteers to achieve your organisation's mission will require you to commit time and resources, and as such you will need to be able to measure the success that volunteer involvement has helped you to achieve. As chapter 15 will explore, being able to measure the effectiveness of volunteer involvement is important both to ensure that you are using resources in the most effective way and to demonstrate to your management team, staff, funders, donors and – perhaps most importantly – current and prospective volunteers that volunteering benefits your organisation and its beneficiaries.

- **Achievable:** while your organisation may have noble, lofty ambitions, it is important that the plan you make to reach them is achievable. That is not to say that it needs to be easy to achieve, but it should be something that a team of volunteers can feel confident they can achieve with your support. This helps to ensure that volunteers stay committed and motivated as they will be able to see that clear progress is being made towards your goals.
- **Relevant:** there are very few limits to what you can achieve with the support of volunteers, but it is important that your volunteers' work is relevant to your organisation's mission. When volunteers approach you with an array of skills and experience, it may be tempting to simply let them run with whatever they think best. While it is important to use the skills and experience that your volunteers bring, it is also important to ensure that all volunteering contributes to achieving your organisation's mission. This balancing act is the heart of effective volunteer management.
- **Time-bound:** it is important to be clear about the timescale in which you want to deliver your specific, measurable, achievable and relevant goals. There are no right or wrong periods – some goals may be deliverable within weeks or months, whereas others might take years. A good plan will include elements of both – some tasks that can be completed fairly quickly and others that will take longer. Even if the tasks you want volunteers to undertake are ongoing, it is still useful to break time down into fixed periods and review the effectiveness of your volunteering regularly.

It is also possible to add **evaluation** and **review** to these to make SMARTER goals, with a focus on evaluating the effectiveness of your volunteer involvement and using the findings to improve the effectiveness of future planning, as is explored in chapter 15.

By following this approach, you should better ensure that your volunteer engagement planning achieves the outcomes you want for your organisation and its beneficiaries.

2.5 PRACTICAL POINTERS

- It is fundamental to volunteer involvement that you locate where volunteers fit into your organisation's mission. Everyone in your organisation – paid staff and volunteers – needs to be engaged in roles that contribute to delivering this mission. Identify what your organisation's mission is and the ways in which volunteers could help you get there.
- Plan how to make volunteers central to delivering your mission. The most enjoyable and rewarding volunteer roles are those where each volunteer can see how what they are doing is helping to deliver, change or maintain something they are passionate about. In short, volunteers must feel like they are in roles where their activities are directly and explicitly related to the mission.

- Setting SMART goals for your volunteer involvement should help to ensure that you involve volunteers successfully. By reviewing how successful your volunteer involvement has been on a regular basis, you can learn from what has gone well and what could have gone better. This will help to deliver the best experience for your volunteers as well as ensuring that volunteer effort helps you to deliver your organisation's mission.

3 Embedding volunteer involvement

This chapter explains how to turn your planned volunteer involvement into action. It outlines what your organisation needs to do in order to organise volunteer involvement, including determining your rationale behind involving volunteers, getting buy-in from paid staff and management, and making sure that everything is in place for successful volunteer involvement.

The Institute for Volunteering Research noted after an extensive survey of volunteering practices in museums in the UK that:

> The old adage that 'one size does not fit all' is perhaps more relevant than ever. Any attempts to develop volunteering programmes should correspond with the starting point of each individual museum and its organisational culture. The culture of an organisation and the personalities within it are significant factors in the success of any volunteering programme. The history of volunteer involvement in an organisation is also important. Investing in a volunteer co-ordinator can move an organisation on a long way in terms of its relationship with volunteers, but only if there is a will within the organisation to do so and an organisational culture which allows the role to develop appropriately.[1]

Therefore, it is important to consider several factors: what has happened previously in your organisation, the support and resources that you currently have, and what you can change and improve. This will help to shape the way in which you can continue to develop volunteers and paid staff and how they work together, on an ongoing basis, in a variety of roles throughout your organisation.

Effective volunteer management is simple in theory but subtle in operation. It has all the complexities of managing paid staff – job development, interviewing, supervision, evaluation of performance, recognition and reward, and so on. Yet volunteer management has complexities all of its own.

Effective volunteer involvement depends upon the creation of a good system for working with volunteers. Volunteer involvement schemes that have insufficient infrastructure, inadequate staff and leadership support, insufficient budgeting, or other defects in management will fail to attract and keep volunteers.

3.1 DETERMINING THE RATIONALE BEHIND VOLUNTEER INVOLVEMENT

The first step in constructing an organisation's plan for engaging volunteers requires determination of why the organisation wishes to involve volunteers. As stated in chapter 2, this should be fundamentally linked with achieving your organisation's mission and thereby should help to bring about your organisation's vision. The rationale for volunteer involvement will:

- determine the types of roles and responsibilities that your organisation will create for volunteers;
- enable your organisation to explain to volunteers how and why they are contributing to its work;
- enable your organisation to explain to paid staff why volunteers are being sought;
- enable your organisation to evaluate whether the involvement of volunteers has been effective.

There are a huge number of reasons why you would want to involve volunteers in your organisation, and these reasons will inform your rationale. Some of the reasons why volunteers might be of value to your organisation include:

- They provide a link between your organisation and the community of place and/or of interest in which it works. Volunteers provide links both ways – they talk to you about the needs and concerns of your beneficiaries, and they talk to people in their social networks about the work your organisation does.
- They can supplement staff resources and experience, bringing skills, knowledge and efforts which add value to your organisation and the work it does.
- They can bring skills and efforts that would not otherwise be available.
- Your beneficiaries can benefit from the more personal touch that volunteers can provide. They may also view volunteers in a different light from paid staff because they are giving their time for free.
- Many volunteers engage with more than one organisation, or have a partner or friends who do, and therefore volunteers can help you to build links to other organisations or groups.
- Volunteers, once engaged, can provide flexibility and allow your organisation to react quickly to changing needs or crisis situations.

There are of course a wide range of other reasons why your organisation might want to engage volunteers. Any reason that includes volunteers in helping you to deliver your organisation's mission is valid, although you should avoid engaging volunteers simply to save money. As this book outlines, managing volunteers is a complex business and is far from free. While in our experience volunteers do strongly resist being considered only as free labour and organisations that fall into this trap risk their volunteer involvement falling very flat. This is an issue Susan J. Ellis and Rob Jackson address in depth in their 2015 book *From the Top Down.*[2]

It is important that your reasons for engaging volunteers are agreed by your organisation's board, senior management and front-line staff. Your rationale for volunteer involvement is likely to be a central part of your plan for how to deliver your mission. It will provide a quick and clear understanding of what benefit the organisation thinks will be derived from the engagement of volunteers, and provide a sense of purpose for involving volunteers. In essence, it should answer the question, 'Why are we doing this?'

Once your rationale for volunteer involvement has been agreed and drafted, it is generally a good idea to ensure all volunteers and staff are aware of it, perhaps by including the information in inductions for all new starters. The Blue Cross offers a good example of a simple but comprehensive rationale:

> Blue Cross welcomes volunteers to join us in improving the lives of pets. We value the unique role volunteers provide working alongside employees, so we can help more pets, raise awareness and generate income together as one team.
>
> Volunteers are at the heart of Blue Cross and are vital to our success, freely giving their expertise, skills and time. Blue Cross gains strength from volunteers, benefitting from a variety of experience and talent to deliver our services more effectively.
>
> We involve volunteers because they:
> - enhance the spirit of Blue Cross with enthusiasm, passion and commitment
> - offer a pool of skills and experience we would otherwise not have access to
> - bring credibility to our work – volunteers choose us and donate their expertise freely
> - expand the diversity of teams, providing a wider perspective in the way we help pets
> - are progressive and flexible, increasing our capacity to help more pets
> - champion our mission and extend our reach in communities
> - represent our values, which are: compassionate, fair and reasonable, integrity, responsible and dynamic.

Getting existing volunteers buy-in for new roles

In this chapter we see your organisation building the strength of its involvement of volunteers through the knowledge and commitment of its paid staff. But in your organisation you may have volunteers who are as well established as paid staff, or even more so, and they would be a resource it'd be wise to draw on in designing new volunteer roles. They could be encouraged to tell you about new jobs which would meet needs or add value, along the lines of the rationale check for staff (see page 27). Their experience of current – and perhaps past – volunteer roles could help rule out some options and indicate fresh ideas.

3.2 STAFF INVOLVEMENT IN PLANNING

Throughout the volunteer engagement planning process, it is essential to involve all levels of paid staff. If volunteers are going to be working in conjunction with paid staff it is vital that staff agree about the purpose and worth of the volunteer roles and the engagement of volunteers in your organisation as a whole.

The key thing to assess when involving staff in planning is to learn what they are trying to accomplish in their work and where they are having problems reaching their goals. You are more likely to get staff to buy into volunteer engagement if you understand their motivations and priorities and seek to meet these as much as possible.

Staff who wish to work with volunteers can be hugely supportive in embedding volunteering in an organisation. There are a number of different ways in which you can canvass staff opinion and seek to get meaningful input and buy-in for your volunteer involvement plans from your paid staff. What approach, or combination of approaches, is most appropriate will depend on the size and nature of your organisation and your own role within it. Following are some ideas for ways to involve staff in the planning for your volunteer involvement, but any approaches not listed here that you think will help you to consult your colleagues are worth trying. This will allow you to develop meaningful roles for volunteers, which will be discussed in chapter 4.

Using a survey

One method of assessing staff attitudes is to conduct a survey. A survey may be particularly appropriate if there are a large number of staff you need to consult or if the staff are spread across several sites. Surveys offer you the opportunity to get large amounts of information to base your plans on, but they generally only allow for one-way communication, giving less opportunity to discuss ideas and plans than more discursive forms of consultation. Surveys can be conducted either through in-person interviewing or through a questionnaire (printed or online), and might seek to explore the following things:

● The level of **experience** of paid staff in working with volunteers:
  – Have they supervised volunteers before?
  – Have they ever worked in an organisation that involved volunteers?
  – Does their job description include managing volunteers?
  – Do they volunteer themselves?

- The level of **comfort** of staff in regard to volunteers:
  - Are there jobs that staff feel that volunteers should not be doing? If so, why?
  - Does anything (such as additional staff training) need to take place before volunteers are brought in?
- Any **fears** that staff might have about volunteer involvement:
  - Are there potential difficulties (such as organisational liability or quality control questions) that should be addressed?
  - Are there worries about loss of paid staff jobs?

Whatever questions you ask, you should collect a wide range of views that can help you to plan effective volunteer engagement and avoid any tensions between paid staff and volunteers.

Undertaking interviews

Interviews are a good way of having a purposeful conversation with your colleagues to canvass their views on suitable roles for volunteers within your organisation and on levels of comfort in working with and leading volunteers. Interviews allow for discussion so you and your colleagues can share your thoughts and ideas and, over the course of an interview, move towards a plan that you all agree on. Additionally, if you have already completed a staff survey, you may want to base your conversations on issues highlighted in the survey results.

In smaller organisations with only a few paid staff, it may be possible for you to spend time one on one with all of your colleagues to discuss how they see volunteers fitting into your organisation's plan for how to achieve its mission. Among a small team, it will hopefully be possible to build consensus around why your organisation wants to engage volunteers and what it would like them to do.

In larger organisations, there may be certain roles where a particular member of paid staff is likely to have more engagement with volunteers or more responsibility for areas in which they work. Equally, there may be paid staff who are likely to work hands on with volunteers. Interviewing these staff one on one enables you to get a range of perspectives and should help you to develop a rationale and a plan which meet the approval of colleagues across your organisation.

Conducting focus groups

In larger organisations, it can be hard to speak to all interested colleagues one on one, but nonetheless it can be useful to engage a wide range of staff members in discussions about the best way to integrate volunteers into your organisation. The key to focus groups is to allow people to talk to each other, while also ensuring that you continue to guide the conversation to ensure it answers the questions you want answered. Sound complicated? It doesn't need to be! Have a plan of what you want to discuss but do not be too prescriptive – if the conversation takes an unexpected turn, give it a few minutes to see where it goes, but don't be afraid to bring the group back on topic if required.

3.3 GETTING SENIOR LEADERSHIP SUPPORT

Volunteer involvement in your organisation will be more effective if it has the support of the senior leadership. This support should take the form of official adoption by the board of trustees, management committee or executive committee; a policy supporting the involvement of volunteers; and/or a position statement on volunteers approved by the chief executive or senior management team of the organisation.

As we discussed in chapter 2, one essential element of this support is that the senior leadership should have a clear vision of how volunteers will contribute to the achievement of the organisation's mission. When contemplating the involvement of volunteers, senior leadership should consider the following key questions:

- How would you describe the mission of the organisation and how do you see volunteers aiding in the fulfilment of that mission?
- What specific goals are envisioned for the volunteers during the next year?
- What kinds of resources is the organisation already investing in volunteers? Is this investment sufficient for the goals you want to achieve and, if not, what more might be needed?
- What does the organisation see as the benefits it will receive from the involvement of volunteers?

The most obvious manifestation of senior leadership support lies in the allocation of appropriate financial resources for volunteer involvement. Volunteering may be freely given but it isn't cost free – like anything your organisation does, the support of volunteers requires some money to operate. Costs include a salary for the manager of volunteers, equipment and materials, recognition events for volunteers and reimbursement of volunteer expenses – all highly reasonable and justifiable.

3.4 ORGANISATIONAL CLIMATE

The overall climate of your organisation will influence how volunteers can be involved. Volunteers will quickly become aware of the overall attitudes within the organisation – whether it is about how well the organisation is doing, how things are done, or who and what is important to the organisation. These subtle cues regarding organisational style will influence volunteers' decisions about whether your organisation is worth the donation of their time.

You therefore need to assess whether your organisation, on first impression and beyond, appears to be welcoming to volunteers. If not, you will need to ask why, and what you can do about it. Since your organisation is your volunteers' place of work, you want to ensure that they have a positive environment. What is needed is a sense of common mission and purpose, and an understanding that productive steps are being taken towards accomplishment of that mission and purpose, with everyone pulling in the same direction.

The development of a good organisational climate where volunteers are included and supported is covered in more detail in chapter 8. However, some key aspects are:

- a clear sense of individual roles, with respect for the roles of others;
- a willingness of paid staff and volunteers to make sacrifices in order to achieve your mission;
- trust;
- tolerance and acceptance;
- open and honest two-way communication;
- a sense of group identity;
- a feeling of inclusion;
- mutual support and interdependence;
- recognition of the contribution volunteers make.

An organisational climate that is favourable towards volunteers will communicate two feelings or attitudes to volunteers:

- **Acceptance:** volunteers are welcomed by and connected with the overall purpose and operations of the organisation.
- **Appreciation:** each volunteer has a unique, recognised contribution to make to the purpose and operations of the organisation.

Achieving a positive organisational climate should help with volunteer recruitment and retention, as well as ensure volunteers are keen to work hard to support you in achieving your mission.

You can communicate your organisation's commitment to the successful involvement of volunteers by ensuring that its policies and day-to-day practices reflect this. You should already have a set of values to which all – staff and volunteers – are expected to subscribe, and this should include an atmosphere of appreciation and respect for volunteers.

Top tips for volunteer planning: checklist

You can assess your overall plan for volunteer involvement by reviewing the following checklist. If you have not completed the items on the list, then you still have preparations to finish before you and your organisation can decide to involve volunteers effectively.

☐ Does your organisation have a clearly defined mission with long-range goals which relate to the community?

☐ Does your organisation have a clear vision for volunteer involvement and a widely understood rationale for why it engages volunteers in its work?

☐ Have paid staff and volunteers been involved in developing the plan to accomplish these goals and have they considered and discussed the involvement of volunteers in accomplishing the mission of your organisation?

☐ Is the volunteer work to be done meaningful? Is it useful and significant to your organisation's mission and beneficiaries?

☐ Can the need for the specific volunteer role be adequately explained to a potential volunteer? Can you describe how this role contributes to the mission of your organisation?

☐ Can the work be done by a volunteer? Can it be reasonably split into tasks that can be done in short blocks of time, perhaps at evenings or weekends? Are the needed skills likely to be available from volunteers, or can people be easily trained in the knowledge and background needed?

☐ Is it cost-effective to have the work done by volunteers? Will you spend more time, energy and money to recruit, orient and train volunteers than you would if you used staff? Are you looking at volunteer involvement on a long-term or short-term basis?

☐ Have staff been adequately trained and is volunteer management reflected in their job description?

☐ Is a support framework for volunteer involvement in existence? Do you have a person ready to act as the manager of volunteers? Do you have volunteer policies and procedures? And has the involvement of volunteers been included in the organisation's plan and budget?

☐ Do paid staff understand their roles in relation to the involvement of volunteers?

☐ Can you identify volunteers with the skills to do the role? Are they likely to be available in your community?

☐ Will people want to do this volunteer role? Is it a rewarding and interesting role or have you simply tried to get rid of work that no one would really want to do, paid or unpaid?

☐ Do you know how you will evaluate success and how and to whom feedback will be given?

☐ In the end, is your organisation committed to the involvement of volunteers or is someone just looking for a quick-fix solution to their problem?

3.5 POLICIES AND PROCEDURES

Supporting volunteer engagement within an organisation requires the creation of formal rules and procedures. After you have determined why volunteers are to be involved, your organisation will need to develop its own set of policies and procedures governing the engagement of volunteers. In particular, the following procedures would be appropriate for a wide range of volunteer-involving organisations:

- **An organisation-wide volunteer policy:** this is an all-encompassing document which sets out your organisation's plan for how to recruit and manage volunteers. It will include, in brief, reference to each of the other elements in this list and (where necessary) signposting to other policies or documents. In short, it is your organisation's one-stop shop for how you want to engage with volunteers and as such should contain all the information that anyone managing or working with volunteers could need to know.
- **Volunteer agreement:** this is a more or less formal document (depending on your organisation's needs) which outlines your commitment to the volunteer and their commitment to you. There are no hard and fast rules about what should be included, but it should be a clear document that is agreed by both the organisation and the volunteer.
- **A volunteer expenses policy:** this document should outline what expenses volunteers are able to claim and what the process is for them to make these claims. This should be shared with all volunteers who are likely to need to claim expenses and should form the basis for all expenses decisions.
- **Budgets for volunteer involvement:** engaging volunteers is far from free, and this document will set out what the cost implications – either in terms of direct costs or in terms of the cost of staff or volunteer time – are of engaging and managing volunteers. It is likely that this will be in internal-facing document.
- **A safeguarding policy:** while safeguarding needs vary from organisation to organisation, it is likely that all organisations will need some form of safeguarding policy. Its length and what it includes will depend on what your organisation does and whom it works with.

These policies will allow the manager of volunteers to develop a consistent pattern of volunteer involvement, and will provide assistance in dealing with problem situations. Both the policies and the procedures by which they will be implemented should be developed in conjunction with paid staff, particularly if the organisation is involving volunteers in a variety of different projects or activities.

Volunteer management also requires some basic personnel-related systems, with the extent and formality of these varying depending on the nature of your organisation and the work it undertakes. Whatever system you choose, you will need to record some key information about your volunteers. Again, this will vary depending on your organisation's needs, but there are some key types of information required by the majority of volunteer-involving organisations, including:

- initial information forms;
- role descriptions;
- evaluation instruments.

The amount of information these include and the way it is recorded will depend on the nature of your organisation – as with so many other things in volunteer management, the approach you take will be guided by the demands of your organisation. In some organisations, role descriptions may be structured like those provided for paid staff, whereas in others they may only comprise one line. Similarly, regarding the evaluation of volunteer performance, in more formal settings this may be a regular and detailed exercise whereas in others it may be as simple as asking, 'Are things going okay?'. You will need to decide, in consultation with colleagues, what will be most appropriate.

As well as these forms, it may also be necessary for records to be maintained for each volunteer, giving:

- biographical and contact information;
- records of roles and training;
- hours contributed and tasks accomplished;
- expenses claimed and reimbursed;
- dates of connection with the organisation.

As previously, not all of these will be appropriate or necessary for your organisation, and indeed it is important that you ensure that you are not gathering information which you do not need. All the information that you gather must comply with the rules set out in the GDPR (General Data Protection Regulation) legislation for countries within the European Union or other national or international laws or guidelines, as appropriate.

Records such as those just mentioned are not only important to the current manager of volunteers; they will also be essential to those who work for them and to their successor. These records provide a history both of volunteer involvement and of individual volunteers that can be invaluable in creating an understanding of what is going on.

You may find it useful to look into whether computer software packages can assist you in record-keeping and day-to-day volunteer management. Software packages are now available (or can be custom developed for your setting) that will greatly aid you in keeping track of the names, skills, interests and availability of your volunteers. They can assist you in performing the paperwork functions of managing volunteers in a way which is tailored and enables you to build your volunteer relationships, conserving your time to deal with those parts of the job that require human contact.

3.6 PRACTICAL POINTERS

- It is important to consider why you want to engage volunteers in your organisation before you begin planning how to do so. There are a huge range of valid reasons why you may want to engage volunteers, and these will vary between organisations. Therefore, for your organisation, it is worth spending time agreeing with senior management, paid staff and colleagues why you are engaging volunteers. This should ensure that you avoid confusion down the line.
- Volunteers will be working alongside paid staff, so make sure to take time speaking with your paid colleagues. Listen to their views on where in your organisation volunteers could make the most difference and how they feel their area of the organisation could be boosted through involving volunteers. Ensure that you hear the voices of both senior management and other paid staff.
- Ensuring that your organisation is well prepared to welcome volunteers should help to ensure that volunteers feel both accepted and appreciated as a core part of the way in which your organisation delivers its mission. Consider what, if anything, you might need to change about the way your organisation operates and communicates in order to ensure that volunteers feel fully integrated.
- Establish clear policies and procedures for how volunteers will fit into your organisation and how they will be supported. The formality of these policies will depend on the formality of your volunteering roles. However, as a general rule, your policies should establish what you expect from your volunteers and what your volunteers can expect from you. They should also be clear about the relevant processes.

4 Creating motivating roles for volunteers

The single most important factor in managing effective volunteer involvement is the design of the volunteer roles. An organisation that has interesting and productive roles to offer will have an easy time attracting and keeping volunteers. This chapter outlines how to design and structure volunteer roles that fit with your organisation's mission and provide enjoyable, motivating and rewarding work. As you may have guessed, there is no one-size-fits-all method of doing this – different organisations will require different levels of formalisation in how their volunteer roles are defined. Therefore, this chapter outlines how to consult with staff about what roles are needed and how to negotiate these roles with volunteers.

Much of this chapter is based on the simple premise that while in the short run many volunteers will agree to do anything that needs doing, in the long run most people will prefer to do things they find satisfying, and volunteers are no different. It is, therefore, fundamental to effective volunteer management that roles are created that allow volunteers to contribute to your organisation and to the delivery of its mission, and in doing so feel a sense of enjoyment and satisfaction. All in all, the need to plan clear and motivating roles for volunteers is not just one of the basic building blocks of volunteer involvement – it is the key element.

4.1 DESIGNING VOLUNTEER INVOLVEMENT FOR STAFF BUY-IN

Chapter 3 explored the importance of getting the input and buy-in of your organisation's paid staff for your plan for volunteer involvement. The views of paid staff who will be working with or leading volunteers are therefore a good place to begin the process of creating motivating volunteer roles. To be effective, volunteers must have the support of staff. A volunteer's work, therefore, must be something that staff want done and that contributes to your organisation achieving its mission.

The role of the manager of volunteers in the development of a volunteer role thus involves consulting with staff, helping them to develop volunteer roles that support their work, and creating roles that volunteers want to do. During the process, the manager of volunteers should use the methods outlined in chapter 3 to determine how paid staff might involve volunteers. This does not consist of merely asking staff what roles they might have for a volunteer. That question is unlikely to provoke a creative response from staff who have had no experience working with volunteers or who have not spent much time thinking about this question. Worse, if paid staff have previously had a bad experience working with volunteers, then they may rule out future options as a result of those negative experiences. For example, if a colleague once worked with a volunteer who broke confidentiality, they are unlikely to suggest roles volunteers might do in the future where they have access to beneficiary data.

Instead, the manager of volunteers should consult with staff members and encourage them to answer the following questions:

- What are some things you would like to see done that no one currently within our organisation has the skills to do?
- What are the parts of your job that you really like to do?
- What are the parts of your job that you are less keen on?
- What activities or projects have you always wanted to undertake but never had time for?
- What are some areas which we have never had the opportunity to develop which would add value to what we do?

The answers to these questions can form the basis for defining volunteer roles that can be integrated with the staff workload and will be supported by staff. In a nutshell, if the manager of volunteers can bring in a volunteer who will add value and provide opportunities to relieve members of staff of some tasks, support them in others and give them time to do things they've always wanted to do, staff have a powerful incentive to make sure that the volunteer has a good experience within the organisation. In addition, by involving volunteers in activities the organisation cannot perform with its paid staff (through a lack of either time or skill), you extend the effectiveness of the organisation, perhaps piloting new ways of working and testing new ideas. There is a long history of volunteers undertaking innovative roles, testing out new ideas and trialling new ways of working. Indeed, many voluntary organisations have their roots in undertaking such innovative activities, and many of the public and voluntary services that we now take for granted were originally seen as ground-breaking.

By designing roles around the types of work that staff lack the capacity or skills to do, the manager of volunteers develops volunteer work that is 'real' (i.e. it really needs to be done) and that will be appreciated by staff. As a consequence, the potential for typical staff–volunteer difficulties, such as staff forgetting to thank volunteers for their efforts or feeling threatened, is greatly reduced.

In order to ensure that what your colleagues would like volunteers to do is realistic, it is important to work with them and to manage expectations. Clearly establishing with staff what volunteers can be asked to do – and what they cannot be asked to do – should save you from being bombarded with impossible requests for volunteers to undertake certain activities. To assist in this effort, you can employ a number of tools to show staff what will be possible. These tools can be used in a 'menu' approach, giving staff lists of possibilities. The tools can include:

- a list of the types of roles or functions that volunteers have done in the past or are currently performing in your organisation;
- a list of types of roles or functions that volunteers perform in other organisations in the community or in similar programmes across the country;
- a skills list and descriptions of available volunteers.

These lists may provide ideas to staff who do not have a clear understanding of the potential ways to involve volunteers within your organisation. They can serve to broaden the perspective and improve the creativity of staff in developing interesting and challenging volunteer roles.

The process of staff involvement should be a continuous one. The manager of volunteers should develop a process for ongoing communication with staff, either by periodic follow-up interviews or through written communication in which the process of developing new roles continues. One method for accomplishing this is to introduce a 'work wanted' section in the organisation's newsletter, intranet or similar, in which volunteer roles are highlighted or in which the skills of new volunteers are announced. The aim of this kind of communication is to create a demand for additional types of volunteer effort.

4.2 DESIGNING VOLUNTEER ROLES FOR RESULTS

Designing roles that people want to do is the cornerstone of all successful volunteer involvement. While paid staff will sometimes be willing to fill a role that is unrewarding because they are compensated for doing it, volunteers will not do so for long. Therefore, to attract and retain volunteers, you must design roles that they want to undertake.

Volunteering is in many ways a leisure activity, insofar as it is a thing that people freely choose to do in their free time. People engage in leisure activities for a variety of reasons, including a sense of satisfaction, challenge, moral or political commitment, reward or accomplishment. To attract and keep volunteers, you therefore must design volunteer roles so that they too provide these rewards. Otherwise, people will do something else with their leisure time.

This is an important point to grasp because it means that your competition for volunteers is not other charities – it's anything people in your community can spend their spare time doing. Your competition is them spending time with family, going to the cinema, watching a sporting event, having a meal out and so on. You need to make volunteering so enjoyable and motivating that people would rather volunteer than do other leisure activities. But how?

In designing volunteer roles, we might learn something from people who design games. Games are activities people undertake in their free time that are designed to be intrinsically motivating. Games are so motivating that people will spend lots of their time and money on expensive equipment and lessons in order to get better at them, something that is rarely true of work. Games are so well designed, in fact, that people will spend lots of money to get to see other people play them. If this were true of work, we wouldn't have to worry about getting funding for our organisations – we could just sell tickets to watch our people do their work!

The point here is not that volunteering should be a game but that it should have the same motivational qualities that games have. All games have four characteristics that work can also have but seldom does:

1. ownership of the task to be completed;
2. the authority to think;
3. responsibility for results or outcomes;
4. the ability to evaluate or measure what is achieved.

When we design volunteer roles, therefore, it is good to try to build in these four characteristics.

Ownership

Volunteers should have a sense of personal responsibility for something, with their role containing something they can point to and say, 'This is mine'. This might be a particular service or event or geographical area. Ownership gives the volunteer something to be in charge of and hence to be proud of. Ownership can be individual or it can be split between teams of volunteers. In these cases, there must be a sense that the team has something that is its own.

The authority to think

An individual or group should not only undertake work but also play some part in deciding how to do it. When a volunteer first joins, they may need support and guidance to help them undertake the role; however, as volunteers learn their role and begin to work out what is going on, it may begin to sap their motivation and dilute their feelings of pride in what they accomplish if they are only doing what someone else decides.

While you need to make sure that your volunteers are all working towards the achievement of a co-ordinated and agreed set of goals, you should involve them in the planning and decision-making process so that they feel a sense of authority over the 'how' of their role. The process of managing this is explained in chapter 8 in terms of levels of authority and the extent of a volunteer's self-assignment versus the manager's control (see particularly section 8.2).

Responsibility for results or outcomes

Make sure that your volunteers are encouraged to achieve positive results, rather than simply for performing a set of activities or 'role duties'. If volunteers are responsible for results or outcomes, they are focused on the end product of what they do, and they get the satisfaction of making progress towards a meaningful accomplishment. When people know what they are supposed to accomplish, they are more likely to do so. If, on the other hand, they are responsible only for the activities rather than the result, they are divorced from that satisfaction. Most role descriptions for volunteers (and for paid staff) are not defined in terms of results; they merely list a series of activities that the volunteer is supposed to perform. This should be strenuously avoided.

Ability to measure success

It is useful to decide how to measure whether and to what degree results are being achieved. Showing volunteers that their endeavours are achieving success can be highly motivating for them. Measuring success is more than simply keeping track of things such as hours spent or miles driven or beneficiary contacts made. These measures tend to lack any real meaning because they do not tell us whether a volunteer is accomplishing anything of value. It may be hard to work out meaningful measures of success, as we discuss in chapter 15. However, after undertaking this work, you will be able to motivate your volunteers by showing them the successful outcomes of their work.

4.3 WRITING VOLUNTEER ROLE DESCRIPTIONS

Many organisations and volunteers prefer that a volunteer role, once created, is written down in some form. While this is not necessary for many short-term volunteer roles – especially those that last a day or less, or those roles which are fairly informal – it is often sensible to have a written role description to refer to when volunteers come up against questions regarding the boundaries of their activities. This role description should ideally be developed jointly by the manager of volunteers and, where present, the staff member who will supervise the volunteer. It could also include input from the volunteers themselves. It should provide a summary of the work and activities to be performed by the volunteer, showing what is expected of them and what is not expected of them.

The discipline of writing a good role description is a useful one to master. In some ways, role descriptions can be more important for volunteers than for paid staff. Paid staff are accustomed to learning their roles by osmosis – coming to work and spending time watching what is happening, and determining what they should be doing and how they should do it. For a volunteer, this learning period may be longer, since ten days of on-the-job learning for a full-time employee can easily translate into several weeks or even months of on-the-job training for a part-time volunteer. Unless the organisation is ready for the volunteer to begin work immediately and has prepared suitable instructions, the volunteer can become discouraged right from the start.

A role description that accurately represents the tasks to be undertaken and the results to be achieved can serve as a method of readying your organisation for the appearance of a volunteer. If you discover that either you or the paid staff with whom the volunteer will be working cannot put together a precise role description, continue to work on it until you have something that is clear rather recruit a volunteer for a role that cannot be properly defined.

A role description should contain the following points:

- **Title:** what the role will be called, or what role is being offered. Note that this does not need to include the word 'volunteer' as that simply denotes the status category.
- **Purpose:** what the role seeks to accomplish and its impact on your organisation's mission. This is the most important part of the role description.
- **Results:** if there are definable results that contribute to the overall purpose, these should be listed.
- **Suggested activities:** examples of what might be done to accomplish the results and thus the purpose. The word 'suggested' indicates that the volunteer has the authority to think and to pursue other approved activities if the supervisor agrees that these might be effective in achieving the result.
- **Measures:** how you will tell whether the result is being achieved.
- **Training:** what training is required for the role and when and how this will be provided.
- **Supervision:** relationships with staff and other volunteers, reporting requirements and supervisory relationships, as well as procedures for monitoring and dealing with problems.
- **Time frame:** estimated number of hours, length of commitment and flexibility in scheduling.
- **Site:** location of work.
- **Benefits:** training, insurance, parking, reimbursement of expenses, childcare provision (if any), events to thank volunteers, etc.

An additional item to include might be the values and philosophy of your organisation, along with the stipulation that the volunteer will be expected to adhere to them.

The precise format of the role description is not important. What is important is that all of the elements are covered and that, in particular, a well-thought-out and attractive purpose is defined for the volunteer.

4.4 NEGOTIATING AND UPDATING DESCRIPTIONS

While the role description ought to be formally constructed before recruiting volunteers, it should not be considered an immutable, finished document. Remember that, for the involvement of volunteers to be successful, they must be motivated to take on a role that needs to be filled. To ensure that this is the case, the role description needs to adapt to meet the needs of volunteers and the organisation.

When first meeting with prospective volunteers, you should seek to match roles to the needs and interests of potential volunteers, and in doing so some negotiation may take place. Further negotiation should happen after the volunteers have been accepted and have begun work. As they gain more familiarity with the actual work to be done, they may make suggestions as to how the role might be modified to make it even more rewarding or impactful.

One of the most frustrating things for those who manage volunteers is when a volunteer is reluctant to use their high-level skills in a voluntary setting. Just because someone uses a skill in their paid work doesn't automatically mean that they also want to use it in their leisure time. Accountants do not necessarily want to spend their evenings and weekends doing even more accountancy! Therefore, you shouldn't be surprised if people with professional skills would rather do something else with their leisure time – something that gives them the opportunity to develop a new skill, enhance an old skill, explore an interest or simply do something completely different. When we build a volunteer role for a working professional, it is important to remember to build something that satisfies their needs (see section 12.1 on how appraisals may prompt revision of the role description).

There will be cases, though, where people *do* want to use skills that are related to their paid work. For example:

- Retired professionals sometimes miss using their hard-earned skills. They may be happy to use them to maintain their sense of professional identity and sense of being productive and useful.
- Unemployed people may be keen to contribute their skills in order to stay current and maintain a track record of professional involvement.

- People working towards entering or re-entering the labour market may need to practise and develop technical or professional skills.
- There are also those who are so committed to your cause that they will, for short-term projects, contribute the skills that they use all day.
- Lastly, you may be lucky enough to find someone who loves their profession so much that they prefer to practise it than to do anything else in their leisure time.

Finding these types of people when you are searching for someone with a professional skill is a recruitment challenge – a matter that will be addressed in chapter 5.

4.5   PRACTICAL POINTERS

- Create volunteer roles that your staff and/or existing volunteers identify are needed. By consulting your colleagues, you will ensure that no unnecessary roles are created and avoid people feeling that incoming volunteers are treading on their toes. This benefits not only your organisation but also your colleagues and your incoming volunteers.
- Try to have as diverse a range of roles as possible to ensure that you can attract the widest possible range of volunteers.
- Take time to develop engaging and rewarding volunteer roles. Remember that your volunteers are giving up their leisure time to volunteer for you. You therefore need to make sure the roles you are offering give volunteers the satisfaction of undertaking a meaningful role and in doing so successfully delivering results for a cause they feel passionate about.
- Be clear on what volunteer roles entail, and have this written down so that paid staff, existing volunteers and new volunteers are aware of what it is that volunteers are there to do.
- Involve your volunteers in this process! While you might have a clear idea of what a volunteer role should entail, each individual volunteer will bring with them skills, experience and ideas which could benefit the work of your organisation. Further, by allowing your volunteers to help shape their roles, you will give them ownership of their work, and this should help to ensure they remain engaged and committed.

5 Recruiting volunteers

Once you have planned for volunteer involvement and established what you want volunteers to do, you will need to recruit your volunteers. The most common reason people volunteer is because they are asked, so effective recruitment is fundamental.

In recruiting volunteers, you should aim to find people who are attracted by the challenge of the role and by the idea of helping to deliver your organisation's mission. You can picture this as a process of matching two sets of needs: those of the volunteer and those of the organisation (which will of course take account of the needs of beneficiaries). In this chapter, we explore how you can undertake this process, identifying potential volunteers and recruiting them to your organisation. Each volunteer is different and the method you choose will depend on the context of your organisation, but these simple steps should help you to recruit the volunteers you need.

It is important to remember that the recruitment process begins with, and in many ways hinges upon, the creation of motivating roles for volunteers (see chapter 4). Attempting to recruit volunteers without first having developed worthwhile roles to offer them is equivalent to attempting to sell a product to people who have no need for it. It can be done, but the buyers may well become unhappy later. And, when volunteers are unhappy, they don't stay around long.

The recruitment process might also be pictured as a filter. It is a procedure that involves identifying and separating from the entire universe of potential volunteers those people who might best fit the needs of your organisation and its work.

Organisations that recruit volunteers may suffer from two very different types of recruitment problems. One problem, which is universally feared by new managers of volunteers, is that of not having enough volunteers. The second problem, which is much more subtle and yet much more common, is not having enough of the 'right' volunteers and, indeed, usually having too many of the 'wrong' ones. In this chapter, we explore how to recruit the volunteers you need and only the volunteers you need.

When planning your recruitment campaign or undertaking ongoing volunteer recruitment, there are five different types of processes that can be used:

- warm-body recruitment;
- targeted recruitment;
- concentric circles recruitment;
- ambient recruitment;
- event recruitment.

Each is quite different in what it seeks to accomplish and in what it is effective in accomplishing. The type you choose to pursue will depend on your needs and the context in which your organisation operates.

The final two sections of this chapter look at two additional important things to consider when recruiting volunteers: how you can recruit volunteers from a diverse range of backgrounds, and how you can be flexible in your recruitment.

5.1 WARM-BODY RECRUITMENT

Warm-body recruitment is a technique for finding people for a role or roles where the requirements are so general and broad that most people (any warm body) can do it. It consists of spreading the message about the potential volunteer role to as wide an audience as possible. It is effective when you are trying to recruit for a volunteer role that could be done by most people, either because no special skills are required or because almost anyone can be taught the necessary skills in a limited amount of time. Examples include handing out flyers or directing traffic at an event. Warm-body recruitment is particularly effective when you are seeking large numbers of volunteers for short-term, simple roles, such as helpers at a special event, a festival or a fun run.

The primary methods of warm-body recruitment are as follows.

- using your website and social media to publicise volunteer opportunities;
- using low-cost or free advertising on websites, on social media, in local newspapers or on local radio;
- distributing leaflets or posters advertising the need for volunteers, and asking staff and volunteers to tell their friends and family;
- contacting community groups, such as a neighbourhood association or a youth organisation, that can provide the necessary person power.

The trick in all of these approaches is to make them engaging enough to attract people's attention (which generally means short), but with enough information to get people to actually pay attention to the message and contact you about volunteering.

Leaflets and posters

Leaflets and posters do not have to be expensively produced. Do not try to include every piece of information about your organisation. Too much detail is not eye-catching and can be off-putting. Instead, direct interested prospective volunteers to visit your website, where you can include far more information, or to contact you.

There are a great number of possible sites for the distribution of printed information. The aim is to place your materials in locations where people are likely to pick them up and read them. Possible sites include:

- job centres;
- libraries;
- tourist information centres;
- supermarkets, cafés, coffee shops and pub noticeboards;
- schools and youth clubs;
- bulletin boards in places of worship;
- community centres;
- volunteer centres and councils for voluntary service;
- hospital waiting rooms, clinics and GP surgeries;
- shop windows.

Those programmes that deliver a service within an identifiable neighbourhood might best benefit from a simple door-to-door distribution campaign.

Advertising and publicity

With an advert on local radio, or a good classified advert in your local newspaper, perhaps only a small percentage of the audience will be interested. But, if thousands of people see or hear the advert, this could result in a decent number of applicants.

The cost of traditional advertising, even locally, may be too high for many charities. In this case, consider free website advertising options, of which there are many. Some of these are national and broad (e.g. Do-It.org), others are national and sector specific (e.g. volunteering-wales.net, VolunteerNow.co.uk for Northern Ireland and VolunteerScotland.net) and some are local (e.g. volunteer centres and local council websites).

As well as websites designed for volunteer recruitment, you can also make use of the increasingly accessible and relatively low-cost advertising options on high-traffic websites such as Facebook, Twitter and Instagram. Each of these offer organisations the opportunity to purchase adverts targeted at both specific locations and people with certain characteristics, often at a comparatively low cost. You will be able to track how many people your adverts have reached and the response rate, and use this data to create ever more effective adverts.

It is important to realise that even if such methods do attract a volunteer, they will not by themselves guarantee that recruitment is successful. You will still need to inspire the potential volunteer individually about the role and the work of the organisation. The mass media techniques will simply serve to get you close enough to the volunteer to make an actual recruitment pitch.

Speaking to community groups

One of the best methods of warm-body recruitment is to arrange presentations to local clubs and other groups. Examples include service organisations (such as Rotary), faith groups and student organisations. Such presentations can serve both to inform the public about what your organisation does and to recruit new volunteers. In following this method of recruitment, be sure to do the following things:

- Deliberately select the groups to which you wish to speak. There are two types which are most helpful: those groups whose members regularly help out in the community (such as Rotary) and those groups whose individual members are likely to have a common interest with your cause. Schedule the latter type of groups first.
- In seeking an opportunity to speak to the group, consider going through a group member. The member can serve as your authenticator to their peers, paving your way to a more receptive audience with the person responsible for making the decision. They can also make it more likely that you will be invited to speak. Many groups have a social secretary who is desperate to find good speakers.
- Try to time your speaking to meet your needs and those of the group. Find out about other projects that the group is already committed to and time your talk to coincide with their need to develop a new project. Determine how much lead time they need and make sure that your request is not too immediate and so difficult for them to meet.
- Pick your presenters carefully. Make sure that the person who is speaking can explain what your organisation does and exactly what is needed from volunteers. If you have the opportunity, you might have a volunteer come along with you and tell their own story. Often one volunteer can more easily recruit another than a paid person can.
- If possible, use a visual presentation (slide-show, pictures, video, etc.) to increase interest. If your presentation is boring, the group may assume that your volunteer roles will be too.

- Be prepared for people to offer their services. Take along leaflets, examples of roles for which they are needed, sign-up sheets, etc. If people express interest, don't leave without their names, email addresses and phone numbers – as well as their consent to hold this information – and commit yourself to following up their interest. Follow up as quickly as possible.
- Be prepared for too much success. You may need to have a back-up plan to handle the entire group wanting to volunteer together, and not just a few individuals. If several group members decide to volunteer, you might want to consider ways in which they might work together as a group while performing the volunteer work, as explored further in section 9.2.
- Remember that at some point during your presentation you should directly and unequivocally ask the audience to volunteer. Very few people will insist on volunteering for you without being asked to do so.

Your website

Your website is an important point of contact between you and prospective volunteers. People who have seen your poster, heard about you on the radio or in the local paper, seen you at an event or heard about you from a friend will all be likely to search for you online. This means that your website will often be the first point of contact between your organisation and prospective volunteers – so it is vital that it immediately makes a good impression!

Consider what your homepage says about volunteering opportunities, and make sure you have a clear and easy-to-find section on your website with details of volunteer opportunities. Make it easy for visitors to your website to get in touch with you there and then – a quick and easy-to-submit form that people can fill in before they click off the page will help to ensure you capture prospective volunteers at their most curious and interested. There is no set way of doing this; if you are unsure, the best thing to do is to look at what other organisations are doing.

Your website is a great place to include testimonials from existing volunteers about how much they enjoy volunteering with you and making a difference. You could also include testimonials from beneficiaries and paid staff about the contribution that volunteers make. These could be simple text or illustrated with pictures and videos.

Make sure that your website has clear contact information so that prospective volunteers know whom to contact and how to contact them.

5.2 **TARGETED RECRUITMENT**

The second method of recruiting volunteers is targeted recruitment. With this approach, you determine the kind of person who is likely to want to fill the role and track them down. Start by looking at your current volunteers in the position to find out whether there are any common factors. Do they have similar passions and interests? Do they have similar backgrounds, qualifications, experiences or occupations? Do they come from similar groups? Did they all hear about the role in the same fashion? Common factors will enable you to identify populations that may be more likely to be receptive to being asked. But remember that *who* you currently have volunteering may be determined by *how* you have recruited in the past. If you want to attract volunteers from different backgrounds or with different interests, it may be that the recruitment methods that have worked for you previously will now be less appropriate.

A targeted recruitment campaign involves answering a series of questions.

What needs to be done?

It is important that you communicate to potential volunteers what roles your organisation needs to be done. All too often this important element is missed out in volunteer recruitment (chapter 4 outlines in detail the steps you should take to develop great volunteer roles). The key point here is to make sure your targeted volunteer recruitment ask is specific to the role required.

Who is the right person to do it?

It is easier to recruit the right person for the role if you have answered this question, because knowing whom you want to attract makes it easier to target your message to the needs of that particular group. When you send a message to the community in general, you often end up speaking to no one in particular.

Ask yourself whether there is a certain type of person who is being sought. In reaching this conclusion in a thoughtful way, you can then begin to target a recruitment campaign to each of these groups, with a slightly different message to each.

The advantage of sending a slightly different message to each group is that you have a better chance of speaking directly to that group's interests and requirements. For example, if you identify newcomers to town as a potential group of volunteers, you might stress roles in which they can meet new people. Your volunteer recruiting efforts could highlight efforts in which people work as teams. On the other hand, if you identify businesspeople as potential volunteers, you might stress roles that can be undertaken conveniently within a busy or unpredictable schedule, or even at home, and which have a fixed end point.

By examining and interviewing your current volunteer population, you should get a good start in developing a list of targets. But be careful not to assume that this list will represent all of the potential groups that might be interested in the role, especially if you are developing a new role and looking for a set of skills different from those of your existing volunteers or paid staff. Once you have developed a list of the characteristics of the volunteers who have enjoyed the role, start thinking about what other types of people are likely to have similar backgrounds or interests, and try to expand the list of potential targets before you begin analysing how to locate and approach each potential target group. You can now target your recruitment!

Where will you find them?

Once you have determined the type of person you are trying to recruit, you need to work out where to find them. By focusing in this way, you can ensure that your recruitment effort reaches those who are more likely to volunteer with you.

There are all sorts of places where you can find people, from professional associations to friendship groups. It all depends on whom you want to find and where they spend their time.

How should you go about communicating with them?

Once you have listed some locations where people can be found, the next step is to consider how you will communicate your recruitment message to them. If you have done a good job of figuring out where potential volunteers can be reached, developing an appropriate message should be relatively easy.

In general, the most effective methods of recruiting volunteers are those in which two-way communication is possible. Your existing volunteers are fantastic people to make the ask as they can explain why they enjoy the role. In some organisations, beneficiaries may also be effective in making this ask.

An effective volunteer recruitment effort might have volunteer recruiters in a variety of different groups in the community at large. Such a network, once established, enables you to use the most effective form of recruitment – face-to-face contact with someone you know – in a systematic and convenient way.

A good way of setting up such a system is to have staff, committee members and other volunteers think about people they know in the various community groups who might be willing to volunteer their time in this way. People volunteer when they are asked and because they want to. Helping people to see that they can do something they want to do is easiest when a two-way conversation can take place.

Recruiting through such methods is a more labour-intensive way of going about it than a one-way communication campaign. This will likely mean involving other people in the recruitment process, including existing volunteers. As such, managers of volunteers need to manage the recruiting effort, not do it all themselves.

What do they need?

It is important that your recruitment message speaks directly to the passions, availabilities, interests and needs of potential volunteers. It must appeal to the reason potential volunteers may want to fill the role. When you identify your target groups, you can then try to work out which reasons for volunteering might be most important to the individuals in a particular group (see chapter 1 for an exploration of why people volunteer). You can then send a message that speaks directly to those interests, availabilities, passions and needs.

What will you say to them?

The next major step is to develop an effective recruitment message. An effective recruitment message has four parts:

1. The need

The need usually refers to something that exists in the community, not something that exists inside the organisation. It should relate to your organisation's mission, as explored in chapter 2. By including a problem statement in the recruitment message, you show people how they can help to solve the problem and meet a need, rather than merely undertake some activities. Often, for volunteers involved in providing a direct service, the need will be that of the beneficiaries to be served.

The problem statement should naturally lead the potential volunteer to the conclusion that the organisation's work is important and worthwhile. Once you get a volunteer agreeing with this, recruitment is as easy as showing them that they could be the person to help deliver this work.

2. The role

Next you need to show the volunteer how they can help to solve the problem. In other words, now is the time to talk about what you want the volunteer to do. By describing these activities in the context of the need, you make your recruitment message more powerful.

When talking to a potential volunteer about a role, the recruiter should attempt to help the potential volunteer to see themselves doing the work. People only do what they can picture themselves doing, so you need to make your description of the role as vivid as possible. The picture you create should stress the positive elements of the role in order to encourage the person to volunteer, but it should also be honest. If a person volunteers on the basis of false information, you will only waste a lot of time in training and trying to motivate a person who probably will not last long in the role.

In addition to painting a picture of the work to be done, you should enable the volunteer to see themselves as part of that picture. When talking to potential volunteers, you should always talk about what 'they' will be doing, not about what 'a volunteer' will do.

3. Fears

For some situations, it will be desirable to address potential fears that a volunteer might have about the role. The best way to deal with such issues is to be straightforward, showing the volunteer that the organisation recognises their fears and then letting them know what steps you have already taken to help counter the problem.

Most volunteers are more afraid of the unknown than of any recognised risk. This means that potential problems are less likely to deter them from volunteering if they are addressed openly, and if the organisation seems to be responsible in dealing with them, such as by providing comprehensive training.

4. Benefits

In addition to talking about the need and the role and seeking to allay fears, the message should talk about how the experience will benefit the volunteer. This fourth part of the message, the benefits, helps people to see how they can help themselves by performing activities that help your organisation to serve the community.

To be as effective as possible, the recruitment message needs to show potential volunteers that whatever combination of needs they have can be met by your organisation. If the recruiter doesn't know the person they are trying to recruit, and if the circumstances allow, they should spend some time with that person to find out what kinds of benefits might appeal. This situation also provides the opportunity to identify some things the potential volunteer is concerned about and enjoys doing, and other clues to what it is they want to do.

If the recruiter learns what kinds of benefits are important to the volunteer, it is important that these be communicated to the manager of volunteers to ensure that the volunteer's needs are met, where possible. Information obtained from effective recruiting can also be used in successful volunteer retention.

How will they know what to do?

The last step in preparing for your recruitment effort is to train those who will be delivering the recruitment message. If you follow the principles described above, this is likely to mean training everyone involved with your organisation! Everybody knows potential volunteers; it's just a matter of getting them to think about asking people they know to get involved and of equipping them to make a coherent case for doing so. In general, training should cover the participant's role in the recruitment process and provide an adequate opportunity for them to practise their presentation of the recruitment message.

Top tips on writing a call for volunteers

Whatever the means of delivery, at some point you have to use words to invite people to volunteer. Here are some top tips for fitting lots of content into a short written message.

Catch attention with a good opening

The opening of your message should be interesting enough to entice the potential volunteer to continue reading or listening. The body of the message should be appealing enough to interest the potential volunteer in considering the volunteering opportunity or, at least, in contacting your organisation to get more information.

Present a complete picture

The body of the message should present information in an order that matches how people will think about the offer:

- **Need:** what is the problem to which this role responds?
- **Solution:** how can this role help to solve it?
- **Fears:** will I be capable of helping with it?
- **Benefits:** what's in it for me?
- **Contact:** how do I get involved?

As a general rule, dedicate more space to the problem than to logistics. People will first decide whether you're worth volunteering for and then decide whether they can fit you into their schedule. Sometimes you can't cover the whole picture, so in those cases selectively choose what you think your strengths might be. These could simply be interests that a prospective volunteer might have. In general, there are four different types of selling point that might be used: the cause, the solution, the type of work and the setting.

Make the message easy to understand

Recruitment messages must be easily understood. They must be intelligible and avoid jargon, unless it is included for a specific reason and will be understood by the intended reader. Messages should be examined for ease of comprehension by someone other than the author of the message. Remember: what can be misunderstood, will be!

Make the message inviting

You want those who read the message to find the idea of volunteering for your organisation appealing. Try to write the message in such a way that prospective volunteers can imagine themselves in the role. One small but significant way to make a message more inviting is to give the name of a person to be contacted, preferably including their first name, not just the name of the organisation. Volunteering is a personal decision and people like to talk with other people about it.

Test the message

The message should be tested on members of the target group at whom it is aimed, to make sure that it is understandable to them and communicates in a way that is likely to appeal to their interests. This testing doesn't need to involve high science – if your target volunteers are churchgoers aged 50 or over, ask some churchgoers aged 50 or over whom you know whether the message is clear. If your target volunteers are people aged 14–18, ask some people of that age, and so on.

Top tips on writing a convincing volunteer message

A really good example of a well-written volunteer message comes from the British Red Cross. This message targeted young people:

Why volunteer with us?

You're young. You're busy. You've got friends, school, family, work, sports, an online life and probably a hundred other commitments. So why spend your precious free time volunteering with the Red Cross?

You'll do great things

Volunteering with the Red Cross is about making a difference to the lives of vulnerable people in your community and around the world. Volunteers are the lifeblood of the British Red Cross. They save and change lives, raise vital funds, run our shops and personify the power of kindness. Without them, we simply would not be able to deliver our services, which help hundreds of thousands of people in crisis every year.

There are a range of time commitments

It's true that some of our voluntary roles – such as providing first aid at events – will involve some initial training and regular commitments, but we also have lots of opportunities for young people that take hardly any time to get started, such as fundraising, working in shops and community reserve volunteers.

In between are a range of roles that help people to live independently, orient themselves in a new country, combat loneliness and isolation and respond to local emergencies.

Perhaps you could be part of a Red Cross University Group, do a 12-week voluntary placement or volunteer for a 12-month placement in a European country?

It looks great on your CV

Employers are always impressed to see prospective employees actively involved in the world around them. The Red Cross is one of the most respected and best-known humanitarian charities in the world. Volunteering with us will make your CV or UCAS application stand out in a crowd.

Use the skills you have and learn new things

Everyone has skills and talents that can be used to help others.

If, for example, you are calm and reassuring, a great organiser, have digital skills or speak additional languages you can use these skills to help the Red Cross help people in need. Whether it's performing first aid, giving presentations, providing welfare at festivals or pricing merchandise, all of our voluntary opportunities give you the chance to develop new skills, have new experiences and gain confidence. You'll also get to see from the inside how charities work and whether you might like to make a career in the charity sector.

You can influence how we develop

We are committed to hearing young people's voices and have young volunteer representatives on panels for each of our services and on our national youth leadership team.

There are awards and accreditation to recognise your contribution

Of course you don't volunteer just to win an award, but we think it's important to recognise the amazing work our volunteers do. We also have our RED (Recognise, Empower and Develop) accreditation scheme, which tracks your development across a range of key skills.

5.3 CONCENTRIC CIRCLES RECRUITMENT

Concentric circles recruitment is an easy and efficient way to always have a flow of replacement volunteers applying to work at your organisation. It works through the simple theory that those people who are already connected to you and your organisation are the best targets for a recruitment campaign.

To visualise the theory of concentric circles, simply think of ripples in a pond when a rock is thrown in. Starting in the centre of contact, the ripples spread outward. Concentric circles recruitment is this in reverse – a flow of ripples into the centre which can draw people into your organisation.

To use the concentric circles theory, first attempt to locate a volunteer for the role by starting with the population groups which are already connected to you, and then work outwards. Former beneficiaries may be receptive to being asked, and likewise former volunteers, while existing volunteers may have friends or family who would be interested in getting involved. This approach will make it more likely that you'll get a positive response, because the group of potential volunteers with whom you will be talking will already be favourably disposed towards your organisation. Such techniques are simple, efficient and cost-effective.

A clear strength of the concentric circles method is that it concentrates on approaching those who may already have a good reason for helping out, either because they have received services themselves or because they have seen the impact of the services on others. They have already become convinced of the need for the services and of the ability of your organisation to assist those with that need; once that has happened, all that remains is to demonstrate to them that they are capable of helping in meeting that need.

A further strength of this approach is the personal testimony of the asking volunteer. During the conversation, the volunteer can say, either directly or indirectly, 'This is a good volunteer role with a good organisation. I know this because I volunteered there, and I think it is worth your time to volunteer there too.' This is a highly credible and persuasive argument that mass media techniques and appeals from complete strangers have a hard time equalling.

Ideal groups around which to structure your concentric circles recruitment include:

- current volunteers;
- friends and relatives of volunteers;
- beneficiaries;
- friends and relatives of beneficiaries;
- former beneficiaries and volunteers;
- staff;
- board members;
- money donors;
- people in the neighbourhood;
- people working in, or retired from, your field or subject.

In short, any population group that has already been favourably exposed to your organisation makes an excellent target for a concentric circles recruitment campaign. All you need to do to capitalise on this receptivity is to start a word-of-mouth recruitment campaign, and a constant trickle of potential volunteers should hopefully approach your organisation. Continually stress to all of these groups that they are essential to your recruitment campaign, and help them in getting to know the types of volunteer you are looking for and the ways in which they can assist in finding and recruiting these volunteers.

Top tips for moving from recruitment to partner engagement

A more sophisticated strategy for making sure that you have the right volunteers to draw upon comes from the concept of partner engagement. There are many possible ways to give the community a stake in the success of your organisation. One is to build a network of people who are interested in your organisation's work, people who can be called upon when their skills or energies are needed. One such strategy is described here. It requires hard work and management buy-in; however, once implemented, it tends to take on a life of its own. It is a linear approach, so the steps should be followed in order.

1. Host an annual event to engage the community as a partner

The exact nature of your event will vary, but the important thing is to establish a body of people who are interested and engaged in the work your organisation does. You could ask your paid staff or existing volunteers to invite their friends, family or colleagues. What you do at the event will depend on your organisation – it might involve opening up your facilities to the community, holding a gala, showing a film or many other things. Ask these people whether you can contact them again for their ideas, and make sure you have their contact information.

2. Make a second contact

Over the next few weeks, call people who expressed an interest to thank them for their interest and ask them for further input on how your organisation delivers its mission. During this call, ask them to tell you a bit more about themselves. Notice their interests and the things they really like to do. Although this will seem like a social conversation, you will be gathering information about what kinds of roles the volunteer would gladly do for your organisation.

3. Design volunteer roles

As described in chapter 6, match the needs of the organisation with the things the person will gladly do.

4. Make them an offer

Call them and mention that you have an opportunity. This could be a short-term or longer-term role. Describe the role and ask them whether this would be something that they would enjoy doing. Alternatively, you could ask the person who brought them to the annual event to make the offer.

5. Thank them for volunteering

Assuming that your offer is successful, say thank you. If the expression of thanks comes not only from you but also from senior managers or trustees, all the better.

6. Keep them connected

It is fundamentally important to build the volunteer's sense of being connected, of being part of the organisation. How you do this is up to you: it could be through a printed or emailed newsletter, a social media account, open days – whatever you think would work best (see section 13.3). The key is to make people feel like insiders, not like unconnected members of the community.

7. Make a second offer

If the volunteer took part in a short-term volunteering role, let a little time go by before making a second offer. How much time depends on the level of enthusiasm they seemed to have for the first experience. If the enthusiasm is high, the time could be as short as a couple of weeks. Then offer them a second opportunity to volunteer. Again, this should be a role which you think they would enjoy, and afterwards you should continue to try and keep them feeling connected.

8. Ask them to bring a friend to the next annual event

And the cycle continues.

Once you have done this for a couple of years, you will have an ever-expanding pool of ready volunteers. Over time, people will feel more and more comfortable about making larger commitments of time. And the community will indeed be a partner in helping your organisation to accomplish its mission.

5.4 AMBIENT RECRUITMENT

Ambient recruitment is a method that does not work for all groups, but it is a highly effective approach if you can find a way to tailor it to your target groups. An ambient recruitment campaign is designed for a 'closed system' – that is, a group of people who have a high existing sense of self-identification and connectedness. Examples of closed systems where ambient recruitment might work include:

- a school;
- a company;
- a profession;
- a faith group or congregation;
- a neighbourhood;
- a military base.

In short, ambient recruitment can be used in any situation where the members of a community view themselves as related to other members and view the values of the community as personally important and meaningful to themselves.

An ambient recruitment campaign seeks to create a culture of involvement among the members of a community, getting them to believe that volunteering is the 'thing to do'. This acceptance of volunteering as a value of the community then leads individual members to seek to fulfil that value by seeking to volunteer because 'it's the right thing to do'.

There are three steps to creating a successful ambient recruitment campaign:

1. **Develop a philosophy of involvement.** You first need to create a statement which explains why being involved is an important part of being a group member. This should outline the value of each group member being involved. Such a statement can take many forms, depending on your organisation's context.

2. **Provide early instruction on your organisation's value.** It is important to educate members about the importance of your organisation and the cause it seeks to serve. This is easiest done early in their membership of the group and is best done by engaging them in a discussion of your organisation's value and meaning. This discussion can be conducted best by others who are clearly identified as fellow members of the group, and it works particularly well if these individuals are opinion leaders within the group.

3. **Continually support involvement.** The final step in creating a system of ambient recruitment lies in building a support system. An effective ambient recruitment campaign gets members of the group to want to volunteer, but it does not tell them where or how to become involved. Rather, it allows potential volunteers to decide for themselves where and how they would like to become involved. Nonetheless, someone must still assist them with the logistics of finding a suitable volunteer assignment and must ensure that the volunteer role is one that will be personally rewarding to the volunteer. Someone must also ensure that volunteers enjoy and succeed in their work.

5.5   MAKING USE OF EVENTS TO ATTRACT VOLUNTEERS

Recruiting volunteers for a short-term event is a relatively commonplace and straightforward practice; lots of organisations engage individuals or groups in short-term volunteer roles. Turning these one-off events into sustained volunteer effort is a difficult, but not impossible, task. Your events can be used to attract volunteers to engage with you more regularly. Following are some tips for approaching this situation. While running and capitalising on events requires a planned and organised effort (see section 9.2), you should find it well worth the time.

Step one: create attractor events

An attractor event is designed to engage the attention and short-term involvement of large numbers of volunteers. It can be organised around a clean-up (of a park, a home or a garden, for example), around community education (such as a shopping centre exhibition or a corporate fair), a 'something-a-thon' fundraiser, or any other activity which meets the following requirements:

- it can involve large numbers of people in a variety of volunteer tasks and projects;
- the volunteer roles don't require any substantial training or preparation;
- the work is fun and exciting and allows people to work with others;
- the activity is photogenic, thus potentially attracting media attention.

The event itself should also accomplish something worthwhile so that participants know they have made a difference. In addition, the event should allow all those who participate (volunteers and the general public) to get an introduction to the cause, beneficiaries and operation of your organisation, with a particular emphasis on the contributions made by volunteers to the work of the organisation. This introduction can be provided via printed materials, demonstrations, photos, videos or whatever medium seems to work in your setting. The key is that current volunteers should be a prominent part of the event.

Step two: operate a scouting process

During the event, outgoing, approachable and friendly current volunteers should be assigned to work with groups of newcomers. Part of their assignment is to manage the work to be done during the event, but another part of their assignment involves explaining to potential new volunteers the benefits of engaging in longer-term volunteering.

Your existing volunteers should be encouraged to:

- establish personal contact with each of the new volunteers with whom they are working;
- give the newcomers a sense of being welcome and appreciated;
- get the names and addresses of those attending – with their permission so as to be compliant with GDPR (General Data Protection Regulation) – so that they can be thanked afterwards;
- ensure that each new volunteer gets some basic information about your organisation;
- champion and advocate about the role that volunteers play in delivering your organisation's mission.

Particular elements to look for in volunteers with a potential for further development are:

- people having a lot of fun;
- people who seem to like organising;
- people who show an interest in your cause;
- people who seem to have some personal connection to your cause.

Your existing volunteers should keep a note of those people they have asked to volunteer and/or those they think have the potential to become volunteers, and a debriefing should be held following the event. The debriefing should discuss who might be receptive to further involvement, what types of volunteer work they have shown an interest in, and the best way to encourage them further into your organisation – consider getting the same volunteers to re-contact them rather than someone they don't know.

5.6 RECRUITING FOR DIVERSITY

Colin Rochester and colleagues identify four important reasons why organisations should strive to ensure they are engaging a diverse group of volunteers:[1]

- **Equity:** by making every effort to be inclusive, organisations can ensure that they do not unwittingly discriminate against any group.
- **Effectiveness:** your organisation will benefit from being able to draw on the widest possible pool of skills, experiences and perspectives.
- **Representation**: it will benefit your organisation and its beneficiaries to reflect the community it serves in all its diversity.
- **Inclusion:** by being as inclusive as possible, organisations can play a part in fighting social exclusion.

Your volunteer recruitment process is one way in which your organisation can broaden its involvement in its community as well as contribute to combating discrimination more widely.

Doing this effectively goes beyond the volunteer recruitment process. It needs to be matched by wider adjustments in the organisation, including examination of staff recruitment practices, changes in the composition of the board, review of priorities in the mission and vision, and reassessment of deeper institutional factors and values. Some volunteers, such as young people or minorities who are already uncertain about their reception by the organisation, will be sensitive to any tell-tale behaviours that might make them feel as though your organisation is not for them, no matter what fine sentiments are set out in public statements.

Nonetheless, research has identified problems in volunteer recruitment affecting disabled people, cultural minorities, migrant populations and others outside the social and economic mainstream.

The *Helping Out* survey of volunteers in England and Wales found that:[2]

- There were some significant differences in the reasons for not volunteering given by respondents according to age, sex and whether they were at risk of social exclusion. For example, while time was the most significant reason for not volunteering for all groups, it was most likely to be identified by younger people and by those not at risk of social exclusion. Not knowing how to get involved was also more of an issue for younger people than it was for older people.

- Older people were more concerned about being too old or ill/disabled, and this was also true for people from at-risk groups compared with those from not-at-risk groups (unsurprisingly, since at-risk groups include people with a limiting, long-term illness or disability). Those from at-risk groups were also more likely to be concerned about threats to safety, being out of pocket and fitting in with others when compared with respondents not at risk.

- Differences in the reasons cited for not volunteering were associated with ethnicity. For example, Black and Asian people were the ethnic groups most likely to identify concerns about not fitting in as a reason for not volunteering. Asian people were the group most likely to identify being worried about being out of pocket and about safety concerns as reasons for not volunteering.

An Institute for Volunteering Research survey in the UK uncovered the following potential barriers to volunteer involvement perceived by populations commonly excluded from volunteering:[3]

- Lack of confidence was a key barrier, exacerbated for individuals who had experienced exclusion in other areas of life, and when volunteering took place in unfamiliar environments.

- Other people's attitudes created barriers. The perception (rightly or wrongly) that organisations would not welcome them put some people off volunteering; this was particularly true among ex-offenders. Prejudices and stereotypes held by staff, other volunteers and beneficiaries put some people off staying involved.

- A fear of losing welfare benefits was a significant barrier to volunteering.

- Over-formal recruitment and selection procedures were off-putting to some people, particularly for those whose first language was not English, for people with visual impairments and for people with low levels of literacy.

- Delays in the recruitment process were particularly discouraging – it was apparent that, without a prompt response, some potential volunteers would simply walk away.

- A physically inaccessible environment created an obvious barrier, particularly for disabled people with mobility-related impairments.
- The failure of organisations to fully reimburse out-of-pocket expenses meant that some people could not afford to volunteer. This was particularly problematic among disabled people and ex-offenders, who were often unemployed or on a low wage.

The Institute for Volunteering Research study noted that solving these potential barriers is not impossible. By ensuring that recruitment processes were user friendly – for example, by minimising form-filling and asking new recruits to come in for a chat rather than an interview – some organisations had successfully made the volunteering experience seem less daunting.

The GoldStar Programme, a Cabinet Office scheme (2007–2008) that sought to encourage organisations to recruit more volunteers from minority groups – such as ethnic minorities, asylum seekers and unemployed people – proposed seven critical factors for achieving greater diversity:

- **Positive action:** targeting under-represented groups is fundamental to developing an inclusive volunteering programme. First, you need to understand who in your community is under-represented. Next, you need to ask what types of activity they might want to get involved in and how you can best recruit them. This may require you to change which types of recruitment method you use.
- **Recruitment:** advertise widely and be clear about what role you want to fulfil, rather than simply advertising for volunteers. People from under-represented groups may not see volunteering as something for them, but they may be interested when a particular role is specified.
- **Matching:** it is important that you understand the needs and motivations of volunteers and ensure that these are met through the volunteer role offered. While you must always ensure that any new roles contribute to delivering on your mission, you can also consider creating roles to fit volunteers' abilities and interests, as explored further in chapter 6.
- **Progression:** make it clear from the start how volunteers can progress, either into paid employment or by learning new skills and developing in your organisation. Regular reviews, supporting volunteers to try new things and helping them to find what they enjoy most can ensure progression opportunities are available and are taken up.
- **Training:** both at induction and on an ongoing basis, you should provide training which is sensitive to individuals' requirements. Ensure that your venues and materials are accessible for all, and consider integrating training with social events. Where applicable, consider providing accredited training so that volunteers can gain formal recognition of what they have learned.

- **Support and supervision:** all volunteers, but particularly those from excluded groups, appreciate friendly, efficient and effective support. This should include regular, clear communication as well as efforts to ensure that all volunteers feel included in and central to your organisation's work.
- **Recognition:** you should ensure that you thank your volunteers, of course, but it is also important to recognise their value by involving them in decision-making throughout your organisation. This should be reflected in your policies and procedures, so it is clear to both paid staff and volunteers that both have a role in ongoing planning.

In some ways, these proposals can be seen as key elements in any good volunteer management practice. However, having considered them, you may need to review the five forms of recruitment we have discussed in this chapter to assess to what extent each of them would encourage people from often excluded groups to join you. A particular issue is likely to be how far each method takes you into different social networks.

When considering diversity, it is important to note that when we talk about volunteering we are referring to formal volunteering – that is, time given through an organisation. There are other forms of volunteering which are more informal in nature, such as self-help, advocacy, campaigning and good neighbourliness. Many groups or people not engaged in formal volunteering may still give their time in these less formal ways. It is therefore important not to assume that they don't volunteer at all and to recognise that they may actually be very active in ways that don't fit a more mainstream concept of volunteering. Assuming that people don't do any volunteering because they don't volunteer with you or other organisations is more discriminatory than having inaccessible paperwork or websites. It is a good idea to understand the ways the groups you want to reach may already be giving their time and to investigate how to adapt your processes to support them to volunteer with your organisation.

5.7   BEING FLEXIBLE IN YOUR RECRUITMENT

You have more chance of success in your efforts to recruit volunteers if you remain as flexible and responsive as is practical. Variations in what you had planned may be necessary where difficulties are encountered in finding adequate numbers of volunteers. There are a number of ways in which you can be flexible.

Allow people to double up

One way to approach difficult recruitment is to break the volunteer role down so it can be done by not just one person, but several. If the difficulty is that the activities are too extensive for a single individual, then the obvious solution is to make them the responsibility of more than one person.

One way of achieving this is team volunteering – the classic role-sharing approach to the situation. Make the volunteer unit a partnership, with two people equally sharing the role, or make the role one filled by a lead volunteer who is given an assistant.

The team can split up the time and work requirements. This approach is especially useful when you are attempting to encourage a volunteer who has particular expertise but is reluctant to volunteer because they don't feel as if they have the time necessary to do all of the work.

While the word 'team' is used to describe this type of role-sharing relationship, it is worth noting that the team should not include more than two people. Role-sharing with three or more people is nearly impossible to accomplish without a huge amount of effort and work, though some organisations have introduced family volunteering (see section 9.2).

Group volunteering

Another way to allow people to double up is to recruit an entire group as the volunteer unit. The group might consist of a club or business. The advantages of group volunteering are various – a group can subdivide the work involved in, for example, running an event. Or they may rotate the leadership to lessen the time burden on any single member and safeguard against burnout. Furthermore, a volunteer group's commitment levels may be higher.

Start the process by recruiting one member of the group who will draw in the others to become involved, making the volunteer role their project. Management of these volunteer clusters may depend upon your focus on this person or other colleagues, as we discuss in chapter 9 (see particularly section 9.2).

Ease people in

People may be reluctant to commit to volunteering if they feel it will be too onerous a commitment or one which they will not be able to be successful in. This may lead volunteers to fear that they won't be able to fill the role well enough. As a result, they may be hesitant to take the role on for fear of letting the organisation down.

These difficulties can be dealt with by introducing the volunteer to the role gradually rather than expecting them to buy into the whole package at once. There are a couple of ways to let a volunteer become accustomed to a more difficult role.

One approach is to offer potential volunteers a short trial period. Invite them to try the role and see whether they like it enough to keep going. This is a great approach because it simultaneously allows the volunteers to see whether they like the role, and the staff to see whether they like the volunteer, as we discuss in chapter 13 (see particularly sections 13.2 and 13.3).

Schedule a review meeting for a month or two after the volunteer starts the role and stress that the volunteer is under no expectation to continue the role after the test period – a no-fault divorce clause. While you will lose some volunteers, you will gain quite a few who have had the opportunity to examine the role without pressure, learned that they liked the work, and decided that investing their time and energy is worth it.

Another approach is to make the volunteer an aide or apprentice to an existing volunteer in that role. Apprenticeships work exceptionally well for leadership roles or roles with large amounts of responsibility that people are reluctant to take on because they don't feel totally comfortable that they will be able to do the work well.

A variation on the apprenticeship approach is the mentor or buddy system. In these cases, the assisting (experienced) volunteer does not supervise the new volunteer directly but serves to provide advice as requested or needed, and often will operate as a coach to the newcomer.

5.8 PRACTICAL POINTERS

- There are a lot of possible ways for an organisation to engage in volunteer recruitment:
  - A **warm-body** campaign is good for when you need a large number of volunteers for an event, or when you are just beginning a programme and need to attract community attention.
  - A **targeted** recruitment campaign is good for finding individuals with specific talents or interests.
  - A **concentric circles** campaign is good for maintaining a steady flow of replacement volunteers.
  - An **ambient** recruitment campaign creates a culture of volunteering within a group.
  - Recruitment **events** allow you to access a number of people in one go, while also creating a buzz around your organisation.
- Each type of campaign can successfully recruit volunteers; the trick is to select the campaign that will obtain the right types of volunteer with the least amount of effort. If you're just beginning within a community, then often you must rely on a warm-body campaign, and then carefully sift through those who approach you. As your programme matures, you will find yourself making more use of targeted and concentric circles recruitment.

- Remember, recruitment doesn't stop once you've identified the volunteer. Indeed, the recruitment process is still in full swing during the initial interviewing of the potential volunteer and it continues throughout the volunteer's future relationship with the organisation. Every morning that volunteers wake up, they are free to decide to stop volunteering. This means that recruitment is an ongoing process, which continues for as long as you need the volunteer.
- Finally, remember that successful volunteer recruitment requires that volunteers never be taken for granted. They are the best champions of volunteering for your organisation, and happy volunteers will champion your organisation to others and use their personal networks to bring others in.

6 Matching volunteers to roles

Once you begin to recruit volunteers, you need to ensure that the right people are undertaking the right roles. This assists your organisation because you get to benefit from the skills and experience volunteers bring, and it means your volunteers will be undertaking roles in which they feel comfortable and useful. In this chapter, we outline how this can be achieved through conducting interviews appropriate to the role in question and using these to assess how prospective volunteers can contribute to your organisation's mission.

Maybe the most crucial distinction between interviewing for paid staff and interviewing for volunteers is that the latter involves evaluating a person for *a* role, not for *the* role. Effective volunteer interviewing does not so much consist of examining an applicant's suitability for one role as it does evaluating the ability and desire of that applicant to productively fit into some position within the organisation. Employment interviewing focuses on the question 'Who can do this role?' while volunteer interviewing should focus on the more creative questions 'Who will want to do this role?' and 'What can this person contribute to accomplishing our mission?'.

6.1 WHY INTERVIEW POTENTIAL VOLUNTEERS?

There are a wide variety of approaches you can take to interviewing potential volunteers. The nature of the interviews you conduct will vary depending on your organisation and the work it undertakes. Nonetheless, whether your interviews consist of simply a brief chat or a more formal structured dialogue, the main purpose remains the same. For all prospective volunteers for all volunteer roles, there are two purposes of conducting interviews.

Purpose one: identifying a fit

Identifying a fit includes determining the interests and abilities of the potential volunteers, determining their suitability for particular roles, and assessing their 'rightness' for your organisation, its style of operation and its mission. An examination of proper fit would include determining the following items regarding the applicant:

- To what extent does the applicant have both an interest in a particular role and the necessary qualifications, experience and expertise to perform it?

- To what extent does the applicant have other interests and abilities that might be used to create a different role for them?
- To what extent is there a sense of 'rightness' about how well the applicant will work in a particular role environment?

'Rightness' refer to the likelihood that the applicant will fit comfortably into your organisation's working environment. In many cases, this will be the key predictive factor for success. Rightness could involve matters of style (relaxed, frenetic), personality (neat, messy; introverted, extroverted), political philosophy (traditionalist, radical) or other factors (such as their personal or professional values). These will affect how the volunteer will get along with your beneficiaries, other volunteers, the organisation in general and the particular staff group to which each volunteer is assigned.

As such, identifying these aspects early will save you lots of effort further down the line. Very often these interpersonal relationship factors become more important than factors of technical qualification, which can be learned if the volunteer is willing to stay with the organisation. Quite simply, a volunteer who is happy in their working environment will deliver; one who is unhappy will not.

Purpose two: completing the recruitment

Completing the recruitment includes answering any questions or concerns that the potential volunteer has. It also involves letting the applicant know that they have the ability to contribute to your organisation and its clientele and that they will derive personal satisfaction from helping.

During the interview, it is crucial to remember that the applicant has not yet been recruited. At this stage they have only been attracted to your organisation. One purpose of the interview is to give the applicant the time to make a more deliberate examination of what your organisation has to offer; at the same time, you get a chance to 'sell' your organisation and its work to the applicant. Equal time has to be given to focusing on why a particular role is important and interesting, and discussing whether the applicant would be right for that role. It is likely that the interview will be your first contact with the applicant, and therefore it is important that the applicant should feel welcomed and wanted during the interview process.

Determining the correct role for a potential volunteer involves questions about qualifications, experience, expertise and temperament. Volunteers must certainly be capable of doing or learning to do the role for which they are selected. But it is equally important that they fit into the work situation for which they are being considered. This means that volunteers must be satisfied with the role being offered, and view the role as desirable and fulfilling. It also means that the work setting (including the timing and site of the role) must be amenable to each volunteer. And, finally, it means that the volunteer must be comfortable with the paid staff and volunteers with whom they will work.

Given the importance of a whole range of contextual factors in determining whether a volunteer will flourish in a particular role, it may be sensible to offer new volunteers a trial period appropriate to their role (see section 5.7). At the end of this period – the length of which will be different for different roles and different types of involvement – you may conduct a review in which both your organisation and the volunteer evaluate whether the volunteering is likely to be successful. During this discussion, either party may request a change of assignment, based upon their additional knowledge of the situation (see section 13.4).

This initial testing period will make it easier to induce prospective volunteers to try out roles about which they are uncertain and will make it more likely that any problems of mismatching will be identified early and corrected quickly.

6.2 INTERVIEWING POTENTIAL VOLUNTEERS

In the majority of situations, a fairly basic interview with prospective volunteers is likely to be sufficient for your organisation's needs. It is nonetheless important to get this basic interview right, as this is your first interaction with your volunteers and therefore your first opportunity to show them how your organisation operates and what it seeks to achieve. There are a number of factors you need to consider.

Picking an interviewer

The staff with responsibility for day-to-day oversight of the role the potential volunteer would be performing must have some involvement in the interviewing process, either helping to draft questions or being involved with the interview itself. If possible, it is best practice to always have two or more interviewers, to bring different perspectives to the interview process.

It is important that the interviewers are able to give a good impression and are capable of making a satisfactory judgement about potential volunteers' fit with your organisation and the skills and passion they can bring. It goes without saying that your interviewers should be personable and friendly, but there are also a number of other desirable abilities:

- knowledge of and commitment to the organisation and its programmes;
- recognition of and commitment to the value of volunteering;
- knowledge of the paid staff;
- ability to relate to the people being interviewed;

- ability to talk easily with strangers;
- ability to listen attentively to what is said and be able to discern the meaning of what is not said;
- ability to ask follow-up questions;
- ability to recruit and motivate while interviewing;
- ability to empathise with other people;
- ability to say 'no' kindly.

If this sounds like a role for a superhuman, it does not need to be! Many of these abilities are ones we all have and use on a day-to-day basis. While conducting their first interview is daunting for anyone, it soon becomes second nature.

Remember that volunteers often make better interviewers than paid staff, as they tend to be better able to build rapport with potential volunteers – after all, they have something important in common (they both thought the organisation was worth donating their time to). The very fact that they think so highly of the organisation that they are willing to interview potential volunteers to work there speaks for itself. They are also likely to be sensitive to the concerns of new volunteers and be able to allay any concerns that prospective volunteers might have.

The interview site

It is important to choose an appropriate site for your interviews so that potential volunteers feel comfortable discussing their abilities and concerns in an open forum. In particular, it is important to ensure that the site you use is accessible, has a friendly atmosphere and is sufficiently private for personal information to be shared without being overhead.

The site for conducting the interview will vary depending on the circumstances of your organisation and how formal an interview you wish to conduct, but it is important during the interview that the applicant feels a sense of privacy and comfort. Do not conduct the interview in a public place or in a shared office, since this will deter many people from offering complete information about their backgrounds and their interests.

Find a location where the interview is unlikely to be interrupted. Besides disrupting the flow of the interview, interruptions give the impression to applicants that they are of lesser importance than your other work. Additionally, remember to turn your phone off!

Remember the old adage: you never get a second chance to make a first impression. What potential volunteers see and feel during the interview may shape their eventual attitude towards your organisation.

Some programmes are simply not in a position to conduct interviews in person. This is not a common situation, but it can make the recruitment process less personal and inhibit both the ability of the organisation to evaluate the applicant and the ability of the applicant to assess the organisation, even if you use video-calling facilities. However, when the reasons are explained to prospective volunteers and the interview is conducted in a straightforward way, this should not inhibit you in forming a rapport with the prospective volunteer.

Pre-interview preparation

The preparation you do prior to conducting an interview will depend on the nature of the interview and the nature of the volunteering opportunities that you have at your organisation. It is worth considering having the following items prepared and ready before the interview:

- It is a good idea to have a **list of possible volunteer roles** with descriptions of the work and skills required. Even if you are recruiting for a specific role, it is a good idea to have alternative options available for prospective volunteers who do not suit the role you are recruiting for.
- A **list of questions** to be asked in relation to each role.
- It may be appropriate to have an **application form** completed by the potential volunteers with background information about them and their interests, although for some less formal roles this may not be necessary. Nonetheless, it is always a good idea to take details of each person's name, how they found out about the role and their contact number. Even with this small amount of information, you can demonstrate that you take their time seriously.
- **Information and materials** on your organisation and its programmes.

This preparation is vital to the success of the interview. A successful volunteer interview is quite different from simply having a pleasant conversation – it has a clear purpose and a plan of how to achieve this.

Opening the interview

The beginning of the interview should focus on:

- **Making the applicants feel welcome:** express appreciation for their coming to meet you.
- **Building rapport:** explain what you would like to accomplish and how they fit into the process. Let them know that their decision about whether volunteering with you would be suitable is the focus of the discussion. Let them feel in charge.

- **Providing information:** give them background information about your organisation and its work and the role of volunteers in delivering its mission. Ask them what questions they have about your organisation and its purpose and programmes.
- **Putting them first:** ask them about their concerns and issues before concentrating on your own.

The key to beginning a successful interview is to start building rapport with the potential volunteer. It is crucial that the interview process belongs as much to the applicant as it does to the organisation. If there is a time limit for the interview, make sure that you have allocated sufficient time for the applicant to express concerns and ask questions. The interview should be a mutual, not unilateral, information exchange process. It is a negotiation, not an interrogation. Make sure that you explain to each potential volunteer at the beginning of the interview that they should feel free to ask questions and express any concerns at any point during the discussion.

Conducting the interview

The major portion of the interview should be devoted to the following points:

- **Exploration of the applicants' interests, abilities and personal situation:** determine why the applicants are considering volunteering and what types of work environment they prefer.
- **Discussion of various role possibilities:** explain the purposes and work situations of the different volunteer opportunities available and let the applicants consider them. Use this as an opportunity to let the potential volunteers discuss how they would approach various roles, which will tell you more about their attitudes, their intentions and their level of interest.
- **Discussion of your requirements:** examples include time expectations, training requirements, paperwork and confidentiality rules. Let the potential volunteers know what will be expected of them.

Remember that you are still recruiting the volunteer at this stage, so do not forget to explain why each role is important to the interests of your organisation and its beneficiaries.

One skill that it is important to possess during the interview is the ability to detect an unexpected talent in the applicant and begin to construct a possible volunteer role for them on the spot. This requires a good understanding of your organisation and its programmes. If you have volunteers conducting interviews, make sure that they have a good background knowledge about the organisation and how its work is organised.

While interviewing, you will be analysing the prospective volunteer to assess whether they are likely to be a good fit for your organisation. You will likely be weighing up a number of different qualities, and the particular things you are looking for will vary from organisation to organisation and from role to role.

Closing the interview

There are a number of different ways in which you can conclude an interview. It may be appropriate to offer the role to the prospective volunteer, subject to taking up references. Or you may have to politely explain that you do not have any suitable roles for them either at this time or in the future (see section 6.3).

There may be situations under current immigration or visa regulations where you realise an applicant who has come from another country is not permitted to volunteer or may require special documentation to do so, such as a visa. In such cases, be clear about what information you will gather and how you will respond to it.

If you and the interviewee both decide that they are suitable to join you as a volunteer, you will need to explain to them what happens next. Depending on your organisation, this may involve:

- making background or reference checks, including when necessary obtaining criminal record checks (see section 6.4);
- arranging a second interview or chat with the specific staff member(s) they will be volunteering with;
- scheduling an induction or training programme;
- arranging a period of limited involvement while references and checks are carried out.

You will need to get the volunteer's permission for references or background checks to be conducted.

For all of these, it is important to explain the process, the time frame and what is expected from the volunteer at each stage.

6.3   TURNING AWAY POTENTIAL VOLUNTEERS

The intention of volunteer interviewing is, naturally, to find a useful and enjoyable role for the interested person. This, however, is not always possible. One of the key responsibilities of an interviewer of volunteers is to identify those cases in which the applicant in question should not be asked to work with the organisation.

There are a number of reasons why such a rejection may be necessary. For example:

- there may be no suitable role for the applicant within the organisation;
- the applicant may have expectations that the organisation cannot meet;
- the organisation and the applicant may not have congruent philosophies – for example, a prospective volunteer for a community-based charity may turn out to be staunchly anti-immigration;
- the applicant may refuse to agree to the organisation's requirements (background checks, time schedules or training requirements, for example).

In each of these cases, rejection should be automatic and is in the best interests of the organisation and the applicant. Rejection, however, may also occur simply because the interviewer makes a judgement that the person should not be accepted for the role, based on responses to questions during the interview about their skills and interests, and on the qualifications, experience and/or expertise that the interviewer knows are required for a particular type of work.

Do not be unsettled when this happens, even if you cannot absolutely define why you are getting a negative feeling about the applicant; go with your instincts, which, after all, you have been developing for most of your life. If you're unsure and are concerned that you may be biased for whatever reason, you might have another person conduct a second interview of the applicant and compare their opinion with yours. As long as you have conducted the interview based on questions that truly explore the fitness and capability of the applicant to perform the work required by a particular role, then you should be comfortable with your assessment of that person, even if you find it testing to describe the nature or cause of your unease.

You might soften the rejection decision by referring the applicant to another organisation for which you believe they would be more suitable or by offering an alternative role within your organisation. You might even, in some cases, accept the applicant on a trial period, but you should be aware that this may simply postpone the inevitable. 'Firing' the applicant down the road (see section 12.4) would be much more traumatic than not making the initial acceptance.

While saying 'no' to another person who wants to help is never a pleasant feeling, try to remember that your primary obligation is to the safety and well-being of your beneficiaries, as well as paid staff and other volunteers.

6.4 FINALISING THE MATCHING PROCESS

Once you and the prospective volunteer have agreed that they intend to volunteer with your organisation, there are a few further steps that you may need to undertake. In general, when someone has agreed to volunteer with you, they will have a desire to begin work quickly. Therefore, you should work hard to smooth and shorten the process for the intake of volunteers.

It is essential to make sure that your systems for screening work efficiently and that, if they do take longer than expected, volunteers are kept informed of what is happening and why the system is taking so long.

Where you have complex systems for screening or potentially long processes for checking records, you should maintain contact with prospective volunteers. While applications are being processed, you may be able to develop ways for involving volunteers on a limited basis (e.g. as observers or trainees) or in tasks which don't involve contact with your beneficiaries.

Reference checks

It may be necessary to conduct a check of potential volunteers' credentials, and you must notify them and obtain their permission for taking up references. What you need to check will depend on the nature and scope of the volunteer role and the beneficiaries.

Note that not all types of references will need to be checked for each volunteer role, and for some roles no references need to be checked at all. For some roles, it may be sufficient to confirm the volunteer's identity; for other roles, you will also need confirmation of their history of employment and volunteering. For still others, you may wish to ask referees about the applicant's suitability for a particular role or their ability to work in certain situations. You should aim to only ask questions that you need to have answered, rather than asking lots of questions on the off-chance that something relevant comes up. Two or three clear and relevant questions will usually be sufficient.

Note that reference checks are not the same as criminal record checks, as covered in the next section. The purpose of obtaining references is to enable you to get a fuller picture of the character and skills of the person in question.

Criminal record checks

For certain volunteer roles, in particular those where volunteers work with children and/or vulnerable adults, it may be necessary to obtain a criminal record check. This is provided by the Disclosure and Barring Service (DBS) in England and Wales, AccessNI in Northern Ireland and Disclosure Scotland in Scotland. Other countries have their own equivalent services (with various names) too. Criminal record checks search police records and other information to let organisations know whether a person has any spent or unspent criminal convictions or has been placed on any barred list which would prevent them from being able to work with children or vulnerable people.

Only organisations that are registered are able to obtain criminal record checks, and it is only possible for organisations to register if they conduct 100 or more criminal record checks a year. This precludes a lot of smaller voluntary organisations from being registered, and if yours is one of these organisations you will need to access criminal record checks through an umbrella body. These vary depending on your type of organisation, but they include sports national governing bodies, church dioceses, councils for voluntary service, volunteer centres and many other types of larger organisation. While criminal record checks for volunteers are often free, umbrella bodies often charge a small administration fee for carrying out a criminal record check.

It is essential to only carry out criminal record checks when they are necessary. The organisations which provide the checks offer guidance on what roles should have a criminal record check undertaken – in general, those which involve regular contact with children and/or vulnerable adults. Many umbrella bodies also offer guidance specific to particular types of organisation. In general, when prospective volunteers appreciate that the role they will undertake involves regular contact with children and/or vulnerable people, they will be happy to have a criminal record check conducted. However, prospective volunteers may be less happy when it seems that these checks are being undertaken in situations where they are not necessary. Therefore, it is important that you carefully consider which roles need criminal record checks and which do not. Carrying out unnecessary checks wastes resources and time – and may be illegal – and create a needless barrier to volunteering.

You also need to be clear that carrying out criminal record checks is not in and of itself sufficient to safeguard children and vulnerable adults from potential harm. They should not replace other methods of safeguarding. You should avoid complacency in assuming that just because a volunteer has a clean DBS check, you do not also need to take further steps to safeguard those you seek to help.

Volunteer agreements

You may wish to consider initiating a process of entering into an agreement with volunteers once the interviewing and matching process has been satisfactorily concluded. A volunteer agreement is not a formal legal document but constitutes an acceptance by both the organisation and the volunteer of a list of the mutual intentions they are entering into. The agreement might specify the work that the volunteer is agreeing to perform, the time frame, and the benefits and support that the organisation agrees to provide the volunteer.

The purpose of the volunteer agreement is to emphasise the seriousness of both the organisation and the volunteer in entering into a relationship. It is not intended to convey a sense of legal responsibility or obligation.

6.5 **PRACTICAL POINTERS**

- It is important to interview potential volunteers for several reasons: to assess their suitability for volunteering in your organisation, to explore what skills and experience they can offer, and to allow prospective volunteers to appraise whether they will fit into your organisation and be able to make the contribution they are imagining.

- Think about who is best placed to interview prospective volunteers, where to conduct the interview and what questions you wish to ask. An excellent way to do this is to consult paid staff and existing volunteers to see what they would like to know about prospective volunteers and what they think people interested in volunteering with your organisation ought to be told.

- Don't be afraid to gently turn away would-be volunteers if you don't think they would be a good fit for your organisation. While it might be an uncomfortable conversation to have, it is easier to have it now than to attempt to explain to someone who has volunteered with you for a few months that it isn't working.

- Once someone has agreed to volunteer with you, get them started as quickly as possible. If there are things that need to be done before they can begin volunteering – such as DBS checks – inform the volunteer of the purpose of these stages and keep them updated with progress so that they stay enthused.

7 Preparing volunteers for success

Now that you have defined roles for volunteers in your organisation, completed your recruitment and matched people to appropriate roles, the last step before they begin is to offer them orientation and training. Again, there is no one right approach, and the orientation and training needs will depend on your organisation and the role being undertaken. It is, however, fundamental that all volunteers are given the induction they need to feel comfortable and the training they need to fulfil their role competently. This preparation falls into two key parts:

- **orientation and initial training:** the process of preparing the volunteer for a clear relationship with your organisation (otherwise known as induction);
- **ongoing training:** the process of preparing the volunteer to perform work for your organisation.

All volunteers should know that they will be required to attend an orientation and/or training session. Orientation may be distinguished from training in that it is usually more general in nature, providing information every volunteer should know. Training is designed to equip volunteers with skills and knowledge required by their specific roles.

It is important that new volunteers feel prepared and able to undertake the role in your organisation to which they have been assigned. In order to achieve this, you will need to provide them with answers to three key questions:

1. Why should I be working here?
2. What will my work here consist of?
3. Where do I fit in with everyone else?

These three questions are crucial if the volunteer is to feel comfortable. A volunteer who does not feel right about these three aspects of volunteering will struggle to feel a part of your organisation. Many organisations experience high levels of early turnover, and this is often due to the absence of a good orientation. Orientation should seal the deal between your organisation and the volunteer, clearly establishing the intellectual, practical and emotional bonds between the two.

This chapter considers what an orientation process should entail and how this will help volunteers to integrate into your organisation; how to meet the training needs of your volunteers, both when they begin volunteering and throughout their time with you; and the provision of training as a 'benefit' to prospective volunteers.

7.1   ORIENTATION

Even if volunteers come to you with all the skills necessary to carry out their role, they will need some orientation to your organisation. Orientation is the process of helping volunteers to understand and feel comfortable with the workings of your organisation. It is designed to provide them with background and practical knowledge of your organisation and to let them understand how they can contribute to the organisation's purpose. If volunteers better understand your organisation's systems, operations and procedures, they will be able to contribute more productively.

Some organisations avoid giving an orientation because of difficulty in getting volunteers to attend. This problem can be solved by a variety of approaches. It might require altering the scheduling of orientations, holding them at weekends or during the evening. It might involve altering the format of orientations, doing them one on one, in small groups, online or in several shorter sessions. It may require making attendance mandatory, even if that means losing some potential volunteers. Make whatever adjustments are necessary and ensure that all new volunteers receive a proper orientation.

Even volunteers participating in one-day events should receive a short orientation focusing on the cause and giving a brief description of your organisation. This will remind them of why they are engaged and open the door to further involvement. And, of course, whoever is managing the work area of volunteers at such an event should provide a social orientation by ensuring that volunteers get to meet and interact with other volunteers. It never hurts if appropriate food is served as well!

Perhaps the best way of understanding the importance of orientation is simply to consider its basic definition. 'Orientation' is the process of learning one's direction and bearings in the world; a person without orientation is, to put it simply, lost.

If your organisation has a volunteer agreement (see section 6.4), this is the place to confirm the contents of the orientation with the volunteer, and discuss and highlight key elements. If you do not have a volunteer agreement, this can be done verbally on a more or less formal basis depending on the nature of your organisation.

To answer the three questions outlined in the introduction to this chapter, there are three main areas that should be covered during the orientation process: the cause, the systems for volunteer management and the social environment of the volunteers. There is no one correct approach to running a volunteer orientation. For some roles, a quick tour of the building and introductions to key staff will suffice. For others, inductions can last a whole day or longer.

Cause orientation

This involves introducing the volunteers to the purpose of your organisation. It should cover a description of:

- the mission and values of your organisation and the importance of volunteers in delivering these, as explored in chapters 2 and 8;
- your organisation's beneficiaries;
- the history of your organisation;
- the programmes and services of your organisation;
- other groups working in the same field, and your organisation's distinguishing characteristics from those others;
- the future plans of your organisation.

The presentation of these items should ideally take the form of a discussion, to allow volunteers to begin to learn and adopt the basic values of your organisation. The goal of this discussion is to allow the volunteers to make a practical and emotional commitment to the basic purpose of your organisation, and to consciously decide that they believe in and are willing to work towards achieving the mission of your organisation. The discussion should make the volunteers feel like they are a key part of delivering the organisation's mission. It should also be designed to give the volunteers sufficient background to explain your organisation if they are ever asked to do so.

This discussion will also give the manager of volunteers an opportunity to learn about each volunteer – this is crucial information in enabling them to understand how each volunteer can best be managed.

System orientation

This section of the orientation introduces the volunteers to the system of volunteer management within your organisation. It is likely to include presentation and discussion of:

- the structure and programmes of your organisation, with illustrations of what volunteers contribute to those programmes;
- the system of volunteer involvement within your organisation: policies and procedures relating to both volunteering and, where appropriate, the wider organisation, as explored in chapter 8;

- an introduction to the person in your organisation to whom volunteers can turn with questions and problems;
- an introduction to facilities and equipment;
- a description of volunteer requirements and benefits;
- an introduction to record-keeping requirements (e.g. how to log hours);
- a description of the timelines of your organisation's activities and key events.

The simplest way to develop the agenda for this portion of the orientation session is to ask, 'What would I like to know about this place in order to better understand how it works?'

The purpose of this portion of the orientation session is to provide an organisational context for the volunteers and help them to understand how they fit into the processes of your organisation. This material is often presented in a factual way, with charts and descriptive handouts, followed by a question and answer period to clarify issues. It can be made more interesting by having different representatives, both paid and volunteer, describe varying aspects of the work of your organisation. This part of the orientation session allows the volunteers to see how the role that they will be playing relates to the work of your organisation. It shows them the basic requirements of that role and how it links to other areas of your organisation.

Remember that friends will ask the volunteers about their volunteer work and about your organisation. A volunteer who fully understands your organisation can serve as an effective communicator with the public about its worth, while a confused volunteer can present quite the opposite picture.

Social orientation

This section of the orientation introduces the volunteers to the social community that they are being asked to join and begins to forge the personal bonds that will sustain volunteer involvement.

Included in this are:

- an introduction to the leadership of your organisation (who might participate in the orientation by presenting or leading part of the discussion on the mission);
- a welcome by staff and current volunteers (through their participation in presenting subject areas or even as a purely social occasion);
- a description of the culture and etiquette of your organisation (matters such as dress and customs).

This part of the orientation session can proceed in a variety of ways. It might be interspersed throughout the other stages of orientation, with official greetings, welcomes and presentations serving to initiate personal contacts. It might begin right after formal acceptance of a volunteer, with the assignment of a personal mentor, buddy or companion who contacts the volunteer, meets with them informally to welcome them to your organisation and introduce them to its processes, and then supports them during their early involvement. It might consist of introducing the volunteers to their future supervisors and arranging for a discussion about how they will be working together. It might consist of a welcome party for new volunteers hosted by paid staff and current volunteers.

The purpose of this part of the orientation is to show the volunteers whom they will be working with and welcome them into the social context of your organisation. Throughout, it is important to show the volunteers that they are a welcome addition to the team.

7.2 TRAINING

Training is the process of providing volunteers with the ability to perform specific types of work. Determining what training volunteers may need requires three questions to be answered:

1. What **information** do they need to successfully perform the work?
2. What **skills** do they need to successfully perform the work?
3. What **attitudes** or approaches do they need to successfully perform the work?

Training to provide this information, develop these skills and engender these attitudes can be provided in three formats: formal training sessions, on-the-job teaching or skills upgrades, and support.

Training is an ongoing process and these three different training formats will be used at different stages of the volunteer journey. Formal training is often useful at the beginning of volunteers' time with your organisation, so that they know the key information to deliver their role properly. However, not even the best initial training will cover everything that a volunteer needs to know, so ongoing training will be useful to volunteers. Similarly, the training session format can only deliver so much – even at their most collaborative, training sessions tend to be fairly one-way affairs. As such, opportunities for training through support sessions – where volunteers can discuss the issues they have faced and their strategies for progressing through them – are useful in many volunteering contexts.

Formal training

Formal training will prepare volunteers for specific roles. Sometimes this training can be quite lengthy, particularly when volunteers are recruited who lack the specific skills required by the role, while at other times it can be fairly brief. For complex roles where the volunteer needs to have a large knowledge base and where the tasks they will be fulfilling need to be delivered with great care, there may be a need for training that lasts multiple days. This can be delivered over weeks or even months to allow time for volunteers to digest what they are being taught.

Training can be presented through lectures, reading lists, discussions, field trips, videos, panel discussions, demonstrations, case studies, simulations and more. Trainers commonly employ a variety of techniques so as to better retain the attention of the audience. Training can be delivered in person or online, or through a blend of the two.

There are two primary content areas to cover in volunteer training, regardless of the role for which the training is being provided. The first area is a description of the functions of the volunteer role, including the following information:

● This is what you **should** accomplish in your volunteer role.
● This is what you **should not** do (e.g. boundaries to the role).
● This is what you should do **if** you encounter the following situations.

The content of the training should provide the volunteer with the collected knowledge experience (both positive and negative) that previous volunteers have acquired. The content should be developed with the assistance of paid staff and volunteers who are familiar with the work, and the session could be delivered by these same staff or volunteers. This need not be as onerous as it sounds – in many cases much of the required information will be common knowledge for those within your organisation and will simply need to be passed on to new volunteers. Where more complex and detailed role information is required, it will be helpful to get input from those who will be managing or working with the volunteers.

The second area might be termed a description of roles and responsibilities. It would include training that communicates to the volunteers the web of relationships in which they will be working:

● This is who you will be working with and this is your role in the task.
● This is their role and how it fits into the task.

This stage of the training will include telling volunteers whom their manager or supervisor will be and informing them of any other staff members or volunteers who will be assigned to work in concert with them. This stage provides a good opportunity to introduce volunteers to the paid staff they will be working with, which is a good step towards building effective volunteer and staff relationships, as covered in chapter 14.

Formal training sessions for more experienced volunteers will generally follow the same format as initial training, but with those being taught assumed to have rather more knowledge. These sessions may also be shorter and more focused than initial training. Often they will set up be in response to internal or external events, such as a new funding grant, a new project, legislative changes or a change in policy.

On-the-job training

Often the most effective way to conduct ongoing training is through on-the-job training while volunteers go about their roles. Effective teaching in this format follows a three-step process:

1. a demonstration of the skill to be learned or improved;
2. observation of the volunteer trying out the skill;
3. feedback and analysis.

The skill can be demonstrated by anyone who is an expert in that area, whether paid staff or a volunteer. While these steps may seem formal, they need not be and indeed often should not be. Rather, the important thing is that volunteers are shown how to do the tasks that make up their role, and given the opportunity, to try them out and receive feedback on their performance. This is commonplace across a range of work contexts and often occurs without being planned or timetabled. Nonetheless, it is useful to consider how best to deliver this in your organisation and to ensure that the relevant trainers are aware of the need to provide ongoing guidance and support.

Support

The goal of support is to assist volunteers in solving a problem by helping them to identify the tasks with which they have difficulty and to take responsibility for their improvement.

When volunteers encounter a problem in their work or during training, they may feel their volunteering is no longer under control. When volunteers encounter issues which they are unable to resolve on their own, they will not be able to fulfil their role to their full potential. Perhaps more damaging in the long term is that volunteers who feel frustrated by tasks they cannot complete may elect to stop volunteering. They might feel a lack of control and get frustrated or feel they are unable to achieve their goals, both of which can lead to volunteer turnover. Therefore, the goal of the support process is to restore a feeling of control in the volunteer's work and alleviate their frustration by helping to find a course of action that will solve the problem.

As with other areas of volunteer management, the principal tool the effective manager employs in supporting their volunteers is the questions they ask. Use questions to help the volunteer do the following things:

- **Identify the problem**
  - What is going wrong?
  - What exactly is happening?
- **Identify the cause of the problem**
  - Why is the problem occurring?
  - What is causing the problem?
  - What factors in the situation are producing the problem?
- **Identify alternatives**
  - What are the alternatives you have in this situation?
  - What else could you do?
  - Have you considered this course of action? (i.e. offer them a suggestion.)
  - What would happen if you tried that?
  - Then what would happen?
- **Identify a better course of action**
  - What are the strengths and weaknesses of each alternative?
  - What can you do to solve the problem?
  - Why do you think that might work?
- **Learn from their experiences**
  - What can you do differently in the future to avoid this problem?
  - What would you do differently if you faced the same situation again?

As indicated above, it is fine to offer suggestions when supporting volunteers – i.e. additional information or ideas about courses of action that volunteers might not see. In doing so, however, you should try to avoid telling volunteers what to do. Your role, in counselling, is to empower them to come up with their own solutions.

7.3 TRAINING AS A VOLUNTEER BENEFIT

Training for volunteers can also serve as a tangible benefit that can be offered to volunteers in addition to the training required for satisfactory role performance.

Such training could involve:

- training in ancillary skills;
- training in career and/or life development;
- cause-related training.

The training might be developed by your organisation or it might consist of providing an opportunity for the volunteer to attend outside conferences or workshops. Attendance would constitute both an opportunity to increase knowledge and a formal recognition by your organisation that the volunteer is 'worth' the expense of sending them for the training and that you have confidence in their being an effective representative of your organisation.

With some volunteers, training can be a significant benefit. For example, young volunteers who come to volunteering as a means of gaining career experience might be offered access to additional employability skills, such as sessions on CV writing or career planning. Older volunteers, too, will see a value in training that may extend beyond the immediate task at hand and reflect a wider desire to develop or consolidate skills and knowledge.

While relevant training is almost always viewed with approval by volunteers, it may be resisted if it begins to impose extraordinary demands on their time. It may also be resisted if it involves new techniques that require experienced volunteers to change the ways in which they have been performing their volunteer work. Some volunteers can also resist training because they think they know it all and don't need training. Simple solutions to this involve not calling it training and developing non-classroom-based approaches to impart the information required. This includes not considering training as something to be delivered in chunks or sessions, but rather as a process of communicating changes and new processes to volunteers regularly and clearly.

It should be noted that you may be advised that organisations should not offer training above and beyond that required for the volunteers to perform their roles. The argument is that, where training is offered which would in legal terms constitute a 'benefit', it could be argued to provide entitlement to status as an employee, and from that would follow being paid the national minimum wage and being protected by employment legislation. While caution should always be exercised where legal issues are concerned, it is important to note that such entitlement is only likely to be claimed if your volunteers have fallen out with your organisation and seek punitive actions against you. While the consequences of this could be serious, you can take steps to minimise the risk, and keeping volunteers happy by offering training which could benefit them beyond their current role may be one way to do this. If this all sounds complex, that's because it is! Take legal advice but also apply good volunteer management to help inform your organisation's approach.

7.4 PRACTICAL POINTERS

- Giving new volunteers a clear and thorough orientation is vital to ensuring that they are equipped to be successful in their new role. At the orientation, you can pass on essential information about how your organisation operates, conduct a tour of your site, assess volunteers' training needs and give the new volunteers the opportunity to ask questions. You will introduce them to the person to whom volunteers can go with issues and problems during their involvement with your organisation. Orientations can be as formal or informal as your organisation's context demands.

- People will volunteer with you because they support your cause and want to have a positive impact on whatever it is your organisation sets out to achieve. To have this impact, they need to know what they are doing and how to do it, and training can help to provide them with this information. Training can be formal or on the job and can take anything from a few minutes to many weeks – it all depends on what you are training volunteers to do.

- Training doesn't stop once a volunteer is in a post. Ongoing training, whether delivered on the job, during training days or via support, is important to ensure that volunteers remain able to undertake their role as effectively as possible.

- If some volunteers are resistant to training, explain to them how it will help them undertake their role more effectively and therefore help your organisation to have more impact. On the other hand, if volunteers are enthusiastic about training, embrace this and ask what you can do to support them in becoming even better at their role!

- It is important to keep up to date on regulatory and legal issues around training, particularly when it could be considered as a tangible benefit or perk of volunteering.

8 Managing and empowering volunteers

So far we have explored how to formulate the mission, strategy and policy for volunteering in your organisation, and how to recruit and equip volunteers for their work. Our focus now moves to managing volunteers. Your role as a manager of volunteers is crucial to providing a rewarding volunteer experience which benefits your organisation, your beneficiaries and your volunteers.

This chapter proposes two pillars of good management for volunteers: the balance between the needs of volunteers, beneficiaries and organisation, and the balance between control and self-assignment in the volunteers' work. Your challenge is how you weigh up those factors and how you track a course for volunteers which enables them to work effectively and develop their potential. Your success will depend on developing an organisational environment which supports you through the clarity of your organisation's policies and values as well as through the understanding and involvement of senior management.

8.1 BALANCING NEEDS OF VOLUNTEERS, BENEFICIARIES AND ORGANISATION

We now focus on how those who manage volunteers can enable volunteers to be effective in serving the organisation's mission and its beneficiaries' needs. The approach we take in this book is to build the volunteering role around the volunteers' needs. Some volunteer roles are straightforward and make little demand on the volunteer beyond their presence and basic aptitudes, while some are more complex and may ask the volunteer to develop beyond the skill set they originally brought to the organisation. Given such a range of roles, the needs of volunteers can vary widely. Yet, even for the most straightforward roles, we believe the manager of volunteers will get the best results by working with the volunteers' needs and making sure volunteers can see goals to achieve, opportunities to become empowered and ways to fulfil their potential.

Successful volunteer engagement is about achieving a balance. If we focus solely on the needs of the volunteers then we risk not creating roles that deliver for the organisation and its beneficiaries. So how do these various needs interact and what can we learn from this? Figure 8.1 illustrates the different needs managers of volunteers have to balance as three circles representing the needs of beneficiaries, the organisation and volunteers.

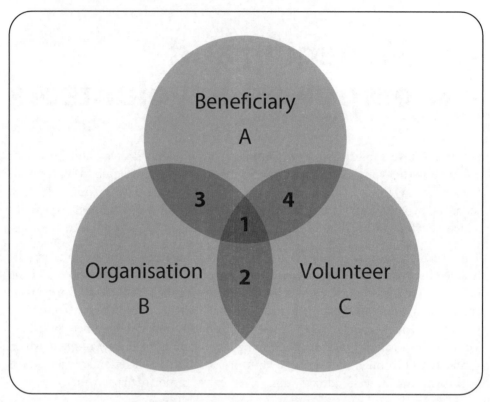

Fig. 8.1 The beneficiary, organisation and volunteer motivational circle

These circles represent the following:

- **Circle A – the beneficiary:** this circle represents the needs of the beneficiaries of the organisation. These may be individuals, other organisations or the community (or natural environment), but within this circle are the requirements that the beneficiary needs to be met, the problems for which the beneficiary needs a solution and the difficulties with which the beneficiary needs help.
- **Circle B – the organisation:** this circle represents the range of services that the organisation is engaged with. It also represents the operations the organisation undertakes to maintain itself, for example fundraising and public relations. Within this circle are activities that the organisation needs to be carried out in order to fulfil its mission (see section 2.1).
- **Circle C – the volunteer:** this circle represents the individual motivational needs and aspirations of a volunteer. These may include anything from a basic desire to help others to a specific need, such as learning computer skills in order to get a paid job.

These three circles represent the basic motivational universe in which the manager of volunteers operates. Success lies in putting the circles together so as to optimise the ability of the beneficiary, the organisation and the volunteer to achieve their motivational needs with the least adverse consequences for the others. To understand this, we have to look at the possible areas of overlap between the circles.

The circles may overlap in various combinations:

- **Overlap 1:** this represents an opportunity for a perfect volunteer role. The beneficiary has an area of need which falls within the type of service offered by the organisation and which also falls within the motivational range of a particular volunteer (i.e. it is a role which the volunteer would want to do because it satisfies some of the volunteer's motivational needs).
- **Overlap 2:** this represents a good area for volunteer roles which support organisational needs directly but only indirectly support beneficiaries' needs (e.g. back office administrative roles where volunteers rarely engage with beneficiaries). The manager of volunteers may have to work a bit harder in order to demonstrate to a volunteer in this area that they are really contributing to meeting beneficiary needs.
- **Overlap 3:** this is an area which indicates the potential for expanding volunteer involvement, probably by exploring with staff the creation of new volunteer roles and then recruiting volunteers with additional skills or interests who could develop these opportunities.
- **Overlap 4 – the danger zone:** this is a very interesting motivational area, one that explains why some well-meaning volunteers do the wrong things. Here, the volunteer's motivation is focused on the beneficiary and their needs but moves outside the range of the organisation's needs in serving its mission and strategy. So the volunteer may start to do things for the beneficiary that fall outside the operations of the organisation, a situation which can create problems not because the volunteer is unmotivated but because their motivation is directed outside the needs of the organisation. Clearly, in such cases, volunteers have to be pulled back into working within the organisation's parameters. However, if you spot a volunteer thinking about moving in such a direction and you can step in and make the situation a matter for discussion, you may be able to turn it into a creative conversation which helps to inspire new activities and develop the volunteer's potential (see section 13.2).

Thus, the manager of volunteers works on the overlap of the circles where the needs of volunteers, organisation and beneficiaries converge. You must balance all three sets of needs to create volunteering roles that deliver for everyone, which is a task that requires skill and leadership.

Managing with the focus on the volunteer

Focusing on the volunteer and their needs necessarily leads to consideration of how the management of volunteers may be different from the management of paid staff.

People often say that managing volunteers is different because volunteers can always walk away; they have a choice about whether to turn up or not, and the manager does not have the power to impose sanctions in the form of pay and notice periods to discipline and control them. Yet the opposite can often be true. Volunteers may be so strongly driven by commitment to the cause that they work unremittingly and risk burnout. Volunteers may see themselves as more committed to the cause than staff, which may lead to tensions. Furthermore, as a result of their commitment – and maybe their direct knowledge of beneficiaries or the problems beneficiaries face – volunteers may feel entitled to use their own judgement to do what they think best.

Volunteers aren't incentivised by a pay cheque or bonuses. For many, their volunteering represents a choice in how they use their leisure time. They may expect a more personal, even friendly, form of management than paid staff, and opportunities to enjoy themselves.

Others may be incentivised by complementing their career needs or satisfying personal or social requirements, and they may expect support and guidance to help them meet those needs. This may require a more businesslike approach, akin to managing paid staff. Or people may volunteer in order to meet their need to serve a cause or to feel they are doing something useful, and want to find their work makes a difference and is taken seriously by the organisations. Volunteers may feel entitled to argue or to present problems to their managers in more affective, emotional even confrontational ways than paid staff. Remember too that for some volunteers in some tasks their needs are not about deep issues of fulfilment but simply about occupying their time doing something useful alongside people they get on with.

Finally, compared to managing paid staff, volunteer involvement may bring a much wider range of people to be managed, from children to those in later life and everyone in between. While elements of employee management are transferrable to working with volunteers, there may be additional and complex needs to consider. This may lead you to thinking afresh about managing staff, as James Kouzes and Barry Posner suggest in *The Leadership Challenge*:

> To get a feel for the true essence of leadership, assume that everyone who works with you is a volunteer. Assume that your employees are there because they want to be, not because they have to be. In fact, they really are volunteers – especially those you depend upon the most. The best people are always in demand and they can choose where they lend their talents and gifts. They remain because they volunteer to stay. What conditions would need to exist for your staff to want to enlist in your 'volunteer' organization? Under volunteer conditions, what would you need to do if you wanted people to perform at high levels? What would you need to do if you wanted them to remain loyal to your organization?[1]

8.2 SETTING LEVELS OF AUTHORITY

Managing with the focus on the volunteer assumes that you are more likely to get good results from people who are empowered than from people who are dependent. By 'empowered', we mean making volunteers more capable of independent action in working to deliver the mission of your organisation (see section 13.2). These are volunteers who understand the needs of your organisation and its beneficiaries, who can identify with the organisation's policies and values, and can make relatively autonomous decisions on how to act as a result.

With such empowered volunteers, the manager of volunteers becomes a source of guidance and not a controller, spending more time thinking strategically and grasping opportunities than making detailed decisions from day to day about what volunteers do.

This is not appropriate for all volunteering situations and all volunteers, of course. There are different degrees of authority which volunteers can exercise in carrying out their jobs. We suggest that it is useful to think of four levels which demarcate how much discretion the manager and the volunteer have in deciding how results are to be achieved (see figure 8.2).

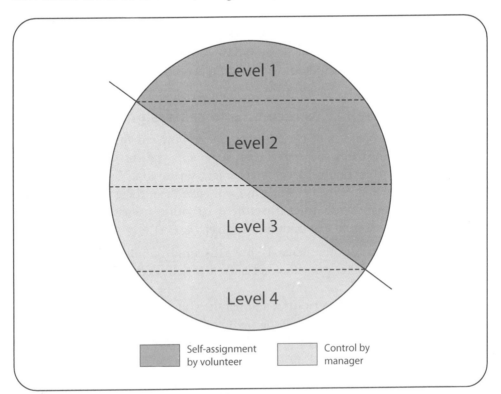

Fig. 8.2 Levels of control and self-assignment

Level 4: no authority for self-assignment

At this level, volunteers have no authority to decide what to do. We'd see this as appropriate in contexts such as:

- **basic, routine roles** where volunteers want to be told what to do and how to do it (typical examples might include data entry, shaking a collecting tin, filing or counting runners at an event);
- **short-term or new volunteers**, who may not know enough about the organisation or the work to make informed decisions about what to do (the volunteer may recognise this very well and want clear instructions);
- **emergencies**, when people need to follow instructions for immediate responses to a situation.

In time, you will find that volunteers will figure out how to do tasks. When this happens, they are likely to find being told what they already know rather irritating and demotivating, even in basic roles. At that point, the manager should switch styles to Level 3 and ask the volunteer how they would carry out the task.

Sticking at Level 4 will produce more work for you as a manager as you spend time deciding and supervising what people should be doing. This style of management may also reduce the number of creative ideas that volunteers provide. Volunteers, who see the work first hand but are not submerged in the day-to-day details of running the organisation, can provide a valuable perspective on the changing environment and the innovations needed to stay relevant.

Level 3: the authority to recommend self-assignment

When a volunteer operates at Level 3, they are empowered to make suggestions about how to do their role while the supervisor retains a veto over the volunteer's ideas. For example, a volunteer might say to you, 'I suggest that I call these people now' and, if that makes sense, you give them the go-ahead to do so. If, on the other hand, you think that there are other priorities the volunteer should focus on, you have two options available:

1. Ask the volunteer for other ideas as to what should be done, encouraging them to consider other priorities and make the right decision. This keeps them at Level 3.
2. Set out how you see the priorities and tell the volunteer what they should do in accordance with your view of the right course of action. This drops the volunteer back down to Level 4 as you return to a directive, non-empowering management style.

At this third level, volunteers should provide regular progress reports, which should include plans for their next actions.

Level 2: the authority for self-assignment, provided the manager is kept advised of progress

The volunteer is now sufficiently experienced that the manager empowers them to go and do their work how they see fit, but the volunteer must report back periodically on what they have done. The key to getting this right is setting clear boundaries so volunteers know the limits of their responsibility.

These progress reports need not be written. An informal chat between the supervisor and the volunteer is sufficient for the supervisor to be assured that things are going well.

The frequency of progress reports depends on how anxious the manager is about the volunteer's performance. A higher degree of anxiety might warrant more frequent reporting – for example, every day the volunteer works.

Level 1: the authority for self-assignment

At this level, volunteers generate their own assignments, identifying and exploring what needs to be done and acting on their own decisions. The role of the manager is to develop a relationship with the volunteer so as to be assured they are doing what is needed by the organisation and the beneficiaries.

Thinking through Level 1 and its implications for the management processes may help you to work out the steps which your organisation needs to take to enable a volunteer to feel empowered and fulfil their potential.

However, it may also offer a caution for when you come across a volunteer who believes that volunteering is all about doing things their way, but you need to exercise authority over their actions.

Level 1 may be appropriate when a new organisation or activity is being developed and the volunteer is formative in its development. Likewise, in all-volunteer organisations, volunteers may be guided by a shared understanding of the cause for which they are working together, more so than by the authority of their manager. The voluntary involvement of trustees and committee members may also be regarded as a Level 1 scenario (see section 10.5).

Establishing checkpoints

One of the most common management mistakes is failure to check progress. Except in particular circumstances at Level 1, you should keep track of what volunteers have been doing. Even where you have discussed in advance what is to be done, it is best to check regularly to ensure that the volunteers are making progress towards the target, rather than waiting until the deadline to be surprised that the result is different from what you expected. Even at Level 1 there should be regular catch-ups about what can be done to enable and support volunteers and ensure information is shared.

An online calendar, shared with volunteers and on which meetings and phone and online conversations are scheduled, is the easiest, cheapest and one of the most effective of all management controls. By requiring regular progress reports, you gain three important advantages.

First, regular progress reports let volunteers know that you are serious about their achievement of results. Volunteers want to make a difference and if they suspect you don't care about what they achieve they will quickly become demotivated and leave your organisation.

Second, regular progress reports help to avoid crises and poor-quality, last-minute work. This is particularly important on long-term projects where volunteers are expected to be self-starters. Most people begin each day asking themselves, 'What is the most urgent task I have to do today?' If a volunteer's project is not due to be completed for, say, six months, it is all too easy for volunteer and manager to put off reports for another day and so let the timetable slip until the deadline is excruciatingly near. But, if the volunteer knows that they have to report progress next Tuesday, they will regard the project with a greater sense of urgency today. By setting regular checkpoints, you ensure that volunteers make regular progress.

A third advantage of regular reports is that they enable you to spot problems in the work while there is still a chance for corrective action. If a volunteer has misunderstood your intentions or isn't clear on the boundaries of their role, for example, you can find this out early, before they have wasted a lot of effort going in the wrong direction.

A common pitfall in reporting progress is when volunteers provide their own assessment of what they did rather than telling you what they actually did. If the volunteer says, 'Things went really well', this does not give you any information about what actually happened. When volunteers say things are 'fine', they are saying things are going the way they pictured them going. Wise managers find out whether things are going the way that they themselves pictured them going – and, if not, can assess on the spot whether the way the volunteer is working is actually more effective and should be adopted by others.

Where you find you need to correct a volunteer's actions, the volunteer may say, 'So tell me what you want me to do and I'll do it.' Be careful! Doing this would mean reducing the level of self-assignment for the volunteer, moving them back into Level 4 and undoing the hard work you have done to make them more empowered.

Instead, you have a choice: you can tell them the thinking which underpins how you – and your organisation – see the job and ask them to follow through on that, perhaps suggesting a way forward. Alternatively, you can ask them to think it out for themselves and come back with some suggestions, thus offering progression from Level 3 to Level 2.

For the second option, you could set out your concerns and discuss what additional information would help the volunteer to think the matter through. Give them the task of gathering the information, clarifying the points or exploring the ramifications, and of doing the thinking and coming back to you with a new proposal that you can discuss and, hopefully, approve. Then, when they work on the project, their actions will be what they decided were the right ones (and which you approved). They will feel more empowered, and your organisation will get more effort and better results from the volunteer.

This method of keeping things under control while simultaneously empowering people works only if those people have clear results to achieve. As a general guideline, you should give everyone the optimum amount of authority you are comfortable with. Every interaction you have with your people about their work takes time that could be spent by both of you doing other things. It may sometimes feel quicker to do the job yourself, but smart managers realise it's not only about their time – it's about giving volunteers the discretion that develops their understanding, effectiveness and potential for the future.

8.3 CREATING A SUPPORTIVE ENVIRONMENT

In the first two sections of this chapter, we suggested that successful volunteer engagement depends on:

- how the needs of the organisation, volunteers and beneficiaries coincide;
- whether the levels of control and self-assignment are appropriate to the task and the volunteer.

As a manager of volunteers, you are involved in balancing these factors for the tasks and the volunteers you manage. How you are able to do this will depend on working in an environment which is supportive for you and the volunteers. The environment should shape volunteers' actions and encourage them to put their efforts and skills into achieving your organisation's goals. It should show volunteers that the organisation has confidence in them, yet also has the means to correct or redirect their efforts and help to improve their skills. Your volunteers should feel valued and empowered to develop their potential.

The working environment is created out of:

- policies;
- values;
- two-way communications.

Some aspects of the working environment are set top down by senior management, whereas other aspects come from the ways of working and behaving together which develop all around you.

Policies and policymaking

Policies are statements about what your organisation intends to achieve and how it operates in working for these achievements. When we talk about policies, we may be referring to statements from two sources:

- formulations of the mission and strategic plan translated into practice, captured in goals and objectives, and resourced;
- rules of working developed out of the need to regulate actions and behaviour.

This section explores each of these in turn.

The first may be handed to you from the top, or you may be in the position of working out how your department or team can turn the abstract language of mission and strategy into practical and observable activities.

Policies in this sense set out how the mission and strategic plan (see chapter 2) are to be turned into practice, with resources allocated and objectives formulated. In doing so, they frame the opportunities and limitations of your volunteers' work, and they should motivate volunteers by showing how their goals contribute to those of your organisation (see section 4.2).

If, when policymaking, you can involve the people who will do the work, you will give them a sense of ownership, which will encourage them to be enthusiastic and realistic in implementing their work. The policy then is more likely to be based on the practical realities your volunteers face and more likely to be effective. As a manager, you can focus discussion in making such policies by asking yourself and your volunteers questions such as:

- Given this mission and strategy, what can we contribute?
- What should we, realistically, be trying to accomplish?
- What should our goals be for the forthcoming period?

While you want to encourage your volunteers to answer these questions, as a manager you should not see yourself as having a purely facilitative role among a group of volunteers. You have responsibility for carrying through the mission and strategy and hence for ensuring that the policies and goals agreed serve this end. You also, as a manager, have an understanding of your organisation, its ways of working and its approach to your beneficiaries' needs – and you hopefully have sound judgement and experience. So, while you are seeking to draw out your volunteers' ideas by putting questions and listening to them, as the discussion progresses you should also offer your suggestions and your own thinking and turn the discussion towards formulating clear statements. The point is to encourage the volunteers to take ownership of the ideas while, at the same time, you show leadership to get effective goals set.

The second way of approaching policy derives from identifying ways of working and behaviours which may be required or prohibited. Here too, as a manager, you may be dealing with policies that are handed down or with issues on which you need to develop policies.

In recent decades, organisations have created – or copied from each other – reams of policies which are handed down to guard against actions, or failures to act, which could be harmful to beneficiaries, staff or volunteers and to the organisation's reputation and legality. Policies on issues such as safeguarding, health and safety, data protection and confidentiality must be promulgated throughout your organisation, and you need to ensure compliance among the people you manage. As a manager, you may be seen foremost as an enforcer, but it is helpful to regard yourself more broadly as the position holder who is best placed to explain the rationale and implications of each policy and to show that it is not merely red tape.

You will sometimes be in a position where you spot things that might go wrong and need to develop a policy. For instance, if you fear that a volunteer might, with the best of intentions, offer medical advice to beneficiaries outside the scope of their role, you may need to establish a policy on what volunteers may and may not do. Or, if you find volunteers interrupt your tasks to ask what they can or cannot do, you may find it useful to discuss:

- What should the volunteers ask permission to do?
- What decisions should the volunteers bring to me to make?

Consider a simple example. When a volunteer says, 'Can I get a pen from the supply cupboard?', what do you consider in making a decision? One such factor might be the expense of the item being requested. Another might be the degree to which the volunteer needs the item to get the job done. Rather than having to make these decisions every time the volunteer asks for supplies, you could create a policy that states, 'Volunteers can get supplies from the supply cupboard when they need them without permission if the item costs less than £5.' Such a policy frees you from being distracted by trivial decisions, and it empowers the volunteers to act within limits and good judgement.

However, some organisations go overboard, writing policies and procedures for every conceivable action, expecting that a wide range of tasks can be precisely formulated and that people will always follow these rules. This reliance on rules can stifle creativity and undermine attempts to develop volunteers' potential;

people assume there is no other way to do things, and expect managers to micro-control their own and their workmates' actions.

So, while rules are crucial, the working environment must also function according to values which all involved share, and which should be manifested in policies.

Formulating and promoting values

Underlying an effective organisation is a set of values. Any effective group must have a shared set of values, otherwise members end up working at cross-purposes. Creating and promoting these values is the responsibility of the organisation's leaders, including the manager of volunteers.

By values we mean a set of principles that guide people's behaviour – a sense of what is right and what is wrong. Having identified its principles, an organisation expects its people to act in accordance with its values, which it may set down as statements of values or may communicate through conversation and personal example. When volunteers have a clear sense of what is right and wrong in their organisation, managers can be comfortable with volunteers taking responsibility for their actions.

For example, let's say a volunteer helping on a project sees two children engaged in taunting each other with slurs referring to the other's faith or ethnic characteristics. The volunteer's response would be guided by values promoting respect for individuals and diversity together with policies on a volunteer's responsibility to act (i.e. whether to intervene in such a situation or to report the incident to a manager for their action).

Values are not empty slogans. Values guide the action of each group member – they are internalised by each person. When the line between what is right and what is wrong is clear, group members know when they are stepping over the line and will refrain from doing so. Managers also have a basis for bringing someone who is behaving inappropriately back to the right side of the line.

Clear values are essential to volunteer empowerment. When people have internalised the values of the organisation, the manager is well placed to empower the volunteer to make decisions, having the assurance that the volunteer will decide to do the right thing.

All this means that the manager should go beyond questions such as 'What are we trying to achieve?' and 'How will we achieve it?' to questions such as 'What do we stand for?', 'What do we believe in?', 'What are the characteristics of our organisation?' and 'What does it mean to be one of us?'. Such questions ought to be current for every leader at every level, and the positive answers to these questions ought to be shared and discussed with volunteers frequently to help create a strong sense of the group's standards and traits.

Fundamentally, the values of an organisation must be based on its mission (see chapter 2). To establish organisational values, begin with your mission statement. Ask yourself and your volunteers:

- Given our mission statement, what problems for our beneficiaries or community are we trying to solve? What kinds of solution are we seeking?
- What philosophy underlies our reason for existence?

The next question to ask is:

- What principles should guide our behaviour in working to fulfil the mission and to respect the spirit of the mission?

This should lead to working out the principles which should guide you and your volunteers as you interact with each other and with your beneficiaries.

Remember that more important than deciding on a collection of abstract principles is helping people to have a clear vision of what those principles mean they are supposed to do in practice. The point is that organisations should be concerned not simply with achieving their goals and objectives but with working in ways that reinforce the values which underlie the goals and objectives. This, we suggest, is particularly important in managing volunteers in that the strength of their engagement may depend on seeing the organisation working in what they see as the right ways, in working according to appropriate values. The likelihood of a volunteer fulfilling their potential for the organisation will be based on the concordance between their own values and the values they see exercised through the organisation.

Reinforcing principles

As a manager, you need to pay active attention to behaviour that is in accordance with the desired values and policies of your organisation. When you observe the right kind of behaviour, you should acknowledge it. You help to establish values by rewarding correct behaviour and acting in accordance with the values that you wish people to exemplify. You should maintain regular connections to and communication with volunteers so you can spot good behaviours to praise, making sure you know the facts in the situation so that the praise is meaningful.

As a manager, you also need support from the commitment of senior management to the role of volunteering in your organisation (see section 3.3). You can reinforce that by informing and involving senior managers so you have top-down support, as we suggest in section 8.4.

Maintaining two-way communications

Managers need to see that volunteers feel a sense of open and ready two-way communication so as to sustain a motivating environment. Volunteers need to find managers available for sharing information and discussion; they need to feel involved and confident about their place in the organisation.

Good communication should be viewed as a web that connects all within the system – it should function up, down, sideways and across, and get the best out of current technology as well as human contact. Consider that, if you don't manage this, people will create their own networks for sharing information, which may or may not include you and may or may not convey the information you'd like them to receive.

There are two key aspects to creating and maintaining effective two-way communication.

Availability

First, volunteers need to be able to meet with, report to and talk with their managers, both on a regularly scheduled basis (as checkpoints – see section 8.2) and at times of the volunteer's choosing as far as is feasible.

Many managers schedule time during which volunteers can make appointments, remembering that volunteers may not always be working during regular office hours. Managers can practise 'management by walking around' so that they can be approached by volunteers. Greeting volunteers when they arrive for work and thanking them when they check out can also offer opportunities for conversation.

Connecting and identifying

Second, volunteers need to feel that they are involved not just in doing the work of the organisation but also in upholding its values. As their manager, you may need to focus on:

- awareness that their involvement is as important as that of the paid staff, whether in terms of participation in decision-making and consultations, team meetings and day-to-day conversations, or social get-togethers;
- open communication through newsletter mailing lists, copying volunteers in on correspondence that involves their work and updating them on what has happened, especially as volunteers are bound to be more often absent than present;
- supporting volunteers in identifying with your organisation and its cause.

Consider too how you converse with volunteers so as to help empower them. Empowering questions focus people on what they can control. They begin with words such as, 'How can you...?' or 'What will you do...?'. If a person makes a mistake, for example, you can ask, 'What can you do differently next time?' or 'How will you approach this kind of problem in the future?'.

In putting such questions, listening to responses and working out how to act, you need to feel confident in yourself and hold the confidence of the volunteers. You must show that you have the confidence to be open to a range of possibilities. You may see this as working more like a consultant than a traditional manager (see section 14.3).

By contrast, an insecure manager may feel they should have all the answers and have instant solutions for all problems. They fear failure if they can't provide an answer to every question, and then make ill-considered decisions or excuses for a delay when presented with complex problems.

Such managers often think it is their job to tell their volunteers what to do and how to do it, and so they tend to foster volunteer apathy and resentment. Volunteers who depend on their managers for all the answers do not grow their potential or enhance their contribution to the organisation and the cause.

8.4   INVOLVING SENIOR MANAGEMENT

Your capacity to manage in the ways we are suggesting will depend, at least partly, on the support of senior management (see section 3.3). You may think of this as a given, but you will need to work on increasing management's understanding, information and involvement.

Understanding

Obtaining a firm commitment from senior management requires that they actually understand the nature of the volunteer involvement which is current or planned for the organisation. They need to understand for themselves why they have volunteers engaged in the organisation. They must be happy with their decision to engage volunteers and recognise how volunteers contribute to the success of the organisation.

There should be a fully accepted rationale for the decision to involve volunteers (see section 3.1). If this does not exist, you would be wise to lead senior staff through a planning exercise to formulate one. Otherwise, you risk having several different, and perhaps mutually exclusive, opinions about why your organisation has volunteer involvement, and you may find that no one in senior management really understands why your organisation does involve volunteers.

Following on from this rationale, senior management should understand what is needed to enable effective volunteer involvement and the investment of finance and other resources needed.

Information

Senior management need to understand what volunteer involvement can accomplish and the associated financial and personnel costs, and they must understand how the benefits outweigh the costs.

Information should be provided to senior management as a combination of facts (statistics, lists, etc.) and stories (anecdotes, case studies, snippets of information, etc.). This information could include:

- **patterns of volunteer involvement:** reports on where and how volunteers are deployed, and what hours, types and roles there are (see section 15.3) – with this information referring back to your SMART objectives (see section 2.4);
- **value of donated volunteer time:** the number of volunteer hours multiplied by estimates of wage rates (see section 15.4);
- **donations:** cash and in-kind donations made by the volunteer and/or their employer;
- **achievements:** evaluations of and reports on what volunteers have achieved and how (see section 15.2).

Involvement

The third element of senior management support involves them knowing – or being told – how and when they can be helpful: i.e. what they can and should do to assist volunteering in the organisation.

Senior managers have a role to play in encouraging staff to value the volunteers' input, in rewarding staff who work well with volunteers, and in persuading other staff that they should work harder to support volunteers. Above all, senior managers should visibly support managers of volunteers to be involved in organisational decisions which have an impact on either volunteers or their work with the organisation.

In larger organisations, the creation of the role of director of volunteering within senior management can both strengthen and complicate the management of volunteers by other managers. The director of volunteering may or may not directly manage volunteers themself, but they will work through managers of projects, teams or departments that do manage the volunteers, often alongside the paid staff. This role may be seen as forming a triangular relationship in volunteer management where the director of volunteering connects both to volunteers and to managers of volunteers (see section 14.3).

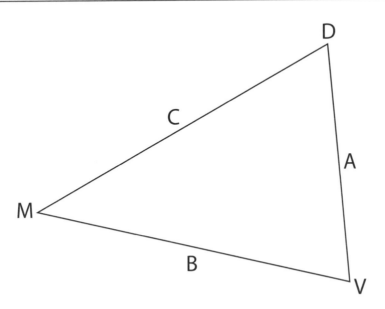

D = Senior manager responsible for volunteering, may be called director of volunteering or director of HR or other title, may or may not be responsible for paid staff as well as volunteering

M = Middle manager, many possible job-titles responsible for managing volunteers, may or may not be responsible for paid staff as well

V = Volunteer

Management relationships between a manager of volunteers with a senior manager and the volunteer can take different forms. The three cases here illustrate some differences among organisations.

Case 1
A – Senior manager directly manages volunteers for whole organisation.

B – Manager supervises volunteers in tasks in their department, team or project, alongside paid staff; and is line-managed by another senior manager for their area of work.

C – Senior manager advises Manager on volunteer supervision, setting strategy and policy.

Case 2
B – Manager manages volunteers together with paid staff for an area of services, with responsibility for breadth of volunteer management functions; and is line-managed by another senior manager.

C – Senior manager provides resource and guidance to support Manager in managing volunteers; and leads on strategy and policy for volunteer involvement, alongside other resource or personnel areas.

A – Senior manager does not directly relate to the volunteer, except perhaps as last resort or point of referral in disputes, and in volunteer recognition events.

Case 3
C – Senior manager line-manages Manager running all-volunteer project, and leads on volunteer strategy and policy alongside other resource or personnel areas.

B – Manager is responsible for breadth of volunteer management functions.

A – Senior manager does not directly relate to the volunteer, except perhaps as last resort or point of referral in disputes, and in volunteer recognition events.

Fig. 8.3 The relationship between the director of volunteering, managers of volunteers, and volunteers

There are several ways in which the involvement of members of senior management can be highly valuable. These include appearing at volunteer orientations, thanking volunteers and giving out volunteer recognition items, reinforcing among paid staff the importance of volunteer involvement and good volunteer management, and meeting with groups of volunteers.

Perhaps the best encouragement that senior management can provide to staff is through example. If the top management effectively involve volunteers in their own work, other staff will receive a clear message regarding the value and importance of volunteers to the organisation.

8.5 PRACTICAL POINTERS

- Work out how you analyse:
  - the overlap between volunteers' needs and the needs of your organisation and your beneficiaries;
  - the balance between the volunteer's self-assignment in doing the job and your own control as a manager.
- Focusing on the volunteer in terms of the needs they have in volunteering – i.e. why they are volunteering – should help you to manage their work in ways that converge with the needs of your organisation and your beneficiaries and so achieve the results you seek.
- You will also need to focus on the volunteer and the task in terms of whether (and how) the volunteer acts independently or whether you specify what they have to do. This should help to achieve the results you seek and, over time, develop their potential and empower them in working towards your organisation's mission.

- In working towards achieving results, you must establish checkpoints when volunteers, whether acting more or less independently, report on their actions and you agree the next steps.
- In managing volunteers, there needs to be a supportive environment, and this requires clarity about policies and values.
- Policies and values will, to some extent, be formulated at an organisational level. However, as a manager, you will need to work on developing and promoting appropriate policies and values, and communicating to volunteers and paid staff how they reinforce the mission.
- Senior management in your organisation need to be clear about the reasons for engaging volunteers and the resources that are available to support them. As a manager, you will need to ensure that senior managers are informed and involved, and understand the benefits of volunteering.

9 Managing at a distance and with groups

In this and the next two chapters, we focus on situations in which managers of volunteers need to adapt their support for volunteers, building on the principles we proposed in chapter 8.

In this chapter, we first discuss situations where contact between the manager and volunteers may be stretched, such as where the volunteer is a long distance away or is supervised by another paid staff member. Second, we consider the differences that need to be kept in mind when people volunteer not as individuals but in groups, including for events and as families.

9.1 VOLUNTEERS AT ARM'S LENGTH

Remote volunteers

One of the biggest challenges in volunteer management is supervising those volunteers who work away from the normal office setting. These workers may be separated from their managers in a number of ways, including:

- being assigned to a field office geographically separated from the headquarters;
- undertaking a role which requires them to work alone away from the office, perhaps matched with a particular beneficiary or where most of their work is performed online or at home;
- working online and/or on a different schedule from office staff, perhaps for an evening or weekend assignment that doesn't overlap with normal office hours.

This separation, even if small in appearance, is significant in practice and affects the kind of support volunteers need. The separation can easily generate feelings of frustration and dissatisfaction, enlarging perhaps minor inefficiencies and misunderstandings. Volunteers might come to believe the central office doesn't understand what the real problems are from their perspective, while those in the central office may believe those in the field are not seeing the big picture.

The challenges of managing volunteers at a distance arise from logistical and interpersonal issues. The logistics of dealing with individuals in locations apart from your own may be formidable. People are harder to locate when you need them; face-to-face communications can be non-existent and dependent on setting up meetings; online communications sometimes distort the message; and people don't have access to the same resources, equipment and support as those in central offices.

Interpersonal problems may arise. As a manager, you may find it hard to have confidence in what you can't see, and you may become anxious about whether volunteers are doing what they are supposed to do. At the same time, volunteers can find it difficult to take instructions from a person who isn't on the front line, so they may not give proper credence to your managerial directives. They may feel left out of the loop in decisions affecting their work.

Long-distance management structures increase complexity across the whole organisation, which may be confusing for volunteers, who generally won't spend their days and nights trying to understand how the system works.

As a manager working with remote volunteers, you must work hard to establish and maintain a working environment that offers a sense of bonding and teamwork, good communication and a feeling of control for all parties. There are three key areas to focus on: connection, communication and control.

Creating a sense of connection

Volunteers work better when they feel closely connected to the organisation and when part of their identity is wrapped up in being a member of the organisation (see section 13.2). People are likely to feel comfortable being supervised by those of whom they have some personal knowledge, rather than a faceless being from above. They are also more likely to work well with managers and team members when they feel they know enough about those people and are confident that everybody is looking out for each other's interests.

A key moment in forming a sense of connection is when volunteers first join your organisation. At this point it is important to give them a sense of welcome and inclusiveness, demonstrating that your organisation truly values them and welcomes them into the group. The behaviour of the volunteer and their attitudes towards others can easily be shaped by how they perceive the culture of your organisation; a volunteer who is going to work remotely needs to be carefully inducted into the group and the culture.

One way for people to get to know each other is to arrange for remote volunteers to visit the organisation's office from which they are managed. A manager can get to know people by visiting them in the field, but this should be mixed with getting them into the office to give them a sense of relating to the larger organisation. It should be noted that such visits should be considered part of their volunteering hours, not something extra you expect them to give.

Identifying colleagues as mentors or buddies can help to establish bonds with the centre of the organisation. Remember that the bonds formed may be stronger with the individual than with the organisation. If the mentor leaves or is dissatisfied with the organisation, this may affect the feelings of the volunteer.

Finally, recognition events are great opportunities for bringing people together and mutual celebration.

Maintaining communication links

Supervising people who work away from your office requires proactive efforts at communication. Volunteers in isolated or separated settings will naturally have different communication problems from those who are in one place. It is important to plan for this and adjust to compensate. Consider the amount of knowledge gained through informal, so-called water-cooler conversations. Remote volunteers do not get this information, and so systematic methods of communication will be needed to ensure this information is shared, whether via planned use of digital messaging, phone or video calls, online conferencing or newsletters. The timing and meaning of communications will differ depending on whether they are sent instantly but briefly through digital media or delayed until a meeting is fixed. Consider organising some communicating time into your working day, or create a volunteer or staff role to keep people informed.

Bringing people together for interaction may look like the best way to involve volunteers in information and decisions, but you have to balance this against volunteers' perspectives on time and travel – and make sure that when they get to the meeting they find something worth hearing and saying. So, you probably need to work out a communications strategy in which face-to-face interaction plays a part, but not the main part.

Maintaining a sense of control

One kind of person who works best in a long-distance relationship is a self-starter. This is a volunteer who is internally motivated rather than externally led, who is proactive rather than reactive, and who makes decisions instead of waiting for instructions. This type of person might be referred to as having an entrepreneurial personality. The challenge with such volunteers is to channel their energies without demotivating them.

Another kind of person who is good in a distant role is the person who just likes to get their head down and get the job done, probably – but not necessarily – as they've been told.

The main tension between managers and long-distance volunteers is between the volunteer's need to decide what they will do and the manager's need to make sure that what the volunteer does is effective. This complicates the balance between level of control and self-assignment (see section 8.2). While you may aim to encourage a volunteer's self-assignment, you would also be advised to establish clear priorities to guide the volunteer's on-the-spot decisions, in order to avoid conflict or unnecessary anxiety.

For the entrepreneurial character, your priorities should provide a clear sense of what is important so the volunteer can see how to focus their time. One problem that you may face at a long distance is that volunteers may stray from the focus of your organisation, possibly entering what we called the danger zone (see section 8.2). To guard against this, clearly set out the results that are required from the volunteer (see section 4.2). Further, ask the volunteer to recommend observable, obtainable goals for set periods of time. These goals should relate to the results that they are responsible for achieving. By agreeing on what the volunteer is trying to accomplish, you will have confidence that the volunteer is going to channel their energies in the right direction.

For the volunteer who just wants to get their head down on their own, you may need to set out the role in more specific terms than you'd like if you're trying to encourage their self-assignment. You will have to judge whether that's the way their personality and aptitudes will prove the most effective for your organisation.

Use the scale of levels of authority (see section 8.2) to provide yourself with assurance that what volunteers do to achieve their goals is likely to be effective. Over time, determine whether each volunteer is capable of working mostly on their own, whether you need to be informed as they make decisions, or whether you need to constantly approve their suggested decisions or even give highly specified tasks. Based on this judgement, allocate your time so as to give more attention to those whom you are less confident can work alone. Maintain communication links, but increase each volunteer's level of self-assignment to free up your own time and encourage their self-development. Set out how you and the volunteer will communicate to agree tasks and report back.

A quick word about online volunteering

Where volunteers take on tasks broken down into very limited periods of time, this is commonly called micro or virtual volunteering, especially when done online. The principles of volunteer management throughout this book should be applied here, with particular emphasis on the issues of managing at a distance, as we have just discussed. In particular, you may want to consider whether these volunteers are of the type who don't want to be tied down in an ongoing volunteer role and, notably, may be driven by a political commitment to your cause. This could affect how you balance your confidence in their self-assignment based on their commitment with the clarity of control you need to deploy them for a campaign or aggregated task.

Resources specific to these forms of volunteering can be followed up in *The Last Virtual Volunteering Guidebook.*[1]

Assigned volunteers

Commonly, volunteers will be assigned to work directly with a particular staff member rather than being under the immediate direction of the manager of volunteers. In this situation, there is a risk that the staff member to whom the volunteer is assigned may not be experienced at volunteer management, leaving volunteers with a feeling of being stranded without any support system.

Some staff may engage in benign neglect: they may appreciate whatever work they obtain from volunteers but not view volunteers as they would a paid employee doing an equivalent job. Some staff may engage in sporadic supervision of volunteers, paying close attention to specific work assignments but avoiding what they may view as the less pressing aspects of supervision, such as periodic evaluations. Others may micromanage volunteers, perhaps because of concerns about their competence arising from never having worked with a volunteer before and not understanding a volunteer's likely needs.

The key to avoiding problems with assigned volunteers is for you as a manager of volunteers to reach a clear understanding about supervisory responsibility with those staff who are assigned volunteers, and to ensure that they are trained and supported to manage volunteers effectively.

Whenever someone is assigned to supervise volunteers, you must make sure that this individual will fulfil their supervisory responsibilities and will provide a link to your organisation and its work. This means that the staff member must accept responsibility for ensuring that the volunteer is provided with work and working conditions that enable the volunteer to both be and feel successful (see the box below).

Top tips on working with assigned volunteers

When working with assigned volunteers, consider asking the following questions about the allocation of responsibilities between the manager of volunteers and a staff member to whom a volunteer is assigned.

- Who will create a role description and who will periodically review and update it?
- Who will interview potential candidates for the role?

- Who will accept the volunteer for the role?
- Who will complete the necessary paperwork and personnel forms?
- Who will be responsible for training the volunteer?
- Who will be responsible for providing work assignments and schedules for the volunteer?
- Who will ensure that the volunteer is kept informed of decisions relevant to their work?
- Who will ensure that the volunteer has a work space and equipment?
- Who will be available to talk with the volunteer if there is a problem with work or scheduling? Or with management processes?
- Who will appraise the volunteer, give feedback on their achievements and take positive action on problems?
- Who is the point of contact for the volunteer when the designated staff member is absent?

Floating volunteers

Occasionally, volunteers may be assigned to various parts of the organisation on a temporary basis, working today with one group of staff and tomorrow with another. While these volunteers will, over time, develop their own links with individual staff members, the manager of volunteers should assume responsibility for most of the supervision of these floating volunteers, either directly or, in some circumstances, by recruiting volunteers to do this.

Staff to whom a volunteer is temporarily assigned can provide supervision of direct job functions but will be unable to do more than this. As the manager of volunteers, you will have to look after the functions of connection and communication (see 'Remote volunteers' at the start of this chapter) even if the function of control (of specific tasks) falls with others. To avoid problems, you should take responsibility for doing the following things:

- Act as the official greeter of volunteers when they arrive at your organisation or are assigned to a team. Check-in with the volunteer at the beginning of each new work assignment and – in person or online – introduce them to the staff with whom they will be working.
- Ensure that there is a flow of work for the volunteer to do, and that this work is not just thrown together at the last minute. One way to encourage this is to send out a reminder to the staff member a few days prior to when the volunteer is due, reminding them that the volunteer is coming and asking them to ensure that something meaningful will be ready for the volunteer to do.
- Serve as an ongoing social and communication link between the volunteer and your organisation. This will mean making sure that the volunteer receives

updates on organisational policy and any decisions that are relevant to their volunteer role. It might also mean creating a small social group of other floating volunteers who meet periodically to keep in touch.

- Provide ongoing evaluation discussions that are based on information gathered from staff with whom the volunteer has worked, and continue to strive to find volunteer assignments that will meet the volunteer's changing talents and needs.

9.2 VOLUNTEERS WORKING TOGETHER

Groups of volunteers

You will encounter different kinds of challenges when you recruit a group of people, such as a club or a team. They will have their own identity and own structure and will view themselves as volunteering as a group rather than as individuals. Keeping control over the actions of group volunteers can be a tricky job, as you have to strike a balance between the volunteers' feeling of ownership and responsibility and your organisation's need for control over what is done in its name.

When events or activities are to be carried out by group volunteers, offer clear, simple, step-by-step guidelines. Make sure that the mission of your organisation is clear. If the project or activity has been performed before, give the group all the information you have about what was done, what worked and what didn't.

If there are any restrictions or requirements that need to be explained, let people know before the start. One example might be any restrictions on the use of the name or logo of either your organisation or theirs. You also need to ensure that safeguarding functions rest with your organisation; if for the volunteering situation you would need a criminal record check and references for individual volunteers, you would need them too for members of a group (see section 6.4).

Clearly outline the allocation of management responsibilities between you, the group and its individual members, remembering the overall legal responsibilities lie with your organisation, including health and safety and safeguarding. Make sure that everyone agrees about who is in charge of what and whom. Also establish reporting dates and a channel of communication between you and the group. If you will be working together over several months, meet more frequently early in the relationship so that you can identify any problems or confusions and be helpful.

Get the group to appoint its own manager or supervisor with whom you will work. This is especially important for a one-off event, such as a weekend construction project or sports event. Work with this person to help with recruitment (see section 5.4), on-the-job supervision and overall management.

In delegating chunks of work to an outside group, you are entering into a relationship with an ally or a partner, and this relationship will be different from other types of management relationships. The group will probably not look at you as its manager but may be willing to look towards you as an adviser who will help the group members to perform their work. Your role is to gain trust and help to define what has to be done so that the result meets the needs of your organisation and beneficiaries as well as the needs of the group and its members.

Family volunteers

Family volunteering is the practice of encouraging members of a family to volunteer together. A family may consist of a nuclear or extended family; parent(s) and child(ren); an adult with their parents; a couple; children and grandparents; adult siblings; people who live together without partnership, marriage, blood or legal ties; and multiple siblings.

They may:

- share in the same task, working together at the same time;
- share in the same task, but working at different times, rotating responsibility;
- work on different tasks, but at the same time or during the same event;
- work together in sharing tasks or events.

The key benefit is the synergy of sharing and working together.

Management of families that volunteer takes place in a variety of formats, partly depending upon the type and location of assignment being undertaken. Sometimes a family volunteering project is created with its own management, possibly including volunteers themselves in management roles. Otherwise, families are integrated into the management system used with individual volunteers, in which case the manager will need to recognise how families may pose some different issues.

Follow all the normal requirements of management, but the following advice may be appropriate:

- Strive to develop self-supervising systems where the families take responsibility for managing themselves, enabling them to be more self-assigning.
- Establish a clear rule that the responsible adult is in charge of the children or young people under their care unless other specific arrangements are made in advance.
- Alert other volunteers and staff as to the presence of children volunteering, and, if your organisation does not otherwise have children volunteering, ensure that appropriate safeguarding policies and procedures are in place.

Matching volunteer assignments to the skills and interests of a family is challenging when multiple individuals are involved. However, it is a key factor in motivating volunteers to perform tasks cheerfully and successfully, and making sure that those tasks meet their needs as well as those of your organisation and beneficiaries.

Interviewing families is different from interviewing individuals in that you are attempting to discover how the family behaves together, as well as learn about members of the family as individuals.

Screening of families follows the same pattern as screening of individual volunteers, including asking both adults and children for referees and getting appropriate criminal background checks of adults.

Finally, beware that families, like all groups, have their own internal dynamics and politics, and these may spill into the volunteer situation – you may end up being a mediator for something that has nothing to do with the volunteer work, or you may decide that the family needs to address its own issues away from your organisation.

Event-based volunteers

Volunteers who do jobs at events, such as sports competitions, are likely to share some characteristics of remote and group volunteers. They may only connect with your organisation on the day of the event and only need that much connection; they support your cause and see their contribution as giving time in this particular way. So, in managing them, you should face up to the responsibilities of connecting, communicating and controlling, as we've suggested above.

In the lead-up to the event and on the day, you should focus on what we refer to as control (see section 9.1), which can be particularly challenging when a large number of individuals arrive, some of whom may feel uninformed about what to do and some of whom may feel like old hands who don't need to be told. In preparation for the event and in feedback afterwards, it is especially important to communicate information and updates about the ways your organisation achieves its goals for your beneficiaries and community, and about how the event is playing its part in the good news (see section 13.3).

These volunteers may come as a group or be so used to meeting up at your events that they feel like a group. Some events volunteers are run as a team by a voluntary organisation or local authority and serve at a range of events. Sometimes a club or a team from another organisation regularly helps your cause by working at events. In such cases, refer to the advice above about the management functions of working with groups and about maintaining connections and communications in between events.

As the manager of volunteers, you will help the paid staff to develop a plan for involving event volunteers, as individuals or groups. Staff will typically either over- or underestimate the numbers of volunteers that they actually need. Work with staff before the event to determine how many volunteers will actually be needed and whether shifts or a rota are required, and ensure that brief role descriptions are available for all the roles. Think through the tasks in terms of the levels of control and self-assignment (see section 8.2), and decide whether the volunteer will be doing a straightforward task or more of a problem-solving role. For example, are they simply opening and shutting a gate all afternoon or do they have to judge whether it's safe to let a race competitor through?

The decision about who manages the volunteers on the day may differ from your organisation's regular volunteer management. You may involve experienced volunteers in supervising teams of volunteers at the event. Or, as discussed above, groups of volunteers coming from other organisations may have their own managers, and then you will channel management roles and responsibilities through them. In both scenarios, you must be clear about who carries which responsibilities in terms of the recruitment and supervision of the volunteers, the preparation and organisation on the day, and thanking the volunteers afterwards.

Help event volunteers to feel successful and have fun. Some volunteers will be evaluating your organisation and deciding whether to volunteer with you again. They are likely to determine this based on whether they felt good about their participation, and the two keys to this are feeling as though they accomplished something and feeling as though they enjoyed the time they spent with you.

Make sure volunteers have all the information and equipment they need – identification badges, forms and information sheets, tickets, machinery, etc. Nothing is more demoralising to a motivated volunteer than to be lacking the basic equipment that is necessary to do a good job, and some volunteers will be ready to cast blame for wasting the time they are giving.

All volunteers at the event should have a clearly identified contact person who will help them in an emergency. Volunteers who are visible at an event are likely to be asked questions that may be beyond their capacity to answer. Always ensure that they know whom to refer questions to and whom to involve when incidents escalate beyond their remit.

Get the names, addresses and contact numbers of every volunteer, even if they come in a group – not just so you can send them a thank you and contact them about the next event, but also because your organisation has responsibility for the care and safety of everyone at the event.

Above all, ensure that colleagues running the event plan for volunteer involvement well in advance. This avoids you being asked to recruit large numbers of volunteers at the eleventh hour, a situation still too common in volunteer management.

Drop-in volunteering

Your organisation may have a facility where those who wish to volunteer can simply turn up, perform a few hours of volunteer work and then leave. Or it may organise an occasional day or weekend to carry out, say, a tidy-up. Volunteers who turn up may feel like a group that gets together occasionally, in which case they may share some of the group characteristics discussed above. Alternatively, they might come as individuals and behave more like remote volunteers.

Key differences in managing them include:

- It has to feel easy – drop-in volunteering only works if volunteers can get involved without having to complete full application forms or undergo interviews, background checks and administrative procedures.
- Nonetheless, your organisation is still responsible for their care and safety and for the staff and beneficiaries they come into contact with, as well as for your reputation and effective work.
- You will need at least a minimal registration form (containing the volunteer's name, contact details and emergency contact information) and information for any other minimum reporting your organisation requires (such as roles filled and time given).
- The volunteers' working conditions must meet your health and safety and safeguarding responsibilities.

It is likely that the balance of control and self-assignment (see section 8.2) will be weighted towards control and specification of tasks, as distinct from giving volunteers scope for self-assignment, and the tasks will need to be clearly communicated. You will need to ensure the volunteers are informed about how what they are doing helps your cause, although you may sometimes find that people just want to get on with doing something useful and aren't terribly interested in the big picture. Likewise, so as to be able to call on them another time, refer to the advice on staying in touch with volunteers over time (see section 13.3).

9.3   PRACTICAL POINTERS

- When volunteers work at a distance from you as their manager or outside your main offices, you must anticipate logistical and interpersonal issues: a lack of face-to-face contact can impede the flow of information and lead to misunderstandings.

- In managing volunteers at a distance, the key factors are:
  - **connections:** enabling volunteers to feel included in the mission and values of your organisation;
  - **communications:** creating a strategy which recognises potential problems and creates a mix of online and face-to-face contacts, meetings and written communications;
  - **control:** working out appropriate levels of empowerment and control for different types of volunteer and tasks.
- In managing volunteers who come as a group, you may be connecting, communicating and controlling the volunteers not directly but through someone from the group who holds a managing or supervising role. You need to be clear about:
  - **planning**, of numbers and tasks;
  - **management**, of communicating, allocating and supervising tasks;
  - **responsibilities**, for volunteers' records and for care and safeguarding;
  - **ownership**, in carrying through your organisation's mission and values;
  - **achievement**, in reporting and recognising successes;
  - **thanking** volunteers, and ensuring that volunteers have a rewarding time.

10 Managing volunteers with different purposes

This chapter considers how, as a manager of volunteers, you should expect to give different kinds of support to different kinds of volunteer. Building on the principles laid down in chapter 8, we explore how younger and older people pose different challenges, especially in terms of meeting their needs as volunteers and matching them with the needs of your organisation and its beneficiaries. We then focus on how some people need additional support to benefit from the opportunities which volunteering offers for making changes in their lives. The last two sections concern volunteers in senior and specialist roles and the forms of support appropriate for them as managers or as trustees and advisers.

10.1 YOUNG PEOPLE AS VOLUNTEERS

Volunteering by young people offers benefits for the young people themselves and for the services or activities in which they are involved. People who volunteer when they are young are likely to volunteer during later stages of their lives, and so investing time and effort in them may show a good return for your organisation and for volunteering in general.

Government data from the Community Life Survey for 2018–19 shows that young people aged 16–24 are among the age groups more likely to engage in formal volunteering, with 35% doing so at least once a year and 21% at least once a month (see section 1.2).[1]

But it is important not to treat them as a homogenous group. Some 16-year-olds may be living at home attending school while others are in work and have children. Some 24-year-olds may be studying and living with parents while others are unemployed and homeless or already embarking upon prosperous careers.

It is also important to recognise that many people under the age of 16 volunteer. Giving time to good causes is an important part of schemes such as the Duke of Edinburgh's Award and other initiatives that seek to grow volunteering by young people through schools and other organisations.

The extent to which young people continue to volunteer varies. Some may be entering into a long-term commitment, whereas others may be looking for short-term opportunities, perhaps seeking useful experience for their CV or potential career. Some will move to another part of the country to go to university, and they may stop volunteering with an organisation at home or seek to continue volunteering with the same organisation in a location closer to their academic residence. They may come back to volunteer at home during the holidays and possibly even after university. Thus, they may present you with some of the same issues as arm's length and episodic volunteers (see section 9.1) in relation to staying in touch (see section 13.3).

Young people who are students may have competing demands on their time during the academic year. Make sure that you support them in trying to balance their studies, part-time paid work and volunteering. Flexibility of scheduling is of prime importance, but you should be careful not to devalue volunteering in relation to a paying job and other pressures in life.

Demonstrate that it is normal for young people to keep to their volunteer agreement, and support them in doing so. If you allow them to always put other things first, they may come to believe that volunteering isn't as important as their other commitments. This devalues their contribution and is likely to make them feel less significant when they volunteer. It is important to help them in the areas of connection, communication and control (see section 9.1), so that their reasons for volunteering and the clarity of their roles and tasks will stand up against other pressures in their lives. You may also want to remember that encouraging young people to volunteer is not just a benefit for today but an investment in the future.

Bear in mind too that some young people, particularly those of school age or coming through a student volunteering organisation, may volunteer in a group (see section 9.2).

Katharine Gaskin created a practical approach to managing young people called FLEXIVOL. Through interviews, Gaskin found that young volunteers tended to ask for:[2]

- flexibility – in work and working times;
- legitimacy – in relation to education and positive image;
- ease of access – in finding out how to volunteer;
- experience – for career and personal development;
- incentives – such as a reference for their CV;
- variety – of work, issues and structures;
- organisation – efficient and informal;
- laughs – enjoyable, satisfying and fun.

A particularly important part of managing young people as volunteers may in some sense seem to run counter to this wish list: safeguarding. You will need a precise understanding of how the safeguarding regulations of your jurisdiction (see section 6.4) affect young people as they move across age boundaries.

A safeguarding policy and whistle-blowing procedures should feature prominently in your procedures for managing volunteering by young people and by the people who volunteer alongside them. You need to make it clear who is responsible for safeguarding within your organisation's management and ensure that all volunteers and staff understand their responsibilities.

You will also need to work in accordance with the requirements of national umbrella, governing and regulatory bodies in your field. These institutions may have specific guidance, advice or requirements about young people and safeguarding, which may be more restrictive than the law.

The basic point to remember in managing young people is that they will almost certainly act responsibly if you give them responsibility. Young people tend to live up or down to the expectations of adults. If adults treat young volunteers in a condescending way or reveal their low expectations or lack of faith in young people, they may be setting up self-fulfilling prophecies.

Young volunteers must, therefore, know that what they offer is valued, respected and sought by staff and other volunteers in your organisation. If they begin to feel inferior, undervalued, overworked or disrespected, they will become dissatisfied with their connection to your organisation. Even worse, damage may be done to their self-esteem, and they may gain a negative view of volunteering that lasts into adulthood. Before you start involving young people as volunteers, staff and longer-established volunteers should be encouraged to regard them as responsible partners.

One of the most powerful things you can do to promote young people's self-esteem is to ask for and implement their ideas, giving them a voice. Sometimes young people can come up with creative ideas nobody else has thought of – or perhaps ideas that have been forgotten. If, however, their suggestions appear ill-considered, try to keep from telling them what is wrong with the idea or rejecting it out of hand. Instead, express your concerns about the idea and encourage the young person to develop a solution that takes into account this additional information.

Young people need to be guided in a positive and supportive manner in order to learn the professional expectations of your organisation. This guidance should come in part from an orientation session for young volunteers (see section 7.1). And, day in, day out, staff and experienced volunteers should demonstrate your organisation's expectations and values (see section 8.3) in their interactions with young people.

Be prepared for young people to challenge why your organisation does things. Sometimes, they will be right and change will be needed! Do not automatically reject their challenges as youthful naivety. But, while you may offer high levels of self-assignment in how they do the work and contribute ideas (see section 8.2), you must always balance this with your grasp of the organisation's strategy and needs.

10.2 OLDER AND POST-EMPLOYMENT VOLUNTEERS

People who have retired from paid employment have always been a large part of the volunteering labour force, and some services depend on older volunteers to volunteer regularly and for more hours per week than other age groups.

People aged 65–74 hold the place as the age group that volunteers the most regularly, with 39% volunteering at least once a year and 28% at least once a month, though for the 75-and-over age group these figures drop, respectively, to 31% and 24%.[3] However, differences in levels of involvement among age groups are only a few percentage points, and don't predict individual behaviour.

Because they tend to have plenty of time available and a high level of commitment, the needs of this demographic group have posed relatively straightforward demands on volunteer management. Their needs to be able to use their skills, feel useful and give back to society have coincided with the needs of organisations for reliability and quantity of volunteer effort. However, social changes have had a large effect on this demographic group and complicated volunteer management.

Whereas historically there were defined retirement ages, government and occupational pensions have been moved later into life by government social policy, and there is no longer a statutory retirement age in the UK. Therefore, people have in recent years been retiring at younger and older ages than previously. Some have given up paid employment during their fifties, whether from choice or compulsory redundancy, and some have reduced their employment hours and entered into volunteering as a preparation for retirement. Some have chosen to stay in paid employment beyond what was previously the retirement age, whether from choice or in response to worsening pension provision. Additionally, people in this post-employment phase of their lives are engaging with other social changes which may divert them from volunteering. Some are spending more time looking after grandchildren and/or elderly parents. Some have life choices made possible through better pensions and investments so that they can take holidays or join in other leisure activities.

Thus, expectations that older people will commit to large amounts of time on a regular basis have to lessen. You will need to consider how your organisation's needs can be met by older volunteers working to differing patterns of time and with flexibility to respond to family issues. They need to be recruited and managed as individuals, negotiating for their time and talents, just as with any other potential volunteer.

Many people in this cohort – and perhaps notably those retiring early – will be skilled and experienced, even though new to your organisation. This has three implications:

- This experience can be very useful, as it will bring additional knowledge and skills to your organisation.
- Such volunteers may be more skilled and experienced than your paid staff. They may want to work at a senior level in the organisation, using their skills for maximum benefit. This can be quite threatening to paid staff and uncomfortable for senior managers who are used to volunteers working below them in the organisational structure.
- As with all other experienced volunteers, you will have to make sure their experience is applied within the context of the specific knowledge your organisation has gained about the best ways to meet your beneficiaries' needs and implement your strategy.

Questions about the health and physical capacity of older volunteers are bound to arise. In recruiting and managing volunteers, you should focus on matching the individual to the role, without peering through a lens of age. The health and physical requirements of tasks and working conditions can be a factor at any age and should feature in your application and selection process for everyone (see section 6.2).

However, there may be adjustments needed if volunteers lose capacity as they get older. Some volunteers shift from being people who give help to others to those who need help themselves, with consequent demands on the time of their managers and other volunteers. People may want to carry on as volunteers in order to fulfil their own needs to feel involved and useful or to maintain the friendships they have developed. You may face difficult issues about how they may be differently deployed or released (see section 12.4) and whether you can set up a pathway of involvement from their volunteering to supporting them in activities.

10.3 SUPPORTED VOLUNTEERS

Some people who volunteer have particular support needs related to their physical, social or intellectual capabilities. They may want to volunteer as a way to overcome the limits society places on their prospects for employment, training or social life. They may seek to gain skills and confidence through volunteering, but it may be that the volunteering role you are envisaging is not suitable for their capabilities. To volunteer, they may need special support. This can take various forms, depending on each individual's needs and preferences:

- clear information about volunteering opportunities and support (in a group or one to one) so as to enable people to make an informed choice about whether to take up an opportunity;
- workshops covering preparation for volunteering, to support people who would like to develop their confidence and skills before they go into new environments and interact with others;
- training in specific and basic skills needed in a particular volunteer role;
- a mentor or personal assistant (voluntary or paid) who can accompany the person to the place of volunteering, perhaps for an introductory period while they gain confidence;
- a personal assistant for the long term to enable the person to interact with other people and/or do the job.

Generally, these kinds of support would be offered by a body such as a volunteer centre or by an organisation dedicated to supporting people with a particular condition. Where a volunteer brings a support worker, you will need to consider in each individual circumstance how you create the necessary functional relationship with the volunteer while, to some extent, depending on the support worker.

If the volunteer would be classified as a vulnerable adult or is a child, you will have to ensure your safeguarding measures, including day-to-day management, are in place and functioning properly.

In deciding when, why and how to accept a volunteer with additional support needs, you should consider:

- whether it is part of your organisation's mission and strategy to serve people with this status or condition, or at this stage of life;
- whether it might be helpful (assuming the potential volunteer is comfortable with the possibility) to place the potential volunteer in a role where their experience or identity would make connections with your existing beneficiaries or their community;
- weighing up the balance between the resources your organisation would gain from the volunteer's involvement and any additional resources you'd have to commit to supporting them.

As a manager of volunteers involved in recruitment, you might have to make a hard-headed choice, given that your objective has to be to serve your cause and your beneficiaries. In most cases, your volunteers are a means to that end, not an end in themselves. So, for example, you may have to resist a volunteer centre which thinks your organisation would be ideal for a hard-to-place would-be volunteer.

In recruitment, you may need to get expert advice on the applicant's ability to do the job and to work with your staff, volunteers and beneficiaries, although it is important to recognise that people are experts in their own situation and so speaking to them about what is required and asking them for their solution is essential. You should check whether they could do well, for both their needs and yours. You don't want to set them up for failure.

Where a volunteer has a clear plan for transition into the workforce, the recruitment process may include some career planning with them. Ascertain what type of work they would like to get into and then help to develop a volunteer role that will give them the greatest opportunity to practise skills and gain confidence. You can further assist their efforts by maintaining records of their work experiences that can be used in letters of recommendation.

As a manager, you have to ensure that each volunteer is doing the work needed, receiving the particular physical or psychological support to do it, and gaining the skills and confidence that they anticipated when they came to you in the first place. This applies to all volunteers, of course, but it has an extra significance for volunteers who are seeking experience to help them changes their lives.

Finally, be aware that involving volunteers with additional needs may increase your management tasks – requiring you, for example, to report on their progress and achievements, especially if their participation is part of a funded project.

10.4 VOLUNTEERS AS MANAGERS

In some organisations, volunteers operate as managers within the management structure (as distinct from being on the management committee; see section 10.5), directing the efforts of other volunteers and sometimes paid staff.

Avoid the most common mistake in selecting management volunteers, which is simply promoting those who are good at other jobs. Many volunteers who are skilled and enthusiastic about front-line work do not want to get involved in administrative work and might make the mistake of agreeing to do it simply because they don't want to disappoint you. Remember that volunteers who have management responsibilities in their paid careers may be volunteering because it gives them something different to do, in which case a management volunteer role will not be for them.

A major issue which must be confronted when placing volunteers in charge of others is what degree of authority they will have. While, in theory, management volunteers should have the same authority as paid managers, you will probably want to restrict their remit to supervision of projects and tasks.

A particular area of difficulty will lie with volunteers who not only manage other volunteers but also exercise authority over paid staff. This may happen when volunteers have particular expertise that paid staff lack or in small organisations where paid staff are in more routine roles. You will need to exercise care in helping to work out potential confusion over the levels of responsibility and authority which the volunteer can exercise, and in ensuring that the staff buy into this. This should be an agreed procedure across your organisation, not a matter of individual negotiation, except perhaps where the volunteer has a special professional leadership role.

If volunteers are to manage other volunteers and/or paid staff, then it is crucial that they be involved in all significant communications and decision-making processes. Volunteers who work with beneficiaries may be able to function without full involvement in all of the organisation's operations, but those who are representing the organisation and managing others need to have full knowledge about what is happening.

One place to engage volunteers in management roles may be in the operational aspects of involving volunteers. Tasks such as recruiting, interviewing and training volunteers may be done better by volunteers who are trained for the function, clear about their authority within your organisation's systems, and supported by you. This will not only free up some of your own time but will also model high-impact volunteer involvement for the rest of your organisation.

10.5 VOLUNTEERS ON COMMITTEES

Volunteers serve as members of governing bodies, committees and advisory groups, and this raises various issues about how to manage them. It may seem like talk about having to manage them is misplaced because these volunteers may be the leaders of the organisation or people whose expertise or political status gives them a position of power. However, we suggest that recruitment and support for their ongoing involvement are treated as management issues so as to optimise their contribution to meeting the needs of your organisation and its beneficiaries.

The roles of managing these volunteers are likely to be undertaken by different functions in the organisation. These kinds of volunteer are generally not regarded as part of a volunteer workforce alongside the kinds of volunteer we discuss in the rest of this book.

Governing bodies

We are talking here about boards of trustees of charities (or equivalent bodies, such as executive councils or management committees), which carry governance responsibilities. These bodies provide an organisation's strategic leadership and keep it accountable to the public, its members and its beneficiaries, with their formal responsibilities depending on the organisation's legal status, nature and tradition.

For you as a manager of volunteers in the workforce, the membership of the governing body may be entirely beyond your scope; you may just have to wait and see who emerges from a ballot or the annual general meeting. In some organisations the chief executive will have a role in advising on membership of the governing body, and they may consult other managers on the skills which need to be added or replenished through new members of the governing body. Alternatively, through your knowledge of the field, you may be asked to suggest – and even approach – potential candidates. If, however, as a result of your commitment to the cause, you feel a need to undertake informal conversations about possible members, you will need to be tactful, discreet and careful.

An area which can be problematic is where members of a governing body are also volunteers working in different roles within the organisation. Outside a board meeting, a trustee should not feel entitled to issue instructions about a job on the basis of being a trustee, and, in mirror image, should not on the board of trustees just speak up for the role they regularly undertake – though their grasp of practical detail may be helpful. A board would also need to be aware of a potential conflict of interest in overseeing tasks in which a trustee has taken an operational role as a volunteer.

How you approach your role in managing this aspect of volunteering will depend on your organisational situation and the ways the governing body shapes your role.

A common mistake is to assume that, because the governing body is commonly the top decision-making body and its members are powerful, the staff are best advised to stand clear and wait for decisions to be passed down. Of course, this isn't the case insofar as the decisions of the governing body depend on the information and papers submitted to it from the staff. But it is also not so because the members of the governing body need, like all volunteers, to be deliberately involved in the organisation. This means employing the three principles introduced in section 9.1; specifically, members of the governing body must be:

- **connected** to the workings of the organisation;
- **communicated to** about achievements and problems in delivering on the mission;
- **controlled** insofar as you make space in which they can perform their role.

In managing trustees, you must ensure that their needs converge with the needs of the organisation and of your beneficiaries.

Advisory groups

Establishing a viable advisory group or committee of volunteers (and sometimes paid staff as well) is roughly equivalent to setting up a quasi-independent volunteer project. The more planning you do up front, the fewer problems you will have later on.

As in our suggestions about working with a governing body, your scope for action will depend on your organisational context. You may decide – or guide others on deciding – what the purpose or goal of the advisory committee will be. It might be to give input and advice to the organisation, or to provide outreach and community representation, or to assist in a specific task, such as fundraising. It might be to make some decisions or to recommend decisions to the governing body or other functions in the organisation. If you haven't determined the rationale for the committee in advance, it will be difficult to enable it to achieve its purpose later. Do not create an advisory committee just for the sake of having one or avoiding another decision, since you will be wasting both your time and that of the volunteers.

You will need to target volunteers who have the skills you need on the committee. Try to get a diversity of people who have sufficient time to devote, who have the requisite skills to assist, and who are devoted to the cause and the task.

The organisation should identify the person who will serve as the primary support for the committee. This person will be responsible for negotiating a viable working relationship between the organisation and the committee and for seeing that its members find their roles worthwhile. In a small organisation, this person could well be the chair or another volunteer, but in a medium or large organisation they should probably be a staff member embedded in its structure.

A key element in recruitment is in picking the chair to lead the group or committee and, where this is not a new body, managing the handover from the outgoing chair. The chair will lead on developing the agenda to achieve the group's purpose or goal and see that clear decisions or recommendations emerge. The chair will be responsible for generating participation from members, but in doing so will probably rely on you or other staff members, again depending on the nature and tradition of your organisation.

Just like other volunteers, members of advisory committees and groups need to learn about the organisation's cause, culture, values, context and conditions. To ask advisory committee volunteers to serve and make progress without a good understanding of the organisation is to invite trouble and bad results.

10.6 PRACTICAL POINTERS

- Do not to jump to conclusions about what different people need when they volunteer and how their needs relate to your organisation's and beneficiaries' needs (see section 8.1).
- Focus on the needs of volunteers, recognising how younger and older volunteers come with different expectations of how they can contribute their knowledge and of what they will gain:
  - **Younger volunteers** may be seeking to develop skills to help them into employment or to have a record of community service on their CV. Yet an issue you may face is how you encourage but contextualise their enthusiasm to change how things are done in your organisation.
  - **Older volunteers** may be looking to contribute the skills they have gained through their paid employment. Yet an issue you may face is how you welcome that but do not let them put such knowledge ahead of the knowledge your organisation has garnered in how to meet the needs of your beneficiaries.
- Consider where you will place each volunteer in the levels of authority (see section 8.2). Might an older volunteer be seeking opportunities to gain a sense of empowerment beyond what their employment had offered them? Might a younger volunteer be seeking a routine which clocks up hours of work experience?
- Consider how changes in external factors affect volunteers' needs. For decades, older volunteers have been a mainstay of caring services with an expectation that they will be happy to give back to society and volunteer regularly. Yet some potential volunteers in this demographic now have competing demands on their time from caring for grandchildren or working longer, or they may have opportunities to use their leisure time in other ways. Their needs in volunteering may now involve different kinds of scheduling and occasional tasks with rewards on a short timescale.
- In recruiting and managing volunteers who need additional support to volunteer, carefully assess how they will match your organisation's needs, whether getting them involved serves your mission and whether you are able to deliver on their goals for volunteering. You may face additional responsibilities in supporting the volunteer in making progress towards their career or social goals.

- Recognise with volunteers in trustee and management roles that, while they may be powerful and high up on the scale of authority, their needs still should be managed. You should still work to connect and communicate with them, so they are informed and involved and so that they understand the needs of your organisation and its beneficiaries.

11 Managing with external requirements

This chapter carries through our theme of how to apply the principles of volunteer management (set out in chapter 8) differently to different situations. Now we turn to programmes where you as a manager of volunteers are, at least in part, responding to requirements established outside your organisation.

First, we focus on schemes where governments have used volunteering as a policy instrument, particularly to tackle unemployment. Second, we turn to volunteering initiatives whose policy objectives focus on rehabilitating offenders. Third, we turn to volunteering undertaken by individuals or teams supported by their employers, including advice on enabling paid staff from your organisation to volunteer in your organisation.

11.1 GOVERNMENT PROGRAMMES FOR EMPLOYABILITY

The evidence that volunteering can help people to gain work skills has prompted a number of policy programmes where governments have encouraged unemployed people to volunteer in order to improve their employability. In parallel, governments have adopted policy drivers specifying that people receiving government benefits should make some contribution to the public good and should commit to gaining habits and skills that will help them to re-enter the labour market. These programmes present challenges for volunteer management.

The primary challenge – which is likely to be handled at senior management level – is whether your organisation wishes to take part in these programmes. Are you willing and able to engage with volunteers on this basis?

Your first consideration should be whether helping people into employment is, of itself, part of your organisation's mission, perhaps as part of a mission to solve problems of social exclusion or poverty. If it is, is a government programme likely to be effective in helping you towards your goals?

Alternatively, you may see an instrumental benefit in working with such a programme because it would recruit volunteers who would help you to achieve other goals. An employability programme could help you to involve not only more volunteers but also people who have not traditionally been attracted to volunteering, and you may find such volunteers continue to volunteer after their placement has been completed. Moreover, you might find the experiences of these volunteers will be useful in working with your beneficiaries.

On the other hand, your organisation may wish to take account of the possibility that people have been pressured into volunteering on such government programmes by incentives relating to state benefits and by sanctions being threatened if they do not volunteer or do not see through their placement. Your organisation may choose to review whether this is the case and, if so, whether these potential volunteers' participation constitutes volunteering and hence whether it is the right thing for the organisation to take on. These programmes have raised fierce political controversy with arguments that volunteer-involving organisations should boycott them, and thus taking part might carry a reputational risk.

Beyond these questions of policy, as a manager of volunteers you will need to be sure what the government's expectations are for obligations such as health and safety, risk assessment and record-keeping. You will need to be clear about systems for reporting if volunteers on the programme fail to attend or do the agreed hours.

Following are some suggestions as to what changes might be needed in your organisation to accommodate volunteers from such government programmes.

Changes in the design of volunteer roles

Two changes need to be made when designing volunteer roles for inexperienced volunteers who will only be with an organisation for a relatively short period of time. The first is an increase in the number of routine volunteer jobs suitable for those who may have little work experience or skills and little time for extensive training. Consider the advice in section 3.2 on involving paid staff in identifying volunteer roles and in chapter 4 on creating motivating roles.

The second change is an increased need for, and reliance upon, roles that are shaped around projects or events (e.g. tasks that multiple volunteers can work on together) and which have definite, often short, time frames.

Changes in volunteer recruitment

Introducing this kind of programme is likely to require three new focuses in your recruiting effort:

- **Changes in how you recruit:** you will need to assess the extent to which people joining the programme are likely to come to you through similar processes to your other volunteers. You may then need to work through warm-body recruitment (see section 5.1) with particular concerns around supporting diversity (see section 5.6). Alternatively, you may need to recruit these volunteers through agencies that assist people in moving out of unemployment, and hence you may need to reach out to these agencies as partners (see section 5.3).

- **Increased need for support from other volunteers:** you will need to meet an increased need to recruit volunteers who can support those volunteers who are on employability programmes. You may need to target people (see section 5.2) who can fill skilled roles involving technical work, supervision or mentoring.
- **Changes to your retention strategy:** you will need to think about how to optimise your engagement with the volunteers on the programme by seeking to retain them beyond their required time. You may need to invest resources and time into building commitment among these new volunteers.

Changes in screening and matching

Volunteer matching practices generally involve learning about the skills and interests of volunteers and then matching them to suitable roles, as discussed in chapter 6. This may become more difficult with volunteers who are being considered to join a government programme, in that they may lack the experience to know what type of job they are interested in or capable of. This means that interviewing these volunteers must expand to contain some sort of basic skills assessment process as well as an inventory of career interests around which volunteer roles might be shaped. You may have to operate as a career counsellor, helping individuals to discover their interests and talents.

Changes in orientation and training

People on government benefit programmes may arrive lacking knowledge about the purpose and operation of your organisation. Volunteer orientation sessions and ongoing communications therefore assume even greater importance, since volunteers may lack knowledge and interest in the cause for which they are to begin working.

If this will be a volunteer's first work experience, orientation will also need to contain sections on the basic protocols of the working environment (see section 7.1). Training may additionally have to cover basic skills, including literacy, use of equipment, customer service and dealing with the public (see sections 7.2 and 7.3).

Changes in volunteer management

Volunteers who are unaccustomed to the demands of voluntary work or are coerced into a placement are likely to need greater attention and supervision than you are accustomed to. Unintentional difficulties may arise out of ignorance of what behaviour or conventions of conduct are expected. Coping with this may require your management style to be more focused on control than self-assignment (see section 8.2), and mentor or buddy systems may be helpful for new volunteers. At the same time, additional training and support may be needed for staff who have no experience of working with this kind of short-term volunteer, and the necessary resources should be built into the budget for the programme.

Top tips for working with volunteers on government programmes

- Don't do it if you don't want to. You are under no obligation to accept or seek volunteers from any government programme. Your organisation will need to decide whether it is willing and capable of involving these kinds of volunteer.
- If your organisation is interested in being a part of any of these programmes, make sure that staff and other volunteers accept the involvement of these types of volunteer.
- Be aware that the basis of such programmes has been contentious in terms of the pressures put upon people to take on and keep roles designated as volunteering, and so you may be subjected to criticism from opponents of the programme. However, if you have done a full assessment of the reasons for your organisation's involvement and your staff and volunteers are behind it, you will be ready to provide an appropriate response and give case studies from the people whom you have helped to get back into work or to gain work experience.
- Get fully informed about the policies and programmes so you are clear about the opportunities volunteers are likely to expect and the objectives they are likely to have. Find out what the government and its agencies require in terms of any obligations and record-keeping, such as health and safety or risk assessments.
- Depending on the particular programme, you will need to be absolutely clear about contractual and funding arrangements and ensure that your costs will be covered by the payments made to you. In some programmes, volunteering organisations become involved through contractors, which are above them in the food chain; in such cases, the volunteering organisations are dependent on the contractors' payments against results achieved in the volunteering programme.
- Volunteers on these programmes may be resentful of having to give their time to receive state benefits and may be unfamiliar with common expectations of volunteering. You will need to work much harder to connect these individuals with your cause, and to convince them that what you are doing is indeed worth their contribution of time.

11.2 PRISONER AND EX-OFFENDER VOLUNTEERS

Volunteering is a tried-and-tested route for the rehabilitation and reintegration into society of offenders, and the primary mission of some charities is to work directly with these goals. However, there are also charities whose primary objectives are not to assist in prisoner rehabilitation or ex-offender reintegration but to find volunteers from among prisoners and ex-offenders helpful in serving their main charitable objectives.

Many prisoners and ex-offenders have experience that is relevant to meeting the needs of an organisation's beneficiaries. Someone who has gone through similar experiences to the person whom they are trying to help may have a credibility which has a beneficial impact on the beneficiary. Some organisations, however, have a policy of not involving volunteers in services which correspond to their offences in, say, drug abuse; any such policy needs to be balanced against the benefit of the volunteer's credibility with beneficiaries.

The benefits should be mutual, with the prisoner or ex-offender meeting their own needs. These may include demonstrating that they can hold a stable role, can be trusted and can give back to society; they may also include gaining confidence and skills for future employment, and accessing training or other volunteering opportunities.

Be aware that if you involve prisoners and ex-offenders as volunteers, you may experience some resistance from staff, beneficiaries and other volunteers who are anxious about associating with them.

Your organisation will need to make sure that it adheres to required statutory procedures. Funders and commissioners may have specific requirements: for example, a particular amount of time may need to have elapsed since the volunteer's offence, or the volunteer may need to have no outstanding unspent convictions.

Your organisation will have to ensure that the necessary security and safeguarding measures are in place. Strictly speaking, your safeguarding systems around prisoners and ex-offenders need be no more rigorous than your systems covering other volunteers, many of whose pasts you will know little about; however, you will need to be watchful for public scrutiny about your procedures.

If you are introducing prisoner and ex-offender volunteers into your services for the first time, you will need to consider how you prepare the ground with staff and current volunteers (see sections 3.2 and 14.2). Your procedures for safeguarding will be part of reassuring staff, but you may need deeper discussions about the opportunities and risks.

Managing risk

Organisations may interact with prisoners and ex-offenders at different stages of their journeys through the criminal justice system, and this will inevitably have an impact on the level of risk management that is required. Some ways in which organisations manage risk include:

- requiring a prisoner or ex-offender to have no offences for a specific period of time before they are able to volunteer;
- adapting the volunteering role to reduce levels of risk;
- providing additional levels of management and supervision for the volunteer;
- identifying whether staff and volunteers need to be aware of any health and safety or personal security issues when working alongside a particular volunteer or a particular type of offender;
- adapting existing risk management policies and procedures to accommodate prisoner and ex-offender volunteers;
- acting on the assumption that if a conviction has been spent then the ex-offender should be given equal opportunities to other volunteers.

For some organisations there may be questions about how far they can be confident the person no longer poses a risk of re-offending. Ensure that your organisation has guidelines in place on how it will deal with situations where an ex-offender does re-offend.

The volunteering setting

Where the volunteering takes place is another factor in deciding whether or not to recruit a prisoner or ex-offender as a volunteer. For instance, in the case of volunteers with custodial sentences, the volunteering may happen in the prison or in the community while the offender is on day release. You may find that prisoners and ex-offenders prefer not to volunteer in the community where they lived when they committed their offence.

Where the volunteering has been arranged in conjunction with a statutory agency such as a prison, your organisation will need to ensure that it complies with any protocols or restrictions that the statutory body has in place. As the manager of volunteers, you will need to be clear about what reports you must make on attendance and progress.

11.3 EMPLOYEE AND PRO BONO VOLUNTEERING

Volunteers supported by employers

For many years, employers have actively supported paid staff who volunteer, either through formal schemes or through more informal means. As the benefits of this form of social responsibility by employers have become widely accepted, it has spread from private sector to public sector employers (including government departments) and to some large voluntary sector organisations.

Volunteers coming to you with the support of their employer may be:

- **in groups:** for example, they may undertake a day-long team challenge in which they carry out a certain task, such as supporting an event or gardening; or
- **individuals:** bringing their professional expertise, perhaps for a few hours at a time over a long period, sometimes referred to as pro bono work.

You could treat groups like we suggested in chapter 9 for other groups of volunteers, although there is a particular need to be clear from the start whether the group is to be led or supervised by one of the group or by you (see section 9.2).

In managing individuals, you are in much the same position as for assigned volunteers (see section 9.1), where the individual is attached to a staff member or department in order to contribute specific expertise but still needs to look to you as the manager of volunteers.

Some employers provide for their employees to have a number of days, often three or five a year, when the individuals can choose where to give their time. You may find they prefer to be connected over time with a department or project, rather than being treated like a drop-in volunteer (see section 9.1) and taking on whatever work needs to be done that day.

What's in it for the employer?

The benefits to the employer are clear: volunteering can help to build teams and refresh teamwork. It demonstrates the employer's social responsibility and community involvement, which can be helpful in recruiting new staff and in retaining their loyalty. Encouraging individuals to give their expertise over time can be a good form of career development when, say, a junior professional is able to take on bigger issues in a small charity than they could in the hierarchy of their own organisation.

What's in it for the volunteer-involving organisation?

How this form of volunteering meets the needs of the volunteer-involving organisation is not always as clear. You may need some repainting or gardening to be done, but setting up the work and managing the team of outsiders for the day may be costly and disruptive for your time, and even lead to regular activities being cancelled. You may also be left wondering whether the team had the skills in painting a fence that you'd hoped for; perhaps you would have been helped more if they'd given you their professional expertise – accountancy or whatever. Alternatively, the actual work carried out may not be as significant for your organisations as building a longer-term relationship, possibly with a view to developing fundraising or local links.

Before deciding to work with employee volunteers, you need to agree the tasks, the allocation of resources and the management responsibilities. You need to talk through what of their offer would be helpful to you and to weigh up how it meets your needs as an organisation. It may have a direct benefit in terms of meeting your beneficiaries' needs if the employee volunteers can work face to face or, perhaps, join in sports or recreational activities. More commonly, employee volunteering is about organisational support, such as a team undertaking maintenance work or individuals providing financial, legal or other professional expertise. Some community organisations will charge employers for providing a location for a team-building event, as well as requiring them to bring the paint or materials.

You need to be clear-headed about the pros and cons and be ready to say this kind of arrangement won't work for you, even though it can be hard to turn away a well-known business.

What's in it for the employee?

Some employee volunteers may look at volunteering as a way to establish credentials, make contacts, and practise or develop their management skills. For others, volunteering may be not so much an alternative to leisure as an alternative to a boring job (see section 8.1). Don't make assumptions, though: ask potential volunteers what they would like to get out of volunteering and design tasks that will give this to them, remembering that people don't always want to use their work skills in their volunteering.

Much of the success in working with employee volunteers lies in developing relationships with their employers and with their staff who run their corporate social responsibility programmes. This is a process of building trust – showing that you care about their people and will work hard to provide them with a good volunteering experience. Like all trust-building experiences, this requires starting small and building from success.

Top tips on working with employee volunteers

■ Research the company to discuss how your needs for volunteers are compatible with its needs for its employees. Assess whether you and the company are envisaging a one-off opportunity – say, for a team's away day – or an attachment for a volunteer who can help you over a period of time. You will also need to establish whether the volunteering opportunity might feed into a longer relationship in which the company may support you in other ways, such as with gifts in kind or funding, or raising awareness.

- Some corporate employees (particularly younger ones on management tracks) may be looking at volunteering as a way to establish credentials, make contacts or practise their professional skills. Others may simply be attempting to do something they feel relates to real life as an alternative to a desk job. A team may come to do a day of practical work for you largely to help build their team skills and loyalty. Don't make assumptions – ask them what they would like to get out of volunteering and design an opportunity that will give it to them as well as meet your needs.
- Many companies will expect a return on their investment, and this is particularly true of those in which groups of employees volunteer for events. The company will provide extensive help, but they will also usually want some share of any publicity generated by any event that is organised. Your job is to make sure that your organisation's needs are met while the company gets good press coverage and sees evidence of impact. Ensure that you establish a good working relationship with the company so you can resolve problems if something goes wrong.
- Discuss what forms of reporting are sought by the employer. They may want an evaluation or impact assessment that shows how the employees' work has helped your beneficiaries or cause (see section 15.1), or they may be happy with a good story and some pictures for a corporate report. Their focus may be as much or more on the impact on their employees and their enhanced skills and loyalty, and the employer may connect the volunteering to its staff appraisal processes. It is not unknown for an employer to ask a host organisation for confirmation that an employee did actually attend for their volunteering time; you should check in advance whether that kind of information might be required to avoid being put in an embarrassing position.
- Be clear about the mutual benefits and the resources needed. For a team challenge day in your centre, you might have to put off regular activities, and you should be able to discuss whether the company would pay you a fee and whether the team would bring the resources and tools needed.
- If you are involving groups of corporate volunteers for event-based projects, design the work so that they are together as a team, at least at some point, so there are photos of their teamwork that can be used for reporting back and publicity.
- If you are involving corporate volunteers as individuals, strive to make the work challenging. The biggest complaint from corporate volunteer programmes about non-profit organisations lies in the uncreative nature of the volunteer tasks that they offer.

Your paid staff as volunteers in your organisation

Sometimes a manager of volunteers will encounter the perplexing question of how to handle their own staff who wish to volunteer somewhere within their own organisation.

This is a tricky area: can, for example, a person both volunteer and be a paid staff member in the same department without totally confusing everyone? When do you talk to them like a volunteer and when like an employee? Do you say thank you differently on the day they're a volunteer? Might they end up being supervised as a volunteer by someone they in turn supervise in their paid staff role?

While this may not be the most frequently encountered situation, it shouldn't be a surprise that paid staff may want to volunteer, and even do so within the same organisation where they are employed. Many paid staff members in volunteer-involving organisations do their work from a deep commitment to the beneficiaries and the cause. Volunteers do not have a monopoly on passion and commitment. Paid staff may see donating time to the organisation as a way of further contributing to the cause, or as a way to advance their own interests, such as pursuing a hobby or gaining skills or experience in a different team. This may make the most sense where a large organisation has different departments and locations so the voluntary role is clearly separate.

Some organisations do not allow it, however. Paid staff volunteering within the same organisation may create the 'multiple hats' problem – an individual who is attempting to fulfil several different roles at the same time. This type of situation commonly creates:

- possible conflict between the roles, resulting in one role negatively affecting the other;
- confusion over which role is being performed at what time – this confusion can afflict the person performing the work and those around them;
- complications to the hierarchical structure that affect communication flow and lines of authority.

Management is already difficult enough, and the more you complicate it the more trouble you are likely to get. Here are some suggestions that may reduce, but not eliminate, problems that may arise when involving staff as volunteers:

- Before accepting an employee as a volunteer, engage senior managers in a discussion of the issue. If the organisation decides to proceed, develop a policy that outlines the circumstances under which such volunteering is acceptable.
- Ensure that any decision to volunteer by paid staff is entirely voluntary and without coercion. You should avoid any organised internal volunteer recruitment campaign which might be viewed as pressure from management to

participate or which requires staff to work as volunteers in what would be their normal business activity. As well as undermining the value of volunteering, it could draw your organisation into legal problems about working hours and wage rates. The most suitable recruitment process would be spontaneous decisions by staff who are volunteering to tell their co-workers about what a good time they are having in working in fresh areas.

- Compare each employee's paid position description with their proposed volunteer role to ensure that they are distinct in type of work, location and time frame. All of these factors should be as different as possible. As the volunteering continues, periodically conduct assessments to ensure that these distinctions remain in place.
- Exercise great care in making sure that being involved in volunteering will not have a negative impact on the staff member's paid work. Before allowing the staff member to submit a volunteer application, require that they consult with their line manager and seek approval for the volunteer work. You may also want to discuss the situation with the line manager yourself.
- Check with the person who will be supervising the staff member in their volunteer capacity to make sure that they are comfortable with this arrangement.

The staff member should follow all the normal procedures like any other volunteer. This includes completing an application, being interviewed, going through orientation and training, and all other steps of volunteer involvement. If background checks are normally conducted on volunteer applicants, they should also be conducted for the staff member.

Be careful about assigning staff as volunteers in departments with which they have a professional relationship. This would include departments with which they work extensively in their paid job and departments where they would have access to information which has an impact on their own paid job (such as personnel information) or on their co-workers.

While it may seem silly to ask a staff member to participate in an orientation session about an organisation where they may have worked for a number of years, this step is important for two reasons. First, it allows the staff member to be introduced to some aspects of the organisation's operations with which they may not be familiar. Second, it is important to remind the staff member that, while volunteering, they are subject to all the rules and procedures of the volunteer programme.

This last point is quite important. You will need to monitor the ability of the staff member to adapt to their new role and to maintain that role while volunteering. This means that they must be able to keep to the status and limits of their volunteer role while interacting with paid staff who are assigned as their supervisors, even though in their employee identity they may have greater authority than those members of staff. They must maintain their volunteer identity while working with other volunteers. Any attempt to pull rank or display a sense of greater importance could be very detrimental to other volunteers and staff.

It is also important to keep good written records on staff volunteers. An up-to-date role description should be maintained, and time sheets of volunteer hours (recording the actual hours worked, not just the total amount) should be kept, even if you do not keep them for other volunteers. Both of these documents could become invaluable if a dispute about employment status ever arises.

Indeed, the primary point is to ensure that the volunteer programme does not become involved in disputes between management and staff, which are not really its concern and which will only harm the volunteering. To avoid such disputes, you may want to consider a requirement that an employee's volunteer role may be temporarily suspended if it conflicts with the performance of their normal work duties.

11.4 PRACTICAL POINTERS

- Before doing anything else, carefully decide whether your organisation wants to be part of any sort of government programme, or whether it would be beneficial to work with employee volunteers. The decision is likely to be made at senior management level, but issues of management will rest with managers of volunteers, and part of the decision should depend on your ability to meet the external requirements of such programmes.
- Be clear about the requirements of the external agency and your willingness and capacity to meet them, concerning matters such as:
  - criteria for recruitment;
  - objectives for the volunteers;
  - health and safety, duty of care, and risk assessment;
  - safeguarding;
  - record-keeping;
  - reporting on volunteers' attendance and achievement.
- Consider how you identify volunteering opportunities (see sections 3.1 and 3.2) and write role descriptions (see sections 4.1–4.3), and to what extent the requirements of the external bodies would lead you to create different kinds of role. This would include weighing the needs of the volunteers against the needs of the external bodies and the needs of your organisation.
- Consider where you would place the volunteers and their roles in the levels of authority (see section 8.2). Might a volunteer who is joining in order to develop skills for employability and thereby to receive state benefits need to be closer to control rather than self-assignment? Might a volunteer who holds a

senior professional position and is volunteering to give pro bono advice expect to be treated as self-assigning? Or might you be jumping to conclusions about each person's role in your organisation?

- Refer back to chapters 8 and 9 to assess in what ways your management of the kinds of volunteer discussed in this chapter should follow the guidance there. Factors to consider include:
  - fitting the needs of volunteers to the needs of your organisation and its beneficiaries;
  - balancing control and empowerment;
  - managing close at hand or at arm's length, individually or in groups.

12 Making a difference

Ongoing support enables volunteers to make a difference to a cause they care about – and probably a difference to their own lives. This chapter explores how your organisation can ensure volunteers make that difference. We offer advice on ways to approach appraisals and feedback constructively, how to deal with problem-behaviour situations, how to take positive management action and, finally, what to do if a volunteer needs to be removed from their role and the organisation. The approach we've taken has longer-term volunteers in mind but the principles hold true for shorter-term and episodic volunteers too.

12.1   PROVIDING APPRAISAL AND FEEDBACK

Most volunteers want to do the best job that they can. They want to make a difference and not have their time wasted. There are two basic reasons for conducting appraisals with volunteers:

- to help the volunteers work at or near their full potential in achieving what your organisation and its beneficiaries need;
- to help your organisation better involve volunteers.

Failing to give feedback to a volunteer sends a clear message that you don't care about the quality of their work and you don't care much about them. Both those volunteers who know they are struggling and those who think they should be congratulated for good work will think less of your volunteer programme, and of the people who manage them.

What you call the process of appraisal in your organisation will depend on the structure and style of its management. For instance, 'appraisal' may sound more like management speak or more like a system for staff, whereas 'progress planning' or 'check-in and review' may sound more acceptable in a volunteering context. For simplicity, we shall use the term 'appraisal' here.

Remember that, while a periodic appraisal can help to shape the overall performance of a volunteer, it cannot replace day-to-day management and support (discussed in chapters 8–11).

Components of a system of appraisal

1. A policy on performance appraisal and review

As we emphasise throughout this book, your organisation needs an overall policy which sets out how it aims to achieve its mission as well as what systems and processes are in place to help it achieve those aims by – among other methods – involving volunteers (see section 3.5). The policy must include the system for volunteer management, which in turn must feature the process for supporting volunteers through appraisal and feedback. Volunteers and their managers should be able to see how it all fits together.

2. An initial trial period

The system for appraisal and feedback should be explained to each volunteer during the initial orientation (see section 7.1).

3. A system for developing and maintaining current and accurate role descriptions

To conduct appraisals, you need role descriptions for each volunteer so you can see what they are meant to be doing (see chapter 4). The role descriptions need to be accurate and updated as your organisation develops and/or as the volunteer's role changes.

The appraisal is a particularly useful time to review the role description. First, this enables you to check whether and how the volunteer is doing what is expected. Second, it is a chance to recognise any divergence between the statement and the job, and then consider how the description should be amended to take account of these.

Possibly the most difficult part of this effort is getting managers to change the role descriptions of volunteers as time passes; it's too easy to think it's just paperwork.

4. Periodic scheduled meetings between the volunteers and their manager

The centrepiece of the system is to hold the appraisals according to the agreed schedule, whether annually or, perhaps, every six months. The appraisal should ideally take place face to face, though there may be some circumstances where it needs to be done by phone or online by video-calling, such as Skype.

The appraisal session should be a two-way meeting. It is your chance (or the chance of the volunteer's manager if this is not you) to talk about the volunteer's performance, giving both positive reinforcement and suggestions for improvement and development. It is also the volunteer's opportunity to talk about how their potential can be fulfilled, and that might include discussing their moving to a different volunteer role.

The easiest method of conducting an appraisal session is to follow this simple approach:

- review the past;
- analyse the present;
- plan the future.

In the process, guidelines to consider include:

- **Don't get overwhelmed by forms.** You can use an appraisal form, but the main purpose of the session is to have a substantive conversation with the volunteer about how their volunteering experience can be improved. Forms may be helpful to prepare for the meeting as well as to structure the discussion and keep a record, but the point of the session is not simply to fill out a form for the filing system.
- **Work from the role description.** Find out whether it, in fact, describes what the volunteer has been doing. Take notes so that you can adjust it to reflect reality. The major issue with highly motivated volunteers is that they rapidly go beyond their role description's scope in their assignments. You don't want to discourage this, but you do want to know about it as you may need to restrain it or officially enlarge the volunteer's role.
- **Focus on the basics.** The conversation should concentrate on the volunteer's performance and working relationships, and a comparison with the previous review.
- **Listen at least as much as you talk.** Tell the volunteer that this is their opportunity to evaluate the organisation and that you want their ideas on how to make things better both for them and for other volunteers.
- **It's not all about the volunteer.** The appraisal may show as much what you and the organisation need to do as what the volunteer needs to do.

Rather than thinking of an appraisal as a way of dealing with problems, you should think of it as a means of confirming and rewarding good work and – if appropriate – opening up new areas or opportunities. The majority of comments can be positive ones, focusing on how the volunteer's work helps to achieve the organisation's mission and strategy.

The session should also be diagnostic, allowing you to determine how volunteers are feeling about their work and about any organisational problems or barriers. For example, volunteers who are in intensive roles may get burned out but not ask for help, since their commitment drives them on. The appraisal can shine a spotlight on whether a good volunteer is feeling burned out or unnecessarily held back. You can also find out about a volunteer's readiness to take on increased responsibility.

Finally, it is always possible that an appraisal will involve consideration of how the volunteer could move into another role in the organisation or explore a larger role in another organisation.

5. A method of following up commitments to change

The policy and processes of the organisation need to provide a clear process for following up what has been agreed or found in the appraisal, so as to ensure that suggestions for improvement are implemented by the volunteer, you as the manager and the organisation. This is likely to be a focus in the regular supervision.

Fortunately, most management experiences with volunteers will be pleasant, and you will spend most of your time assisting dedicated volunteers to optimise their performance. It is good, however, to be prepared for the exceptions, since it is one of the clear responsibilities of a manager of volunteers to protect their organisation and the other volunteers by dealing with problems quickly and conclusively. Otherwise, it gives a clear sign to staff and other volunteers that you are not willing to enforce standards of quality.

12.2 TACKLING PROBLEM BEHAVIOUR

Since volunteers are people, you will sometimes encounter difficult behaviours. We will examine this type of situation in some depth since it may occur for a variety of reasons.

Analysing poor performance

Broadly speaking, poor performance results from either a lack of skills relating to the task or a lack of motivation for the role. This leads to four different types of situation:

- The volunteer is both motivated and skilled.
- The volunteer is motivated but not skilled.
- The volunteer is skilled but not motivated.
- The volunteer is neither skilled nor motivated.

1. The motivated and skilled volunteer

If the volunteer both is motivated and has the necessary skills, problems will probably be caused either by unclear performance expectations or by difficult personal relationships with paid staff or other volunteers. In the former case, staff may think the expectations have been communicated clearly, but they may not have been. To take a simple example, a volunteer who is frequently late for a shift may not be aware that it matters whether they are exactly on time. In the latter case, where the problem is interpersonal, your role as the manager of volunteers is to counsel and engage in conflict negotiation or, if that fails, to shift the volunteer to a setting where the conflict does not exist. (See also 'How a good volunteer may create a problem' in section 12.3.)

2. The motivated but unskilled volunteer

If the volunteer is motivated but does not have the skills for the work, you could tackle the problem through training, counselling or upgrading skills (see chapter 7). This may require getting staff involved who have the abilities needed to upgrade volunteers' skills. Make sure you support and train the staff on ways of transferring their knowledge and skill to the volunteer.

In some cases, a volunteer may be recruited to provide a service for which staff do not have the required skills. For example, you may take on a volunteer to do public relations work for your organisation where staff lack such expertise. If you then find that the volunteer turns out to be less effective than you hoped, you might recruit a more senior person from a public relations firm (or whatever is appropriate to the specific case) to volunteer and give them advice and supervision.

3. The skilled but unmotivated volunteer

If the volunteer is skilled but not motivated, your role as the manager of volunteers is to see how the volunteer can be placed in a more motivating set of circumstances. Consider the following points:

- Is the volunteer placed in a role that they want to do?
- Is that role designed according to the principles described in chapter 4?
- Does the volunteer see the connection between their work and the mission of your organisation?
- Has the volunteer received adequate recognition for the work they have done (see section 13.5)?
- Does the scope of the role offer the volunteer opportunities to fulfil their potential, perhaps by empowering them to make decisions (see sections 8.2 and 13.2)?

If the answer to any of these questions is 'no', then remedy the situation according to the principles discussed in this book. This will include considering whether, in advertising or interviewing for the post, you or the organisation did not communicate accurately about the role.

4. The unskilled and unmotivated volunteer

The fourth possibility is that the volunteer is neither motivated nor skilled to do what needs to be done. In such a case, you could try to find or create a role that will meet the volunteer's motivational needs and is more suited to their skill level. If no such role is available in your organisation, you may find the easiest course is to refer the volunteer to another organisation where their skills will be more appropriate. This may involve releasing the volunteer, which will be discussed later in this chapter (see section 12.4).

Regardless of the cause of the problem, you must insist on the volunteer meeting your organisation's performance expectations. If the volunteer is not meeting those expectations, you must intervene for the good of the organisation and the other volunteers.

Identifying the problem

Having brought the problem into focus, you need to answer the following questions:

- What is the extent of the problem, and how significant is it?
- What factors – and people – are involved?
- How did the problem arise?

There are some common indications of approaching problems in working with volunteers, such as:

- the quality and quantity of work begin to decline – the volunteer makes mistakes;
- the volunteer was previously reliable but starts arriving late;
- the volunteer simply does not show up for assignments or meetings;
- there is a lack of enthusiasm;
- rarely, if ever, does the volunteer make suggestions or show initiative;
- a normally verbal and open volunteer becomes silent and closed down;
- the volunteer consistently avoids parts of their role, especially those that are more complex or disagreeable to them;
- the volunteer blames others for their own errors or shortcomings;
- the volunteer is less agreeable, affable or co-operative – they complain regularly;
- the volunteer avoids interaction with colleagues and makes sure that they are unavailable for any social interaction;
- the volunteer ignores timelines and due dates for projects;
- co-workers and direct supervisors complain about the volunteer and their performance;
- the volunteer bad-mouths the organisation, the programme or key leaders;

- the volunteer loses their temper over insignificant instances and their reactions are out of proportion to incidents;
- the volunteer projects an attitude that nothing is right.

You should consider the demonstration of *any* of these behaviours as a warning that something is wrong. A combination of *several* of these behaviours needs to be seen as symptomatic of a serious underlying problem.

Depending on the severity and nature of the problem, you will need to take one or more of the following steps and responses:

- **Meet with the person in private.** Describe what exactly has been observed and ask them whether there is an underlying issue that needs to be discussed. Do not offer an interpretation of their observed behaviour; allow them to explain it if they will.
- **Avoid rushing to judgement** on their response or explanation. Listen attentively, do not interrupt, and allow silent spaces in the conversation to give the volunteer time to gather their thoughts and consider how to express themselves. Encourage them to respond fully through your body language, attentive listening and avoidance of defensiveness.
- **Determine the issues producing the behaviour:**
  - Has something changed in their personal life that is forcing a shift in priorities, energy allocation, concentration, etc.?
  - Are they a victim of misinformation? For example, does the volunteer believe changes are being made which they won't like?
  - Are they upset about a specific incident and thus fighting back by reducing their productivity?
  - Have they burned out? Volunteers may feel unable to take a break because of their high level of commitment.
- **Ask the volunteer for their input.** What do they see as an effective response to their issues? What would be best for them? A time-out or leave of absence to regain their old enthusiasm? A move to a different assignment? A release from the role and perhaps from the cause, giving permission to leave?
- **Agree on a time frame for the resolution of the problem.** If leaving is the chosen option, select the time frame that is best for the organisation. Allowing a disgruntled volunteer to stay on for a month when you feel that they will continue to contaminate the work climate is unwise, even in the face of the volunteer's assurances that they will be positive and productive.

When behaviour becomes abnormal or negative, consider the volunteer's actions (or inaction) as symptoms and warnings of problems about to erupt, and take steps to intervene swiftly. Remember that the problem may be the person involved, but it might also be a specific situation or the relationships between several people that is the root cause.

Exploring misunderstandings

Very often, particularly in less significant problem behaviour, there will be no real villain. Two people in the organisation might just not be getting along, or they may even have a simple misunderstanding in which neither is actually at fault. These innocent situations often create larger difficulties, however, if unaddressed.

A good manager of volunteers can sometimes intervene and assist the parties to look for their own solution to the situation before things get out of hand. This is likely to mean talking with the parties involved on an individual basis and getting them to describe their version of the difficulty as well as what they think they could do to address the problem. Note that the solution offered here is not for the manager of volunteers to act to solve the problem, but rather to encourage and assist the involved parties to identify what they themselves can do to resolve the difficulty.

Not becoming part of the problem

It is worth noting that you could become part of the problem by how you approach the situation. Here are some common ways for a manager to exacerbate a problem situation:

- **Personalising the problem.** Some managers deal with problematic behaviour or performance as though it were a matter of inadequate character or personality traits, rather than a thing which the manager and the volunteer can work on.
- **Overreacting.** Some managers explode at petty situations, lashing out at others, especially when they are harbouring some resentment for past transgressions.
- **Whinging.** Some managers spend their time complaining to others about a problem rather than directly dealing with the person involved.
- **Lecturing.** Some managers treat the person whose actions or performance are problematic as though they were a child, lecturing them rather than talking with them.

Managers can also become part of the problem by avoiding dealing with difficult volunteers. Here are some common reasons for this avoidance:

- They don't want to admit that they have a problem because they think it reflects badly on them and their supervisory skill.
- They don't want to confront the volunteer out of niceness and because they think that, as a volunteer, the person should be allowed some latitude.
- They are friends with the volunteer and don't want to appear to be criticising them.
- They are focused on their own work and don't need any more problems to deal with.

- They feel sorry for the volunteer, judging that the lack of performance is not really their fault.

12.3 **TAKING POSITIVE MANAGEMENT ACTION**

If the approaches suggested above don't work, you will face a choice between taking decisive corrective action and releasing the volunteer (see section 12.4).

The positive corrective approach

Taking corrective action means setting up a face-to-face meeting with the volunteer. The basis for enabling this encounter to be productive is to plan and organise your interaction so that you focus on what the volunteer can do differently. Statements about performance should focus on specific behaviour for which you can provide evidence from your own observations or reliable reports from others. You should not generalise, refer to hearsay, or offer your interpretations of behaviour or motives. The positive corrective action approach contains four basic steps. These steps place you (as the manager) in the role of helper rather than accuser, and they make the volunteer responsible for making the changes happen.

1. Get the volunteer to describe the unacceptable behaviour

The interaction should begin with a brief statement of the problem in the volunteer's action (or inaction) and a question such as, 'How would you describe your performance or actions (in this situation)?'. Sometimes talking about it like this will clear up the performance problem.

On the other hand, sometimes the person will not be able (or willing) to describe the problem behaviour at all. In such cases, you will have to do that for the individual. If it comes to this, make sure you concentrate entirely on what the person did or did not do. Describe the behaviour without judgement.

2. Divorce the behaviour from the individual's self-worth

In talking to people about their unacceptable performance or actions, make sure they know that you are talking only about what they did, not what kind of person they are. Suppose, for instance, you identify a problem with a volunteer's offhand responses to colleagues: you're not likely to achieve positive corrective action by starting off with, 'I feel like you're really grumpy.' If you instead refer to a specific incident along with the words and manner the volunteer used, you should have a basis for identifying problems in the work situation and in the volunteer's relationships with other volunteers. From here, you can begin to discuss solutions.

3. Say something positive about the volunteer's contribution

One of your purposes is to sustain the volunteer's sense of self-worth so you can maintain their motivation to volunteer and help them to build up their skills and potential. You will need to defuse the defensiveness that is a likely response to a corrective action encounter. It is hard to get people to change when they are defending their unacceptable behaviour. Here you should recognise the volunteer's positive contribution and validate their potential for your organisation and its cause. During the meeting, the volunteer might come to confirm they have difficulties in interacting with colleagues, and you might identify the expert knowledge they have developed and applied through their volunteering in your organisation.

4. Ask the volunteer for a plan for improvement

Ask the volunteer, 'What will you do next time?' or 'What can you do to fix it?'. Make sure the plan they give you is clear, specific and easy to visualise. Get details. If they can't clearly picture themselves doing something different, they won't be able to improve. Listen to any excuses but insist on the expectation of performance. Ask how they will make sure they meet that expectation in the future. Although the plan must be acceptable to you, it should come from the volunteer.

In summary

These four steps will generally improve people's performance, but that may not always be the case. If so, we recommend going through the four steps again but also letting the volunteer know that you must see improved performance in the future. Make sure that the volunteer knows you are serious. If they still perform at an unacceptable level, you need to consider how to release them from the role and the organisation (see section 12.4).

How a good volunteer may create a problem

Sometimes even the most dedicated and committed volunteer can get into difficulties: they want to do too much for the beneficiaries and go beyond the boundaries of the organisation (see section 8.1). Their own high level of motivation pushes them to break the rules. The urge to meet their motivational needs can conflict with the operation of the organisation, causing volunteers whose behaviour is otherwise good, if not exemplary, to behave in seemingly destructive ways.

For instance, an organisation working in the health and social care field cannot solve all the needs of its beneficiaries. It was founded and has developed a strategy to address some specific issue, such as a need for hot food via a meals-on-wheels programme, or a need to enhance literacy via a tutoring programme. The volunteers tend to identify with the beneficiaries and develop motivational satisfaction out of performing work to assist them. They establish a relationship with the beneficiaries in order to run an effective service, perhaps coming to like, respect and bond with the beneficiaries. The volunteers and beneficiaries do, in a sense, become friends. So, what could be more natural than a volunteer seeing some additional task they could do for a beneficiary, such as doing some shopping or advising on other services?

To the volunteer this seems to be absolutely the right thing to do. However, the unfortunate thing is that, while what the volunteer is doing is needed and worthy, it doesn't conform to the strategy of the organisation and may be outside its legal powers, its charitable objects, its competences and its willingness to tolerate risk. It might also lead beneficiaries to expect a service which the organisation is not going to provide.

So how do you restrain these powerful and natural instincts of volunteers without destroying their motivation to continue volunteering? Here are some suggested tactics:

- Adopt and communicate to all volunteers a non-abandonment policy regarding beneficiary needs that they encounter that do not fall into the normal work of your organisation. Urge volunteers to bring these needs to you and let them know that you will work to find some way of meeting the needs, usually through referral to another department or organisation.
- Stress to the volunteers that your organisation is committed to the well-being of your beneficiaries and to linking each one to the support they need. It is crucial to maintain open communication with the volunteers regarding these issues, and it is equally crucial to get them to know that you are on the same side as them. If a volunteer ever gets the impression that your organisation doesn't care about the beneficiaries, they will be much more likely simply to act on their own and may eventually stop volunteering for your organisation.
- Provide each volunteer with a clear explanation of why actions have been prohibited. Do not simply cite rules and refer to policies. Explain why your organisation has chosen not to provide some types of service. There are two generally accepted reasons: that the organisation isn't capable of doing a good job in the area and that some other organisation exists to provide this kind of support. You can also point out that, in order to accomplish its specific mission, your organisation has had to make choices about the extent of coverage it can provide.
- Provide clear rules and procedures, with specific examples of prohibited actions, and build these into 'What if?' training scenarios for all volunteers – and consider whether a specific policy has been broken or a new policy needs to be formulated (see section 8.3). A volunteer is most likely to stray when they

meet a new situation which has not been covered in any organisational discussion, so they may then act in a way they might in their personal or social life. You can create an ethic of keeping within the organisation's boundaries and working to its values (see section 8.3), maybe telling stories of the volunteer who 'restrained their natural inclination to help' and who 'got the appropriate action taken'.

- Build a sense of personal connection between your organisation and the volunteer that will counterbalance the relationship between the volunteer and the beneficiary. This can be done by making the volunteer feel part of your organisation, including them in decisions, and fostering their sense of identity with your organisation's operations and values. It can also be done by developing trusting working relationships between staff and volunteers.
- Develop bonds between volunteers. If volunteers relate to one another, they will tend to reinforce good behaviour patterns, because individuals will not want to let their colleagues down.

What all this indicates is that the high motivational levels that initially cause people to volunteer have some potentially negative sides. High motivation can lead to burnout. It can also lead to disillusionment if expectations cannot be met in your organisation's setting. And, as discussed here, it can also lead an otherwise 'good' volunteer to sometimes engage in behaviour that is 'bad' from the perspective of the organisation, but which is entirely rational from the viewpoint of the volunteer, who is determined and eager to help a beneficiary they value. Volunteers have always been known for being willing to do a little extra, but that doesn't necessarily make it right.

Dealing with changes in volunteers over time

A person's motivational needs will vary depending on their changing life situation. Throughout life, we all find ourselves in situations where we need more information or support in order to cope successfully. The mix of needs that primarily motivates a volunteer to engage in activities may change. For example, a person whose spouse dies may experience a greater need for contact with others. They may have been happy doing a volunteering role on their own, but now may want something to do that they can do with others.

When a volunteer encounters a change in their life situation, you may need to change the volunteer's job, hours or type of engagement. You will need to be flexible about the volunteer experience so that they get the motivational reward they find satisfying.

Difficult volunteer situations may be taken as indicators of some mistake in volunteer management; they usually result from difficulties in interviewing, placing or supervising a particular individual. As such, these incidents, while painful, provide opportunities to examine and refine your system for involving volunteers and allow those involved to put measures in place to avoid similar future occurrences.

That said, this is not always the case, of course. Sometimes people are just unpredictable – and in such cases it is your job to keep them on track.

12.4   RELEASING A VOLUNTEER

This chapter generally assumes that you want to retain volunteers or, as we discuss in chapter 13, stay connected so you can draw on their time and skills on another occasion. But there are some volunteers you might want to release – for instance, those who:

- lack the skills or commitment to carry out the role or the tasks you need;
- have lost the capacity to carry out aspects of the job through decline in physical or mental health, perhaps as a consequence of a chronic medical condition, increasing disability or reduced faculties with ageing;
- break the rules of your organisation, offend against its mission, or abuse beneficiaries, staff, other volunteers or members of the public.

These categories need to be considered differently, but there are common aspects to be borne in mind.

Principles and framework

To reject someone's willingness to give time and help may run against the ethos of engaging with volunteers. It may also be demoralising to the individual. However, sometimes it has to be done.

Your primary responsibility is to the mission of your organisation: you must deliver an effective service to your beneficiaries, and the involvement of volunteers is a means to that end. However, you may also have a responsibility to your stakeholders and need to maintain good relationships with volunteers and ex-volunteers in order to sustain the reputation of your organisation. You want to be seen as enabling people to be involved in your cause, and, where this is no longer possible, enabling them to leave with dignity.

Some organisations require volunteers to step down from jobs such as committee or management posts to make space for other volunteers to get involved. In such cases, you may be asking volunteers to give up roles which they want to retain and are capable of performing, but you have to give precedence to a wider benefit for your organisation.

Remember that, apart from in the case of disciplinary issues, the decision to terminate the relationship between your organisation and a volunteer is best regarded not as a judgement of the volunteer and their character, but as a recognition that the relationship has reached a point where it is no longer productive. Just as the volunteer may reach this determination and quit, so the organisation can reach a similar determination and ask the volunteer to leave. The underlying cause of the situation may, in truth, be the fault of the organisation or of the volunteer, or both. Often, however, it is the fault of neither – things just didn't work out. Not all volunteers can fit into all settings. Not all organisations can offer productive settings for all volunteers.

Telling a volunteer they have to leave can be one of the most difficult tasks for a manager of volunteers – and one of the most upsetting things for a volunteer to hear. Some volunteers may be so committed to the cause, to the people they work with and to their own self-identity that being released may be very distressing for them. Moreover, if volunteers feel they have been badly and unfairly treated, they may be more distressed to find they have no rights or procedure for a review of the organisation's decision or appeal against it.

Two of this book's editorial team were part of initiating and administering the Volunteer Rights Inquiry with Volunteering England (2009–11);[1] the inquiry produced the 3R Promise, which proposed that organisations should commit to a framework of support. We suggest that its principles – getting it right, offering reconciliation and accepting responsibility – may be useful for developing policies and procedures as appropriate in different organisations (see box 'Top tips: the 3R promise').

Top tips: the 3R promise

We will endeavour to get it **RIGHT** from the beginning

- Our organisation will follow guidance on good practice and ensure it has up-to-date policies and evidence this in appropriate reports.
- Our organisation will ensure that concerns of volunteers are listened to and given due consideration.

We will offer means to achieve **RECONCILIATION** if things go wrong

- Our organisation recognises that sometimes things go wrong and makes sure that everyone in the organisation knows how to deal with it.
- Our organisation will identify a trustee or equivalent to become a volunteering champion.
- Our organisation will appoint an individual who will monitor volunteer complaints and encourage rapid resolution in emerging conflicts. Volunteer complaints will be reviewed by directors/trustees on a regular basis.

- Our organisation will explore independent alternative conflict resolution when necessary.

We accept our **RESPONSIBILITY**

- Our organisation explains and accepts its responsibility for its volunteers and their well-being and respects their wish to always have a fair hearing if a conflict arises.
- Our organisation will work... to share lessons and improve standards.
- Our organisation will report publicly on the implementation of its 3R promise.

As developed by the Volunteer Rights Inquiry (2009–11)[2] and amended by its Call to Action group (2011–14).[3]

Performance management processes

We have already discussed in this chapter how the organisation establishes processes for reviewing and supporting the performance of volunteers (see section 12.1). We have offered advice on a regular appraisal process for volunteers, in which those volunteers whose performance is unsatisfactory are told of their shortcomings and guided on improving their work, with their progress tracked in subsequent supervision and appraisal meetings. Regardless of these efforts, the volunteer may still fail to produce the required quality of work over time, which brings us now to considering grounds for terminating their involvement.

There will be occasions when a volunteer's behaviour requires an immediate management response – there is no time to schedule the intervention for a supervision or appraisal session. This may lead to a decision to end a volunteer's involvement, as we describe below.

Generally, though, our advice would be not to rush to frustration and despair about a volunteer's performance. As we saw in section 12.2, the cause may lie as much in your organisation's processes as in the volunteer's motivation and skills. We therefore suggest that you first look for opportunities to adjust the volunteer's role specification, change their line management and/or provide training and development opportunities to focus on improving their skills and motivation (see 'Top tips on remedies and adjustments').

The cause of the behaviour may be linked to some failure in management on the part of the organisation, such as failure to:

- provide a clear standard for behaviour or performance in this area;
- place the volunteer in a role for which they are suited and qualified;

- provide adequate information or equipment for the volunteer to perform their work;
- give supervision and feedback to the volunteer.

Nonetheless, on some occasions, the volunteer is just not going to match up to the job; perhaps they never could – you got it wrong! – or perhaps they can't be bothered to try. Really, the only option you have in such cases is to move them on before they damage your organisation's work and the morale of other volunteers.

Top tips on remedies and adjustments

Many situations that appear to warrant releasing a volunteer may actually be remediable by less stringent methods. Before contemplating releasing a volunteer, see whether any of the following approaches may be more appropriate and less painful.

Resupervise

You may have a volunteer who doesn't understand that rules have to be followed. This is a common problem with young volunteers, some of whom test the rules as part of their self-expression. Explaining and enforcing the rules may end the problem.

Reassign

Transfer the volunteer to a new role. You may, on the basis of an initial interview, have misread their skills or inclinations. They may simply not be getting along with the staff or other volunteers with whom they are working. Try them in a new setting and see whether that helps.

Retrain

Ask them to step back for further training, perhaps a fresh induction phase. Some people take longer than others to learn new techniques. Some may require a different training approach, such as one-on-one mentoring rather than classroom lectures. If the problem is lack of knowledge rather than lack of motivation, then work to provide the knowledge.

Revitalise

If a long-term volunteer has started to slip up in their performance, they may just need a rest. This is particularly true with volunteers who have intensive assignments, such as one-to-one work with troubled beneficiaries, and they may not realise or admit that they're burned out. Give them a sabbatical and let them recharge. Or temporarily transfer them to something that is less emotionally draining.

Refer

Maybe they just need a whole new outlook on life, one they can only get by volunteering in an entirely different organisation. Refer them to a volunteer centre or set up an exchange with a sibling organisation.

Retire

If the above remedies are not effective in a particular case, then the next step to consider is for the volunteer to retire. Recognise that some volunteers may no longer be able to do the work they once could or may have lost their enthusiasm. They may have become a negative factor in a team or even be a danger to themselves and to others. Give them the honour they deserve and ensure that they don't end their volunteer career in a way they will regret. Assist them in departing with dignity before the situation becomes a crisis.

Lost capacity

One area upon which there has been particular focus is where the organisation has an ageing pool of volunteers, some of whom have lost some capacities for helping beneficiaries but want to keep volunteering to meet their own needs for social support and a sense of purpose. Staff may feel that these volunteers are like an extra beneficiary group, needing staff assistance and management. This may raise problems of effectiveness of the individual or their team or of safety.

The very high motivational levels of these dedicated volunteers can make it difficult for them to resign from volunteering. How can they abandon the cause to which they have given so much of their lives? How can they not see their friends? How can new volunteers be relied upon to do the job?

You need to be clear what the difficulties are and not jump to conclusions about individuals' capacity, age or health. Some indicators may be an evident drop in the effectiveness of the skills of the volunteer, increased time off because of health problems, resistance to innovations or resistance to offers of assistance. You may hear reports of difficulties from other volunteers and staff.

If you have suspicions that difficulties exist, you should have a frank conversation with the volunteer, probably after checking with their supervisor or team leader. You should determine the possible risks if the volunteer continues in service. Are there risks to beneficiaries due to a volunteer's diminished skills or possible danger to the volunteer from inability to work safely or from personal health problems?

You may not be competent in judging the volunteer's condition, and they themselves may not be in a position to do so. In this case you must turn to outside help – for example, taking advice from charities that work with people with this condition and/or refer the volunteer to a health professional for assessment.

A loss of capacity is not necessarily related to old age. Organisations may have younger volunteers who suffer from conditions that will progressively affect their ability to volunteer. This becomes an especially significant area when the organisation is an advocate for the rights of those who have the condition and must work with practical problems presented by their own people.

A problem may also be imposed on you by external regulations or expectations, rather than the actual capacity of volunteers. For some tasks, such as driving vehicles, there may be limitations in insurance policies about age of drivers, or policies with good intentions for health and safety may limit what entirely capable individuals are allowed to do.

After clarifying what difficulties the volunteer is having, minor adjustments should be considered. One example would be changing the way that instructions are given to the volunteer, to adjust to sight or hearing difficulties. Another might entail partnering them with another volunteer who can provide assistance or support.

You can determine what other roles the volunteer can fill and whether the person feels such roles would be right for them. Some roles may involve making use of the skills and historical experience the volunteer has acquired (such as to move into a mentor role), whereas others may involve transferring the volunteer to work that has fewer physical requirements. Creating an emeritus advisory group may allow retired volunteers to maintain a sense of status, connection and self-identity, while releasing them from the obligations of physical work.

The volunteer may be reluctant to raise these issues themselves. They may feel guilty about letting down the service. You may also find that their high degree of motivation is linked to a sense of identity which it is hard for them to give up. However, after a proper conversation, they might welcome being given *permission* to resign. This conversation could centre on working with the volunteer to identify what kind of volunteer might take their place, so the volunteer feels comfortable that their replacement will do a good job and that their experience has counted.

Evidence and documentation

As you see a situation emerging where it may be necessary to let a volunteer go, you would be well advised to make careful notes which can be used as evidence on the volunteer's actions and behaviour, your guidance and, especially, your agreements with them about what would help them improve. In an ideal world, you would keep similarly precise notes about volunteers whose performance raises no problems, but in reality you will probably now have to sharpen up your act in this respect.

You will need your notes so that:

- You can give the volunteer factual feedback on where and when they have fallen short of the job in terms of tasks and performance.
- You are not reduced to trying to find and blame aspects of their character or demeanour.
- You have evidence you can cite in the event of them challenging the decision to terminate their involvement.

Key in this documentation are records of:

- shortfalls in the volunteer's performance, giving notes of specific, observable behaviour;
- occasions you spoke to the volunteer about their conduct or performance, with indications of the steps they agreed to take to correct the problem within a time frame, and any consequent change in behaviour;
- training and development opportunities, and their impact;
- statements by others about the conduct or performance of the volunteer, preferably signed by the individual giving the testimony;
- steps in the supervision and appraisal processes, including warnings to the volunteer, performance agreements, formal appraisal forms, etc.

The grounds on which a volunteer's involvement is terminated should be supported by information on your organisation's files. However, you may find that records from before you took on the job are incomplete: if this is the case, you should be cautious and take the time to see what action is warranted.

Procedure for ending involvement

If the decision is made that your organisation no longer has a place for a volunteer, you have to accept the responsibility of a face-to-face, direct conversation which sets out the decision and the reasons. Someone has to convey the decision to the volunteer. This will never be a pleasant experience, but here are some tips that may help:

- **Conduct the meeting in a private setting.** This will preserve your dignity and that of the volunteer. The volunteer may, according to your organisation's rules, be able to bring a friend. You may also want a witness or note taker, and, in extraordinary circumstances, security.

- **Be quick, direct and absolute.** Don't beat around the bush. It is embarrassing to have the volunteer show up for work the next day because they didn't get the hint. Practise the exact words you will use, and make sure they are unequivocal. Do not back down from them, even if you want to preserve your image as a nice person.

- **Announce, don't argue.** The purpose of the meeting is simply and solely to communicate to the volunteer that they are being separated from the organisation. The meeting is not an opportunity to re-discuss and re-argue the decision, because, if you have followed the system, all the arguments will already have been heard. You should also avoid arguing so as to make sure you don't put your foot in your mouth while venting your feelings. Expect the volunteer to vent, but keep quiet and do not respond, especially emotionally.

- **Do not attempt to counsel.** If counselling were an option, you would not be having this meeting. Face reality; at this point you are not the friend of this former volunteer, and any attempt to appear so is misguided. Giving advice demeans the volunteer and makes it more likely that they will experience additional anger.

- **Be ready to end the discussion.** Allow soon-to-be-former volunteers some time to vent their emotions, but at some point you may need to announce that the discussion is over and that it is time for them to depart.

- **Follow up.** After the meeting, write a letter or email to the volunteer reiterating the decision and informing them of any departure details. Make sure you also follow up with others. Inform staff and beneficiaries of the change in status, although probably not of the reasons behind the change. In particular, make sure that beneficiaries with a long relationship with the volunteer are informed of the new volunteer to whom they will be assigned and work to foster that relationship as quickly as possible. The intention of these actions is to ensure that interactions which involve the former volunteer and your organisation or its beneficiaries are less likely to happen.

Procedure when a serious breach has taken place

There will be occasions when you need to terminate a volunteer's involvement because they have broken rules or behaved abusively, and you cannot allow them to continue in the organisation.

Your volunteer policy or agreement should be clear about actions, or failures to act, which would give rise to dismissal. These actions and non-actions may be the equivalents of what would count as gross misconduct in your organisation's disciplinary procedures for employees. You may have precedents for how your organisation acted in similar cases involving staff or volunteers, which could be taken as setting out expectations.

1. Policies and framework

Volunteers must be given adequate information regarding the expectations and policies of the organisation, so that the disciplinary process operates on the basis that:

- volunteer policies include procedures for suspending and terminating volunteering involvement;
- volunteers are informed in advance about these policies and procedures in their volunteer agreement or volunteer handbook – and the volunteer induction should point out the policies and procedures and the requirements about behaviour, even though you don't want to come over as negative at the start.

2. Investigation and determination

You need to have set up a process for determining whether and how the volunteer has broken the rules. You (or a management colleague) must take the time to examine the situation and produce a report with evidence of what the volunteer has done wrong.

The organisation needs to have a procedure to suspend a volunteer while the issue is investigated. If the offence is serious enough to warrant dismissal – or raises that possibility – you can't allow them to carry on volunteering; for instance, the risk where someone has been accused of abusing a vulnerable adult or a child is too great.

You need to assemble evidence that could be cited in your interview with the volunteer and potentially in any appeal or legal review. As noted above, you need to have documentation of the volunteer's actions and/or behaviour and of the procedures you have followed, including previous supervisions or appraisals where they have been given guidance on inappropriate behaviour.

The evidence might include testimony from other volunteers, staff or beneficiaries, but you might find people are unwilling to be quoted as evidence. This may be a deterrent to assembling a case and taking action against the volunteer. In such circumstances, you might:

- make a judgement that off-the-record accounts are strong enough to assure you and colleagues that you have good grounds and are ready to be accountable in the context of the organisation's governance;
- use off-the-record accounts as leads into material which gives stronger evidence of the wrongdoing and can be cited.

It may be tempting to wing it without citing evidence, relying on the probability that the volunteer won't resist dismissal, but that would be unwise.

You may find you cannot process the matter as a disciplinary issue and so have to explore whether you or a colleague could have a frank conversation with the goal that the volunteer agrees it would be better to leave. This runs the risk that you will not be able to explain – to other people within your organisation or externally – why the volunteer was encouraged to leave. And, if the ex-volunteer has a strong sense of grievance and this is widely communicated (perhaps even in the media), you may find yourself in a difficult situation. It is therefore best to avoid this approach if at all possible.

3. Application

Any disciplinary process requires equal and fair application of the rules and the review process, so that any decisions made are not, and do not look like, personal ones. The rules should assist you in reaching the right decision and in feeling comfortable about making that decision. The system should be fair to both the volunteer and the organisation.

Additionally, the disciplinary process helps to develop a case for dismissal that can be used to explain the decision within your organisation's management and governance structure. A side effect of this systematic approach is that a volunteer with problematic behaviour may voluntarily decide to resign rather than face the seemingly inexorable conclusion of a dismissal process. This allows the volunteer to save face, which will make it much less likely that their frustration will lead to further reactions against the organisation.

The points we set out above for the final interview apply even more strongly here. Though it may hurt – yourself as well as the departing volunteer – it's your job to be clear and decisive.

12.5 **PRACTICAL POINTERS**

- Start from the assumption that volunteers want to do the best job they can, make a difference and not have their time wasted.
- Ensure you have a system for appraisal and feedback which helps:
  - volunteers to work closer to their potential in achieving what the organisation and its beneficiaries need;
  - the organisation to better involve volunteers.
- The system should include:
  - organisational policies, including on performance management for volunteers;
  - introductory periods for volunteers to trial the organisation and the role;

– accurate role descriptions which are reviewed and updated;
– scheduled appraisals between the volunteer and their manager;
– follow-up of the actions planned in the appraisal.
- The appraisal is not all about the volunteer; it's as much about the organisation and how its management of the volunteer can be improved.
- Be prepared to identify problem behaviour and take positive management action, recognising these possibilities:
– the volunteer is both motivated and skilled;
– the volunteer is motivated but not skilled;
– the volunteer is skilled but not motivated;
– the volunteer is neither skilled nor motivated.
- Ensure you have clear procedures for releasing volunteers, recognising that you are entitled to do so on the basis of evidence that the volunteer:
– lacks the skills needed for the role and the tasks;
– has lost capacity to perform the role and the tasks;
– has broken disciplinary rules or been abusive.

13 Building and maintaining relationships with volunteers

Happy, effective volunteers are a great resource for your organisation and a resource you will be keen to sustain through ongoing good management. An important part of that is understanding why people continue volunteering and why they stop volunteering. We propose throughout this book how you can create the conditions for volunteers to be satisfied with their role, and in this chapter we suggest ways of enhancing their satisfaction so they continue volunteering.

But your relationships with volunteers should not necessarily mean you try to keep people volunteering for as long as possible. Sometimes it is both natural and sensible for volunteers to move on, and many people choose to volunteer for occasional and small-scale opportunities. Thus, you may face issues relating to how to stay in touch with large numbers of people over time.

As an overview of managing people's ongoing commitment to your organisation, this chapter plots the typical life cycle of a volunteer. This information could enable you to plan how you focus on the issues which are likely to be significant in your volunteers' relationships with you and your organisation.

A major feature of encouraging volunteers to stay involved is how you recognise or reward their contributions. The thanks you give to volunteers show them that you are serious about supporting volunteers, and it enhances the chance that they will stay with you or, after they leave, will come back to volunteer again.

13.1 INDIVIDUAL NEEDS AND CIRCUMSTANCES

Successful volunteer engagement happens when the needs of volunteers are met. They want to do the work that the mission and management of your organisation needs to be done (see section 8.1). They will be motivated when their needs are satisfied by doing things that are productive for the organisation and its beneficiaries.

Volunteers have different combinations of needs and will do better in the settings which suit them (see section 1.3). For instance:

- Some volunteers are most motivated by gaining experience and skills to assist with their prospects for paid employment; in such cases, give them the opportunity to learn skills and get accustomed to working conditions.
- Some are highly motivated by the desire to meet new people; in such cases, place them in a setting where they can work with others.
- Some have a burning passion to work for the cause; in such cases, make evident to them what a meaningful contribution they make to helping others and serving the organisation's mission.

Changes in a volunteer's needs over time may call for adjustments. For example, a volunteer may start out working well on an independent project, finding satisfaction in achieving results. However, if they lose family or friends in their life, their need to be with others may become more important; ideally, you will be alert to this and transfer them to a group project so as to retain their contribution.

The art of motivating volunteers lies in being able to work out what set of needs a particular volunteer has. You could ask them to indicate which factors are important to them in volunteering, as shown in the box 'Top tips on motivations for volunteering'. Their response will give you a better feeling for why they want to volunteer, what kinds of involvement might suit them, and how you can recognise and support them.

Top tips on motivations for volunteering

Consider asking volunteers to think about why they volunteer with your organisation. Which of these factors are important for them? Ask them to tick the ones that matter most.

- ☐ To put my skills to good use
- ☐ To spend quality time with friends or family
- ☐ To get out of the house
- ☐ To keep busy and active
- ☐ To make new friends
- ☐ To give back to the community
- ☐ To feel useful
- ☐ To make business contacts
- ☐ To be part of a prestigious group
- ☐ To make a transition to a new life
- ☐ To gain new skills or fresh experience

☐ To gain work experience to help me get a job
☐ To fulfil a moral or religious duty
☐ To have fun
☐ To make a difference
☐ To feel I belong here
☐ To achieve the mission or cause of this organisation
☐ To work with the beneficiaries of this organisation
☐ To work with animals or the natural world
☐ To take responsibility for something
☐ To be part of a group or team
☐ To gain approval from my employer

While their needs are what motivates a person to volunteer, the reasons why they stay or leave will generally not be related to the level of their initial motivation. Their burning passion to start volunteering is not what keeps them from stopping.

Volunteers stop volunteering for a number of reasons. Some are beyond the control of an organisation or of the volunteer, such as changes in personal circumstances, moving house, a new relationship, new employment or starting a family. Some are within the control of the organisation, such as the volunteer feeling that their time or talents are not well managed or that they are not being thanked.

The *Helping Out* survey for England and Wales found:

By far the most common reason for stopping volunteering was time, and particularly a lack of time due to changing home or work circumstances, identified by 41% of respondents.

The second, third and fourth most commonly identified reasons for stopping volunteering... were, respectively, because the activity was no longer relevant, health problems or old age, and moving away from the area.[1]

The most common reason people give for stopping volunteering is a lack of time, often relating to changes in other parts of their lives. However, our experience is that when people really want to do something, they make the time. People may offer conventionally acceptable excuses ('I don't have time to volunteer') to avoid being negative about their experience or about the people they volunteered alongside. When people are questioned in depth about other factors that led them to stop volunteering, two factors that are often mentioned are poor volunteer management and poor use of volunteers' time and talents.

A study in the USA undertaken by the United Parcel Service Foundation found that the reason given by 26% of people who had stopped volunteering was that the organisation was not well managed. It concluded:

> Poor volunteer management practices result in more lost volunteers than people losing interest because of changing personal or family needs. The best way for volunteer organizations to receive more hours of volunteer service is to be careful managers of the time already being volunteered by people of all ages and from all strata of our volunteer society.[2]

In short, a major factor in why volunteers stop volunteering is within the scope and resources of your organisation and your work as a manager of volunteers. Your job is to meet volunteers' needs by designing motivating roles and creating environments which enable them to meet their own needs.

In creating motivating roles, you – and your past and present colleagues – will have:

- set out clear objectives, grounding volunteering in the mission and strategy of your organisation (see chapter 2);
- based volunteering roles firmly in your organisation with a clear rationale, backing from staff and senior management, and a supportive organisational climate, policy and procedures (see chapter 3);
- designed volunteer roles which your staff see as needed and which produce the results your organisation and beneficiaries need – and you will be alive to negotiating and updating the role descriptions (see chapter 4).

This structure will then have been turned to good effect by the processes through which you have engaged people for these roles:

- appropriate methods of recruitment (see chapter 5);
- selection interviews and appointments to match volunteers to roles (see chapter 6);
- induction and training which prepare volunteers for success (see chapter 7).

Your volunteers should then be ready to get going, and you will be working day to day and within monthly or yearly schedules to manage them so they feel their time is well spent in a working environment congruent with their values.

This book suggests that, when deciding on the processes for managing volunteers, you should work out:

- how to balance the needs of volunteers with the needs of your organisation and of its beneficiaries (see section 8.1);
- how to set levels of authority for management control and volunteers' self-assignment (see section 8.2);

- how to create an environment of supportive policies, values and communication (see section 8.3) with the involvement of senior management (see section 8.4).

How you manage different sets of volunteers will depend on factors such as:

- whether they work close to you and other supervisors or at a distance, and whether they carry out their roles as individuals or groups (see chapter 9);
- whether they are younger or older, need additional support, or are in management or governance roles (see chapter 10);
- whether you have to meet requirements set outside your organisation (see chapter 11).

Your management of volunteers will work through frameworks for:

- supervision and appraisal, to enable you to check on progress and to plan further action (see chapter 12);
- engagement of staff in working with volunteers (see chapter 14).

If all of this sounds complex or overbearing, bear in mind our working assumptions are that:

- clear and known frameworks enable you to create productive person-to-person relationships;
- you can adapt these structures and processes to your organisation, its cause, its nature and its history.

All this does, also, come with an awareness that volunteers may be resentful if their volunteering is managed like paid work – you don't want them to feel like their volunteering is a grind. In most cases, the hours volunteers give come out of their leisure time, and management styles should reflect that.

13.2 NURTURING FOR THE LONG TERM

While the structures and processes presented above should provide the means for satisfying volunteers' needs and retaining their involvement, you may want to go further in one of two directions:

- for volunteers who have joined with a view to medium- or long-term involvement, you could support them to enhance their satisfaction through building their self-esteem and through encouraging them to push on to fulfil their potential;
- for volunteers who have signed on for a short-term task or episode, you could work on how to draw them into staying involved.

This section offers some guidelines for these purposes before tackling the issue of maintaining relationships with people who are seeking only short-term opportunities.

Creating an environment that fosters self-esteem

An individual's self-esteem may be regarded as a key factor in their commitment to their volunteering role. A volunteer's self-esteem might be about how through their volunteering they are held in respect and gain self-respect, attaining a sense of confidence and rightness in their actions and about their place in your organisation. It may be a step towards their fulfilment of their potential in their volunteering role and their life beyond.

For developing volunteers' self-esteem, we have found it helpful to refer to the work of Harris Clemes and Reynold Bean.[3] Although their studies and advice are based on children and teenagers, they offer useful propositions on building self-esteem through creating certain conditions. The most important of these conditions, in our view, are a sense of connectedness (or what the authors originally called 'connectiveness'), a sense of uniqueness, and empowerment (or what the authors originally called 'a sense of power').

Connectedness

When people feel connected, they feel a sense of belonging and of being part of a relationship with others. In the volunteering context, this could apply to their connectedness to the organisation, its cause and beneficiaries, and their colleagues among volunteers and staff. Positive feelings of connectedness may be enhanced in volunteers by management's actions (discussed in chapters 8 and 9) and by volunteers' awareness of the part they play in achieving results (see section 4.2) that contribute to the organisation's mission (see section 2.1).

An essential factor might be the sense that staff and volunteers are pursuing goals together. As the manager of volunteers, you should ensure that staff and volunteers are treated equally and have their say in decision-making. Be on the lookout for inadvertent behaviour that makes volunteers feel like second-class citizens. For instance, volunteers may not be invited to team meetings simply because no one thought to give them the option to attend (although in some situations there may be good reason for staff to meet among themselves, without volunteers being present).

Likewise, you should avoid setting performance standards for volunteers that are too low. If the expectations are too easy to meet, people will not feel satisfied by their achievement – you will have lost an opportunity to help them feel a sense of pride in their contribution to the organisation. The standards you require of volunteers may be different from those you require of paid staff, but they should not be lower.

You should encourage your organisation's leaders to celebrate the accomplishments of volunteers and their contribution to the organisation's mission. Leaders should talk about the values of the organisation and what it means to be part of the group of volunteers.

You should be on the lookout for comments volunteers make about their expectations. If people say things like, 'I'm just a volunteer' or 'What do they expect for free?', it should cause alarm bells to ring. What positive ideas can you generate so as to improve the situation?

You should also look for opportunities to promote interaction among group members. This is particularly important where there are few naturally arising opportunities for people to share their common experiences (see section 9.1). Effective managers, knowing how a volunteer can feel lonely, take pains to bring their people together for training and events and to share stories.

Uniqueness

A second characteristic of people with high self-esteem is a feeling of uniqueness – a feeling that 'there is no one in the world quite like me'. Managers of volunteers build feelings of uniqueness by recognising the achievements of individual members of volunteer groups and by praising them for their individual qualities. They encourage individuals to express themselves and give them the authority to think about and explore alternative ways to achieve results.

People's sense of uniqueness can be enhanced by giving them challenging assignments that take advantage of their individual strengths, enable them to learn new skills and give them increased competence in doing the job. You might organise for volunteers to go to conferences and workshops to enhance their knowledge about the latest developments in their fields.

This need to feel unique is sometimes in conflict with a person's need to feel connected. All of us tend to make compromises in our uniqueness in order to be connected, and we sacrifice some connectedness in order to feel unique. In a truly positive climate, people feel safe to be who they are. They can behave in an individual manner and yet feel supported by the group; people respect each other for their unique strengths and eccentricities.

Empowerment

Empowerment tends to be linked with being able to be effective and a sense of making a difference. This feeling can be stifled by some volunteer roles. When people work on menial tasks where they can't see the connection to the outcome, they are unlikely to feel they are making much of a difference. To feel effective, volunteers need to work on things they can see matter. If they are engaged in support activities, such as stuffing envelopes or painting a fence, they should be able to see how they are working towards a bigger purpose. You must communicate the results achieved from the task and how it contributes to the organisation's vision and mission.

Part of feeling empowered is feeling in control of one's life. As a manager, you can take this away from people by trying to overly control their behaviour. Rather than defining results and allowing people a say in figuring out how to achieve them, managers too often simply tell people exactly what to do.

You can produce feelings of effectiveness by making volunteers responsible for results (see sections 4.2, 8.2 and 13.4). Volunteers then have the sense of being in charge of something meaningful, and you can allow people to control their own behaviour by giving them the authority to think.

Fulfilling potential

You might choose to take the above three principles forward with some volunteers, moving from their self-esteem in given tasks and building towards the areas of their self-actualisation and fulfilment of their potential.

How you recruit and manage volunteers may be not so much about defining a role for them to fill as about exploring how a role can be built around them. How can they introduce new solutions in tackling problems for your organisation and its beneficiaries?

In exploring this possibility with a volunteer, you will need to hear about:

- the skills, knowledge and experience they bring from aspects of their professional life and/or academic studies;
- the relevance of their life experience to that of your beneficiaries;
- skills and knowledge they want to develop, perhaps with the view of making changes in their career or personal life, or perhaps simply for interest's sake;
- their follow-through on things they have achieved in your organisation;
- things you didn't previously know about them.

During this conversation, you should look for opportunities for the volunteer's self-assignment (see section 8.2) – that is, opportunities to put in place appropriate ways for them to plan their own actions and report back to you (see section 13.4).

Turning short term into long term

The previous two subsections focused on volunteers signing on for the medium or long term. However, increasingly people are coming forward to volunteer with a view to participating in just one event or task, seeing the experience as an episode in their lives. Section 13.3 discusses how it may be best to let them go, but here we consider how you might want to encourage some of these short-term volunteers to stay with you.

Once volunteers are working in these short-term roles, you might encourage them to be involved for longer. The process of strengthening involvement necessarily varies from role to role and from volunteer to volunteer, but some factors are common to almost all situations. You could consider three key ways of improving volunteer roles to make them more interesting and involving over the long term:

- **Give volunteers a great place to work.** Provide volunteers with a rewarding experience, where the working facilities are satisfactory and the social relationships are positive. What is important for each volunteer role will vary. However, a good place to start is to consider benefits that volunteers feel to be of value to themselves, which may include their satisfaction or pleasure at having helped others.
- **Give volunteers what they don't have.** Another way of making a role more interesting is to look at it from the perspective of the potential volunteers. What is it, for example, that they want out of their role that they aren't getting from their current paid job or other parts of their life?
- **Give volunteers a good time.** To help move people from short-term to longer-term commitments, develop ways to let them have a more rewarding experience. You could analyse your volunteer roles to strengthen their offer of enjoyment.

Beyond these steps, you could rethink aspects of your volunteering offer. You could develop a series of entry-level, short-term roles which are useful and satisfying in themselves and offer volunteers the opportunity to see how they like working with your organisation, its staff and its clientele. You may see one-off roles for sports events or community celebrations in this light (see section 9.2).

Individuals' decisions about how much time they have available may be specific to their circumstances and life planning. They may be open to offering a weekend every so often or they may only look at an opportunity which engages them for a defined period of a few weeks or months.

You could review your volunteering roles and schedules to see where your organisation could be more flexible about times and regularity, about locations (what might be done from home or online rather than in person?) and about possibilities for sharing roles, so as to accommodate people's varying pressures and preferences. More simply, does the same team of volunteers need to come every Tuesday afternoon?

And you could think through how to make the most of volunteers who come and go, as we now discuss.

13.3 STAYING IN TOUCH

In recent years, attention has shifted to people's changing attitudes to volunteering. For many, volunteering is now something to be slotted in around other commitments, not something that they want to do in the same location and at the same time week after week. This presents challenges and opportunities for you as a manager of volunteers. It means:

- you may be better off not devoting all your energies trying to hang on to volunteers for as long as possible – it may be more productive to let them leave;
- you may be managing relationships with people with whom you seldom, if ever, have face-to-face contact, as volunteers may work online spread across the world.

Additionally, people may prefer sporadic and short-term volunteering rather than a long-term commitment. For some this may involve trying out opportunities until they find the volunteer role they want to stick with. For some it may be because their commitments to paid employment and/or family life do not allow a regular and predictable schedule for volunteering. Others may simply be time poor and have to seize occasional opportunities to give their time.

If you let people go happily, they are more likely to come back because they know they won't be pressured into staying. In such cases, your approach to retaining volunteers should thus be one of serial involvement, where people come back over and over again for short-term assignments. The key is to keep the volunteers feeling connected to your organisation between assignments with both your and other organisations.

Behind this recognition of volunteering in more occasional or episodic forms may lie more fundamental factors to understand about the importance of volunteering in people's lives and in society.

According to Jeffrey Brudney and Lucas Meijs, volunteering as a whole may be usefully thought of like a natural resource which many organisations and people can draw on, rather than just an aggregation of chunks of time.[4] So, rather than concentrating on retaining volunteers within your organisation, you should think of volunteering as a movement which, as a manager of volunteers, you will help to sustain.

Volunteers will come and go for your organisation and for others. When they leave, you want them to think positively about what they got from volunteering so they are likely to volunteer again in future – for someone else if not for you!

This approach means you will need to work on how best to stay in touch with them across what may turn out to be years. You want to keep these people feeling connected to your organisation. While they were volunteering, your policies and organisational climate (see chapter 3) should have made them feel connected as an insider rather than an outsider, and after they leave you should aim to keep them feeling connected with your organisation and its mission.

One way to keep them feeling connected could be to ask a few weeks after they have left for their suggestions on:

- how their volunteer experience could have been better;
- how your organisation could serve its mission more effectively.

Longer term, you might seek to continue their sense of involvement with a variety of strategies (see Top tips on ways to keep short-term volunteers feeling connected).

Top tips on ways to keep short-term volunteers feeling connected

- Set up a volunteer page on a social networking site and invite past volunteers to visit it and participate in discussions there.
- Work out which social media work best for your organisation in terms of staying in contact with past volunteers to give them news and information about future opportunities.
- Enable them to keep records or scrapbooks online.
- Keep them on your email newsletter circulation (subject to their informed consent) to fill them in on what has gone on since they left, including plenty of pictures.
- Invite them to social occasions.
- Give them an item of branded clothing, such as a cap or sweatshirt.
- Send them birthday and other holiday greetings, perhaps with photos and messages from people they worked with during their volunteer job.
- Keep your eyes and ears open for opportunities to engage them in doing things they really love. When you find one, get in touch and offer them the opportunity to get re-engaged.

■ Include developing these relationships in your organisation's communications or public relations strategy and work plan. When a past volunteer sees a mention of your organisation on social media or in print media or catches your organisation's name on the TV or radio, you are reinforcing their connection with your organisation.

You might encourage staff and volunteers with whom they worked to contact them occasionally to ask how they're doing and tell them what is going on, but equally you might just want to give them space and recognise their freedom to volunteer as and when they choose.

Basically, this is all about building and maintaining relationships. We should emphasise, however, that it is not simply about building a relationship between the volunteers and their manager. It should be a relationship between the volunteers and the organisation. It is about building a sense of identity, a sense that the volunteer is part of an effort to accomplish the mission of the organisation. If the relationship is only with the manager they know, this can be disastrous for the organisation when that person leaves.

13.4   THE VOLUNTEER LIFE CYCLE: CRITICAL POINTS

Where a volunteer is in a long-term role within your organisation, there will be critical points at which the volunteer will review their decision to remain. These points seem to be predictable to some extent, in terms of both time of occurrence and the content of the factors that will influence the volunteer in either leaving or staying.

This situation is complicated by the fact that the volunteer's motivations, reactions to their volunteer work and need for adjustment to other life factors will tend to change over time. Each of these changes can lead to the volunteer re-examining their commitment.

This section summarises these critical points and suggests ways for you as a manager of volunteers to positively influence a volunteer's engagement.

Initial contact

We focused on the process of bringing volunteers on board in chapters 5 and 6, but it is helpful to stress again here that success in keeping volunteers is often rooted in their first impressions of an organisation. For instance:

- their encounter with the organisation's website;
- the information and materials promoting volunteering;
- their initial call asking about volunteering;

- their first meeting or interview with a manager of volunteers;
- the orientation session;
- their first day in their volunteer role.

During each of these moments, the volunteer is forming opinions about whether the somewhat risky move they are considering (offering themselves to an unfamiliar organisation) is a wise choice. At this point, any feeling of discomfort is likely to be magnified in the mind of the potential volunteer, and any sense that the organisation is indifferent or uninterested is likely to result in them ending the relationship. At this early and fragile point in the relationship, the potential volunteer is highly attuned to any signs of welcome or rejection.

First few weeks

During their first few weeks, the volunteer is learning about the role to which they have been assigned. You should always view the initial match between a volunteer and a role as a hopeful but occasionally inappropriate experiment, commonly based on a relatively short interview in which each participant operates with a great deal of ignorance about the other. As a result, you will need to keep close contact with the volunteer during this initial period.

The primary factor influencing the volunteer during this critical time is one of comfort in the role: do they feel capable and interested in the work now that they are actually learning what it is really about? Reality has replaced the role description.

You can reduce the risk of the volunteer leaving during this period by scheduling a review interview to take place a short time after the initial placement. This interview, arranged at the time of initial placement, should be presented to the volunteer as an opportunity for them to truly decide whether they like the role or not. The first month then operates as a test drive for the volunteer.

First few months

During the first few months, the volunteer has an opportunity to examine and consider their developing relationship with the organisation. There are several critical factors.

- **Reality versus expectation:** does the situation in which the volunteer is now engaged meet their expectations in a positive way? Is the volunteer getting what they thought they would get out of volunteering? Is the volunteer work vastly different from what they thought it would be or what was described to them during the initial orientation and training? Do the beneficiaries and work environment meet the volunteer's expectations?

- **Role fit:** do the overall aspects of the work (beneficiary relations, work process, etc.) match the volunteer's interests and abilities? Does the volunteer feel equal to the work and capable of achieving some success in it?
- **Life fit:** do the volunteer work and its time and logistical requirements fit comfortably into the rest of the volunteer's life, work and relationships? Is the volunteer work too demanding or too intrusive?
- **Social fit:** does the volunteer feel as if they are becoming an accepted part of the organisation's social environment? Do they feel respected and part of the team? Are they finding friends and colleagues?

Possible ways to help a volunteer reach a positive conclusion during this period include:

- Create a buddy or mentor system for new volunteers. These colleagues will assume responsibility for answering any questions the volunteer has, helping them with their new role and introducing them to the social fabric of the organisation. Experienced volunteers make excellent buddies.
- Assume that you will need to allocate more time for communication with new volunteers, and plan your schedule accordingly. Don't assume that a volunteer will come to you; create opportunities to talk with each volunteer, even if just a social call.
- Schedule a six-month review. This is not so much an appraisal (see chapter 12) as it is a chance to talk with the volunteer in a formal way about how they are feeling and whether they are enjoying themselves. If the volunteer has a staff supervisor as well as reporting to you as a manager of volunteers (see section 9.1), this review can explore the three-way relationship.
- Give the volunteer symbols of belonging to the organisation. This can include name badges, branded clothing, necessary equipment, and (depending on the role) an email address, business cards, etc.

Make sure that the volunteer has a realistic view of what is possible. Misperceptions are common among volunteers, who will often anticipate that their work will be more exciting, more glamorous or more immediately successful than is likely. The earlier you can bring these expectations in line with reality, the better your chance of helping the volunteer avoid unnecessary disappointment.

First anniversary, or end of initial term or commitment

This can be one of the most critical points in the volunteer life cycle. Often at this point there is a meeting for reflection or a formal review, probably as part of an appraisal (see chapter 12). This is likely to lead to a discussion of whether the volunteer wishes to carry on or seek a new volunteer opportunity.

There are several key factors for the volunteer at this time.

- **Bonding:** has the volunteer developed favourable personal relationships with others in the organisation? Does the volunteer have friends among the staff and other volunteers?
- **Accomplishments and expectations:** in reviewing their period of volunteering, does the volunteer feel that they have accomplished what they thought they would accomplish in their role? Does the volunteer feel successful, or do they feel that they have failed to achieve what they wanted? Can they see how their work and results connect into the organisation's mission and the cause to which they are committed? Does the volunteer's self-review accord with how their manager sees their achievement?
- **Opportunities for growth:** in contemplating the continuation of the volunteer work, does the volunteer look to the future with anticipation or do they feel that the work will simply be more of the same, or even boring? Does the volunteer feel that they have opportunities to be continually challenged and fulfil their potential in their role?

For this first-year appraisal, you should consider how to do the following:

- Celebrate what the volunteer has accomplished and how they are appreciated. Be prepared to cite evidence and examples.
- Make sure the volunteer has an opportunity to see the results of their work and of the overall work of your organisation. Always remember that the ultimate impact on beneficiaries or the community is part of a volunteer's motivation, and it is difficult to feel motivated when you never know the results. Inform the volunteer about the results of monitoring and evaluation focused on their area of work.
- Talk frankly to the volunteer about whether they are still enjoying their work. Many volunteers will be reluctant to tell you this, either out of fear of seeming to let the organisation down or out of fear of seeming to criticise those with whom they work. Strive to reach an understanding with the volunteer that this discussion is not about failure but about renewal – an opportunity to fulfil their potential in the future.
- Prepare a number of different options for the volunteer that could serve to rekindle the sense of excitement they once had. These might include a change to a new role, greater responsibilities in their current role, or even, after time, a sabbatical to step aside from their volunteer work and gain a new perspective or just a feeling of reinvigoration.

The longer term

In the longer term, individual volunteers will face additional critical points. These are not always predictable, as they occur at different times for different volunteers. Here are some of the factors that will create these incidents:

- **Work adjustment:** if the volunteer's role changes in any substantial way, the volunteer can experience disruption. This can include a change in the beneficiary to whom the volunteer is assigned or a change in the staff with whom the volunteer is working. It can also very often include a change in the status of a colleague to whom the volunteer has a close attachment (e.g. a fellow volunteer may move on to a new role).
- **Life fit:** over time, the volunteer's own life and needs will change. You should stay attuned to how the volunteer's life is going more broadly, since major changes in it will create critical examination of the volunteer's involvement.

Two strategies are crucial in ensuring that volunteers remain committed during these changes:

- Give volunteers a sense of empowerment in shaping their volunteer work (see section 13.2). While this isn't true for everyone, generally speaking, if volunteers know that they can discuss their work and will have opportunities to redesign it to fit a changing situation, they are more likely to remain.
- Discuss with volunteers how they can adapt their role to gain a greater sense of fulfilment in applying their potential, while maintaining the constraints which are needed by your organisation's mission and strategy for volunteer engagement (see section 8.2).

Look at your volunteers on a longitudinal basis, remembering that, like all of us, they are likely to grow and change over time. Since volunteering depends upon meeting both the needs and the individual circumstances of the volunteer, it makes sense that volunteer management will need to adjust to changes in those needs and circumstances.

Bearing all of the above in mind, there are two final important points to note in this section. First, there is a tendency at present towards shorter-term volunteer placements (see section 13.3). The processes in this section assume you will be working with longer-term volunteers, so for shorter placements some of these processes would need to be amended, with the time frames contracted. Obviously you cannot hold an annual appraisal with a volunteer who is only with you for a few weeks.

Second, keeping people volunteering for a long time may not be an approach you want to follow. Aside from giving people more flexibility in their volunteering, you may want to place your emphasis on enabling people to move on – and therefore on recruiting new people. This would enable you to have a greater number of connections with volunteers who give their time occasionally, in small parcels or over the internet. Your decision will depend on your organisation's mission and strategy as well as the roles you want volunteers to fill, the people you need and their needs.

13.5 **RECOGNISING VOLUNTEERS**

Volunteers must receive a sense of appreciation and reward for their contribution. This sense can be conveyed through both formal and informal recognition systems.

Formal recognition systems

Formal recognition systems consist of awards, certificates, plaques, badges and recognition events that honour volunteer achievement. Many organisations hold an annual ceremony in which individual volunteers are singled out for their achievement, often during Volunteers' Week (in the UK, 1–7 June).

Formal systems can be beneficial to your organisation because they provide a simple infrastructure which ensures volunteer recognition doesn't fall into the gaps between your systems. It also sets up a place to bring senior management into the volunteer sphere, and it provides a public platform to show your organisation's support and advocacy for volunteering.

Formal systems are helpful mainly in satisfying the needs of volunteers who seek recognition or approval, whether from a public body, the local community or other volunteers. Systems of certification may be linked to educational awards or be useful in developing careers, especially among young people. Sometimes an important thing for a volunteer is the status or celebrity of the person who presides at the ceremony and shakes hands in giving out the certificate. Long-service certificates or ornamental gifts may carry much significance for some volunteers, even if their monetary value is not large – and they can be a relatively uncomplicated form of showing appreciation.

However, a lavish ceremony may have a negative impact for volunteers whose primary focus is helping your beneficiaries. They may very well feel more motivated and honoured by a system which recognises the achievements of 'their' beneficiaries and/or the contribution volunteers collectively have made towards achieving the mission. Finally, long-service awards may seem fairly meaningless for volunteers on shorter, or more episodic, placements, and may be counterproductive in valuing only those who are able to give large quantities of time.

In determining whether to establish a ceremony such as a formal meal or reception, consider the following points:

- Are you truly doing it to say thank you or just so your organisation can fulfil its obligation to formally recognise volunteers?
- Will it really be seen by the volunteers as a welcome and enjoyable honour, or as yet another call on their time and perhaps more like a way to satisfy the staff's need to feel they have shown appreciation for volunteers?

- Would the volunteers feel better if you spent the money on the needs of your beneficiaries rather than on an obligatory luncheon?
- How will you make the ceremony have a sense of celebration and of building team identity?
- How will the ceremony help to embed volunteering within your organisation and its external relationships?

Informal recognition practices

The most effective volunteer recognition occurs in the day-to-day interchange between the volunteer and the organisation, through the staff – and other volunteers – expressing sincere appreciation and thanks for the work being done by the volunteer.

This type of recognition is more powerful, in part because it is much more frequent – a once-a-year dinner does not carry the same impact as 365 days of good working relationships.

Day-to-day recognition may include:

- saying thank you;
- staff knowing volunteers' names;
- involving volunteers in decisions that affect them;
- showing an interest in volunteers' lives outside your organisation;
- making sure that volunteers and staff are treated as equals;
- enabling volunteers to increase their skills by attending training for their roles;
- recommending volunteers for advancement to more responsible roles;
- celebrating volunteers' anniversaries with your organisation;
- giving regular and honest feedback;
- passing on thanks and success stories from beneficiaries;
- inviting volunteers to relevant meetings and social get-togethers.

The intention of informal recognition is to constantly convey a sense of appreciation and belonging to volunteers. This sense can be conveyed more effectively by the thousands of small interactions that compose daily life than by an annual event. Nonetheless, you can overdo it: saying thank you every time a volunteer does anything can feel patronising or irritating, and risks endorsing poor performance as well as good.

Recognition can begin quite early on in the relationship. A welcome card sent to a new volunteer, or a small welcome party, conveys an immediate sense of appreciation.

Rules for recognition

Whatever mix of recognition systems you make use of, remember the following rules.

1. Give it or else

The need for recognition is very important to most people, even if some volunteers say they don't want it. If volunteers don't get recognition for productive participation, you may have to face up to negative consequences. The most straightforward consequence is that they feel unappreciated and drop out, but they may also harbour a grudge against you and tell their friends and wider networks.

2. Give it frequently

A common complaint of volunteers is that they don't get enough recognition from paid staff. Staff are usually surprised by this and can often cite examples of when they have given recognition to volunteers. The reason for this discrepancy of perception is that recognition has a short shelf life. Its effects start to wear off after a few days, and, after several weeks of not hearing anything positive, volunteers start to wonder whether they are appreciated. Giving recognition to a volunteer once a year at a recognition event is certainly not enough.

3. Give it through a variety of methods

One of the implications of the previous rule is that you need a variety of methods of showing appreciation to volunteers. Fortunately, there are hundreds of methods. Recognition can be categorised into four major types:

- **From a staff member for work the volunteer did.** Examples include saying, 'You did a great job on this', writing a letter or email to that effect, or posting news about the volunteer's project on social media.
- **From a staff member for being part of the organisation.** This is expressed through appreciation of the volunteer as a person. Examples include birthday celebrations or personal compliments such as, 'I'm impressed by how you always have such a positive attitude.'
- **From the organisation for work the volunteer did.** Examples include an award recognising the volunteer's work on a project or being honoured as Volunteer of the Month.
- **From the organisation for being part of the team.** Examples include an award commemorating years of service, or featuring the volunteer in a newsletter article that states interesting personal facts about them but is not written due to any particular incident of good job performance.

All of these types are valid. Certain types appeal more to some people than to others. Try to make sure that you use a mixture of methods.

4. Give it honestly

Don't give praise unless you mean it. If you praise substandard or mediocre performance, the praise you give to others for good work will not be valued. If a volunteer is performing poorly, you might be able to give them honest recognition for their effort or attitude.

5. Give it to the person, not to the work

This is a subtle but important distinction. If volunteers organise a fundraising event, for example, and you praise the event without mentioning who organised it, the volunteers may feel some resentment. Make sure that you connect the volunteer's name to it. It is better to say, 'Ali did a great job of organising this event' than to say, 'This event was really well organised'.

6. Give it appropriately to the achievement

Small accomplishments should be praised with low-effort methods; large accomplishments should get something more. For example, if a volunteer tutor teaches a child to identify colours, you could say, 'Well done!'. If they write a grant proposal that funds a new piece of work, a letter of appreciation might be more appropriate.

7. Give it consistently

If two volunteers are responsible for similar achievements, they ought to get similar recognition. If one gets their picture in the lobby and another gets an approving nod, the latter may feel resentment. This does not mean that the recognition has to be exactly the same – rather, it should be the result of similar effort on your part. Otherwise certain volunteers will come to be regarded as 'favourites', a stigma they may grow to dread.

8. Give it on a timely basis

Praise for work should come as soon as possible after the achievement. Don't save up your recognition for the annual banquet. If volunteers have to wait months before hearing any word of praise, they may develop resentment due to the lack of praise in the meantime.

9. Give it in an individualised fashion

Different people like different things. One might respond favourably to tickets for a show-jumping competition, another might find them useless. Some like public recognition while others find it embarrassing. In order to provide effective recognition, you need to get to know your people and what they will respond to positively – but remember to treat people who work together the same (see rule 7).

10. Give it for what you want more of

Too often, your staff will pay the most attention to volunteers who are having difficulties. Unfortunately, this may result in ignoring good performers. This is not to suggest that you should not show appreciation of less dynamic volunteers, just that you must make sure that you praise the efforts of those who are doing a good job.

13.6 PRACTICAL POINTERS

- Previously highly motivated volunteers stop volunteering for a number of reasons:
  - Some factors are beyond the control of the organisation – and maybe of the volunteer – such as changes in personal circumstances, moving house, a new relationship, new employment or starting a family.
  - Some are within the control of the organisation, such as the volunteer feeling their time or talents are not well managed or they are not being appreciated.
- People who drop out commonly say it's because they don't have time. Consider whether this is an excuse. Are they covering up dissatisfaction with the way they have been managed?
- Strengthen volunteers' engagement through an environment which fosters their self-esteem and their feelings of connectedness, uniqueness and empowerment.
- Encourage volunteers' sense of fulfilment and engagement by building a role and tasks around their potential.
- Volunteers' needs in volunteering change over time. What keeps them volunteering is not usually the passion which originally brought them to your organisation.
- A general presumption may be that you want to retain volunteers for as long as possible. But this is not necessarily so. Increasingly, people are seeking short-term placements, perhaps as a try-out, or taking up episodes of volunteering to fit in with the rest of their lives. Let them go happily, so they come back because they know they won't be pressured into staying. Think of it as serial involvement.

- As a manager of volunteers, you have a responsibility to other managers of volunteers to see that volunteers will volunteer again – even if not necessarily with you!
- Maintain communication with volunteers after they leave and between assignments, so they know how to come back when the time and the project is right for them. (Make sure you have volunteers' informed consent to contact them.)
- Say thank you to your volunteers. But think about the appropriate ways to do this for different sets of volunteers. What would be right for a particular group? A ceremony with a celebrity giving out certificates – or a rose bush? A sit-down lunch – with or without wine? A quick thank you whenever they pick up a broom? Informal day-to-day appreciation may be most effective in many working situations, but some volunteers will expect formal recognition. Treat people who work together equally. And don't forget any of them.

14 Building staff and volunteer engagement

The relationship between volunteers and paid staff in your organisation is crucial in ensuring they can all make the difference they want to make – and the difference you need them to make to succeed in your organisation's mission. But, if working relationships between volunteers and staff aren't good, the problems can be among the most testing for you to resolve, not only in terms of organisational effectiveness but also in terms of personal feelings.

It can be hard to understand why there is a problem. Isn't everybody here working for the same cause? Aren't they all good people committed to making the world a better place? So, how is it that you can see paid staff trying to marginalise or undermine volunteers? How is it that you have grumpy volunteers, resentful about how staff are treating them? Why is everyone complaining to you?

Our approach would be to try not to be too surprised. The political and economic environment is full of tensions which play out on all of us working within it. The situations in which staff and volunteers are placed are changing, raising various pressures and producing different responses among people who are trying to do their best.

Throughout this book, we consider management issues from the perspectives of volunteers and managers of volunteers. However, in this chapter, we focus on paid staff and how they may be negative about working with volunteers, and how you as the manager of volunteers, alongside your management colleagues, may tackle these problems.

The fourth section of this chapter extends the problem area by focusing on the issue of volunteers replacing (or being feared to be replacing) paid staff and, vice versa, problems about volunteer roles being replaced by paid staff. This connects to deeper questions about the place for volunteering.

14.1 CHANGING PROBLEM SITUATIONS

Immense changes have taken place in patterns of volunteer involvement in past decades. In the 1960s and 1970s, as voluntary organisations became more significant in social policy and service provision, most volunteer programmes operated almost as organisations within organisations, with a manager of volunteers (either paid or unpaid) who supervised volunteers engaged in a variety of projects or activities. In many cases, these volunteers were engaged in activities that were somewhat separate from the other operations of the organisation. Managers of volunteers were responsible for almost all recruitment, job development and supervision of 'their' volunteers. In some cases this could result in rather strange management systems where one manager of volunteers was in charge of hundreds or even thousands of volunteers, operating a situation akin to one human resources specialist managing all the paid staff!

As volunteer involvement became more sophisticated, this picture changed considerably. Volunteers came to be diffused throughout the structure of the organisation and became a more integral part of the work. Volunteers began to work more in partnership with staff and, commonly, worked under managers who led teams composed of paid staff and volunteers.

Over the decades, some services which had been initiated and run by volunteers gained public or charitable funding, and jobs were taken over by paid staff on the assumption that they would provide a more regular and expert service. Some professional staff came to regard volunteers as having only ancillary roles, and volunteers seemed less central to the quality and scale of provision. Indeed, on a large historical canvas, this could be seen as the story of the evolution of social services and other mainstream public services.

However, in the twenty-first century, faced with cuts in funding from central and local government and the effects of austerity on public provision, some organisations have seen how social problems might be better tackled if volunteers take a larger and more direct role. Volunteers – or, at least, some kinds of volunteer – may better understand the issues faced by beneficiaries and may place the emphasis on advocacy and social action to tackle problems, rather than service provision. Moreover, volunteers may cost less than paid staff, and so, reversing to some extent the story of the evolution of social services, new developments may be carried out by volunteers. And, in some services, as we note below (see section 14.4), existing paid roles have been taken over by volunteers.

Within this environment, your organisation has not been a free agent. It has been shaped by needing to work within policies and funding systems set by others (for example funders, national and/or local government and their agencies and so on) in seeking to best serve its own mission and commitments. It has made its way through ideological and political debates about providing services through state, market or voluntary organisations and through paid staff or volunteers, sometimes maintaining its own convictions and sometimes compromising.

Staff concerns

Thus, there has been space for anxieties to grow about people's roles, both among paid staff and among volunteers. Tensions between staff and volunteers can run deep through debates and anxieties about roles, status and ethos, and sometimes these will blow up into difficulties in working together.

The concerns felt by paid staff may be of various natures:

- anxieties about the quality of work, that volunteers are unreliable or won't turn up for work, that they don't understand legal or regulatory requirements, or that they lack professional training and expertise;
- resentment about managing volunteers and hence about increased workload, especially if the staff member doesn't have experience of managing volunteers or has previously had a bad experience of volunteers;
- anxiety about loss of status if the staff member's job can be done by an unpaid person, or about loss of satisfaction if elements of the job they enjoy are taken over by a volunteer;
- fears that paid jobs will be replaced by volunteers and colleagues made redundant, or that when post holders leave, their jobs may be given to volunteers.

These are not abstract anxieties. They are entirely reasonable things to worry about when people care about their job and their livelihood and don't feel secure given the external pressures on their situation.

These concerns may be complicated when volunteers bring quite different approaches to work and to the cause. Volunteers can occasionally be pious about the strength of their motivation and commitment to the cause, compared to staff who are paid for a working day. Or, in some circumstances, volunteers may regard staff as the people who do the donkey work which allows volunteers to shine in more public or interesting roles. There is plenty of room for contention.

14.2 BRINGING AND KEEPING STAFF ON SIDE

The essence of engaging staff with the involvement of volunteers is to work alongside staff to appreciate how they see the pros and cons and to encourage them to develop their perspectives and proposals for creating and improving volunteering opportunities. This means facilitating two feelings among staff:

- a sense of benefits being greater than the difficulties or problems;
- a feeling of empowerment over the situation.

Staff are more likely to be satisfied with the volunteers with whom they will be working if they can perceive that the return to them is greater than the effort involved, and if they believe that they will be closely involved in making decisions that affect how they are to work with the volunteers.

You can't simply instruct staff to work with volunteers and expect good results. There are too many grey areas and nuances of working relationships, which may be complicated by a perception that volunteers have more freedom of movement and are more loosely managed than paid staff. There are too many ways for staff to sabotage volunteer efforts; even indifference of staff will quickly communicate itself to volunteers, who will equally quickly decide not to be where they are not wanted.

Nonetheless, where an organisation has a policy that it needs volunteers to achieve its mission and strategy, it will require staff to work with volunteers as part of their role, and this may even be written into their job description. Implementing the requirement for paid staff to work with volunteers will have to be handled with great care in order to make it effective. You will need to explore how to overcome problems and optimise working relationships, and that means listening and exploring rather than telling people how it's got to be done.

That still doesn't mean that managers can simply issue instructions about good working relationships. As a manager of volunteers, you will need to work through any resistance of employees to working with volunteers and clearly communicate the benefits to be gained.

Orienting staff

Staff need to understand the reasoning and processes behind volunteer involvement within your organisation, along the lines we set out in chapters 1–4 of this book. This would include ensuring paid staff are informed about:

- the rationale for involving volunteers;
- a brief history of volunteer involvement;
- an explanation of the types of volunteer and the roles they do;
- a description of the difference volunteers make;
- the roles of paid staff in all aspects of working with volunteers.

This orientation might in practice be provided in different ways and at different times. Part of it might be given to each new staff member, and then another part of it might be given as staff begin to be involved with volunteers. It may be given in either a formal or informal setting in a team workshop or one on one, and basic information may be provided in writing. It would be effective to include managers and other staff with good experiences of volunteers as co-presenters during these sessions.

Committing the organisation

In orienting paid staff, you must work within your organisation's policy on volunteer involvement, expressing why the organisation involves volunteers (see chapter 2). You might refer to reasons such as:

- to provide community outreach and input;
- to tap into the skills, resources and connections of the local community;
- to supplement the expertise of staff;
- to involve people who are able to do things paid staff cannot;
- to allow involvement of beneficiary groups;
- to demonstrate community support or leadership;
- to advocate for funding;
- to provide a personal touch in services to beneficiaries;
- to run services and activities your organisation could not resource through its funding.

The policy should provide a clear rationale which can be used in explaining to staff and to potential volunteers why and how volunteers are involved in your organisation. It should indicate to staff that involving volunteers is not just an emergency measure that was dreamed up one weekend by a desperate senior manager, but rather an approach that fits within the mission and vision of your organisation (see chapter 2). The policy should be seen to have been:

- adopted and supported by trustees (or the equivalent committee or governing body) and the senior management team (see sections 3.3 and 8.4);
- integrated into the overall organisational strategy and budgets (see sections 3.4 and 3.5).

The policy should demonstrate that staff members' engagement with volunteers is a requisite feature of working in your organisation, just as working with paid staff colleagues and managers is not an optional aspect of employment.

Creating and managing volunteering roles

Before introducing additional volunteering roles or a new volunteering programme, as we advised in chapter 3, you should explore with paid staff:

- their views about the need for volunteers, and their fears or recommendations about what jobs would be appropriate or inappropriate for volunteers (see section 3.2);
- their know-how in managing and working alongside volunteers;
- their experience of volunteering, as volunteers themselves or as staff in an organisation that involved volunteers, or perhaps as beneficiaries on the receiving end of volunteering.

This survey and questioning should:

- help to demarcate which roles are undertaken by volunteers and which by staff, or where there may be overlaps;
- inform you about what paid staff already know as a basis for your work to help them develop their skills;
- reassure paid staff that working with volunteers will bring benefits and will be informed by their views and knowledge.

For volunteers to be involved effectively, paid staff need to understand and be adept at managing and working with volunteers. Staff need the capacity to comprehend the variety in the volunteer workforce, recognising how volunteering jobs can be imaginative and meaningful. And they need the skills to lead, supervise and/or collaborate with volunteers. We dare to suggest they could have the opportunity to dip into this book!

A potential problem where staff can seem to resist involvement of volunteers may simply be that the staff recognise their own inexperience in working with volunteers, even if they do not wish to admit it. In such situations, you can assist by helping staff to work through what will need to be done to have a successful experience in supervising or working alongside volunteers. The best time to do this is when the staff member will first be working with a volunteer, but you will probably need to return to the topic when issues arise.

There need to be structural ways to support staff – for example, you could create a 'users' group' or forum for staff who supervise volunteers. This can allow a space for discussion of problems and triumphs and may assist in developing policies and shaping the direction of volunteer engagement across your organisation.

Getting feedback

Looking ahead, you will need to be able to report back to paid staff on the benefits – or not – produced by involving volunteers (see chapter 15), so as to confirm and adapt the ways your organisation is involving volunteers.

14.3   MANAGEMENT WORKING TOGETHER

To be in the position to support paid staff members' involvement of volunteers, you will need the backing of senior management. This backing will need to carry across all aspects of volunteering policy and practice in your organisation (see sections 3.3 and 8.4).

It is important, then, for everybody who manages volunteers in your organisation to work together. There may be a number of paid staff who have management or supervisory responsibilities for volunteers, such as:

- a team leader who supervises one or more volunteers alongside paid staff;
- a line manager of a department or project who manages a mix of volunteers and paid staff;
- a manager who runs an all-volunteer project or team;
- a senior manager, sometimes with a job title such as 'director of volunteering', who leads on volunteering across a big organisation, directing and advising how other managers (as above) manage volunteers in their departments or teams (see sections 1.1 and 8.4). Such a role should be part of a senior management team with strategic responsibilities, and might be integrated with human resource management or community engagement.

The people in these different roles need to work together to prepare staff to work with volunteers and to sustain effective relationships with volunteers.

Where there is a director of volunteering, they are responsible for the system of volunteer involvement within the organisation, working closely with other people who manage volunteers. They are a resource, offering expertise in volunteer management to help other managers and paid staff in their teams involve volunteers more productively (see figure 8.3). Often you can think of this role as like a human resources department for volunteers.

A line manager or team leader will be happy to accept the responsibility for managing and supervising volunteers, providing they are supported by the director or manager who leads on volunteering. Together they will need to work through differences between managing volunteers and managing paid staff and analyse ways of tackling problem situations.

There needs to be clarity about the web of relationships between the volunteers, the paid staff, and all managers and team leaders who manage and supervise volunteers. The extent of a line manager's or team leader's involvement in managing or supervising volunteers will vary, depending on the structure established in your organisation (see chapter 8, figure 8.3). In some cases a manager of volunteers manages the whole scope of the volunteer's involvement and tasks. But in others the overarching responsibilities rest with a director or manager of volunteers so that a project manager or team leader is just focused on supervising the volunteer's tasks. If so, they should be helped to feel part of the whole management team for the volunteer and kept informed not only about their volunteer but also about general issues in managing volunteers.

A manager of volunteers must understand who is in charge of what, who is responsible for what, and what should happen if things go wrong. Who, for example, is in charge of releasing an unsatisfactory volunteer (see section 12.4)? Is it a unilateral decision or a joint one? And who does the paid staff member talk to if they have a problem?

In working with paid staff who present problems about working with volunteers, you (as the manager of volunteers) would be well advised to act like a consultant; as we indicated in section 14.2, commanding staff to work with volunteers is not likely to be effective. This means that you should seek to draw out staff members' views and experiences in working with volunteers by asking questions, summarising and reflecting on the points made, and exploring what solutions people see to the problems. This should be an iterative process in which you establish and test the steps that may be made. It is a process through which you need to keep your cool, especially when the going is against you.

Your natural tendency may be to tell your staff what is wrong, but it is usually more effective to work with them to improve things by asking questions and leading them through a conversation. By doing so, you help people to gain a feeling of being empowered throughout the process (see 'Top tips on getting staff on board' on the next page).

It may be useful to have an external consultant or someone who is not part of the specific management structure to facilitate the discussion. Or, where there is a director of volunteering, they may have sufficient status to preside over an argument without becoming part of it.

Overcoming resistance

In dealing with the concerns of paid staff, you should not take their resistance personally; your natural instinct may be to fight and win, but that is usually disastrous. Instead, you should attempt to work with staff in a consulting capacity, helping them to solve whatever problems with volunteers they encounter or foresee.

Staff who are uncertain about the value of volunteers will be reluctant to invest much in testing their value. However, as the manager of volunteers, you need to help them get past this and trust your advice. A staff member may resist your help because they aren't confident you are capable of helping to solve a problem or meet their needs. They may, for instance, feel that:

- you don't have enough influence in the organisation to help;
- you don't understand the needs of their department or team;
- you care more about volunteers and volunteering than them and their work.

They may also not know about your knowledge or qualities, or they may have had a bad experience with your predecessor.

To deal with this resistance, you need to reduce the personal barriers between you and the staff member. It may be helpful to ask what they need to know about you and your past experience, as well as about your perspective on the future and the options for how to deal with the situation.

One often overlooked factor in this issue lies in whether as manager of volunteers you are a good role model in the involvement of volunteers: if *you* don't involve volunteers in helping you do your work, why would anyone trust your recommendation that *they* should involve volunteers?

Top tips on getting staff on board

1. Begin by recognising that staff will have concerns about the use of volunteers. Some of these concerns will be about what is involved in working with volunteers and whether it is worth the effort. Some concerns will be based on past experiences, and new managers of volunteers should always do some investigation of the history of volunteer involvement in their organisation to identify any past disasters.

2. Other questions, especially if you are a new manager of volunteers, will be about you, your background and knowledge, how you work and the real purpose of your offer of assistance. In a nutshell, staff may be thinking, 'You're new. What could you possibly understand about what I do?'

3. Quite often, staff will not be willing to directly admit their concerns or ask the questions at the heart of their anxieties. What they are concerned about will vary across organisations and among the staff within an organisation. Think about your organisation's staff, in general, or about particular staff and see whether you can identify what concerns they might have about working with volunteers and about following your lead on the matter.

4. Once you have your list of possible concerns, you will need to build proactive answers, working with staff and management colleagues. You probably need to address these concerns without directly confronting staff about whether this or that is their concern; they may not be prepared to acknowledge it and so may close down the discussion. You can adapt your approach to act like a consultant, circling the issues to encourage people to express their concerns and work jointly in coming up with solutions.

5. A key lies in the wording you use to introduce your understandings and prompt people to respond. Some samples of how to phrase your points include:

    ■ 'I hear...'
    ■ 'People have wondered...'
    ■ 'A concern voiced by staff in other organisations has been...'
    ■ 'Here's an example of how I would work with people to...'

    A key element is to avoid pinning anxieties and concerns on the person you are talking with and to leave it open to them to develop their responses.

6. Some consulting skills that will help you build ways ahead include:

    ■ looking – and really being! – open to hearing a range of views;
    ■ talking in terms of 'we' and shared conversation;
    ■ learning something useful and sharing it at the meeting;
    ■ giving staff members time to vent and expressing your understanding;
    ■ summarising staff members' concerns and solutions;
    ■ paraphrasing those concerns and solutions in ways that help to do something tangible about them;
    ■ starting with small wins and building from there.

Top tips for beginning to engage with volunteers

Supervisors or managers who are just beginning to work with volunteers may have a different perspective from an experienced manager. Whereas an experienced manager could adopt the top tips on getting staff on board (see above), someone new to the task may need a different approach to working these issues through with paid staff. These tips may help to overcome initial obstacles and develop full engagement with volunteers.

■ Recognise that staff members in your team – and perhaps you – may have concerns about involving volunteers in delivering your team's activities or services. They may wonder whether it is worth the extra effort of explaining the task and its context to someone who is new. They may also be concerned about working alongside people who may not be professionals.

■ Be open and accept that these kinds of concern are legitimate and may be a consequence of staff members' commitment to the job – they are not just being awkward.

- Brief yourself on your organisation's policy and reasons for involving volunteers, and how those relate to the external environment and the mission.
- Brief yourself on the support available to your team or department, and on the kind of leadership the senior management and board of trustees (or equivalent) give in relation to volunteering.
- Discuss with senior managers and management colleagues your own sense of the opportunities and difficulties, and how managing volunteers may be different from managing paid staff.
- Discuss with your team how volunteers may help your team to be more productive, perhaps with more capacity to enlarge your scope of action, or perhaps by enabling you to get closer to beneficiary groups.
- Take the suggestions from your team into account in your plan for involving volunteers, also collaborating with management colleagues.
- Be consistent in your processes for managing volunteers, and be ready to hear problems and adapt ways of working.
- Be prepared to take problems to senior management or a manager who leads on volunteering across the organisation.
- Record examples of good work and success, celebrate with your team and tell your organisation's leadership about your team's achievements.

14.4 REPLACING PAID STAFF AND VOLUNTEERS

Replacing paid staff

One area which can be contentious and create larger negative reactions among staff is where volunteers are perceived to have been recruited to replace posts previously held by paid staff. Sometimes called 'job substitution', this often happens when paid staff posts are made redundant (or not filled when staff leave for other reasons) and the organisation gets volunteers to do the work. Paid staff are likely to feel threatened about losing their own livelihoods, and they may be angry that volunteers are prepared to work for no pay and put colleagues out of paid employment. They may also believe that volunteers will work to lower standards, downgrading the quality or professionalism of their service and perhaps risking damaging what paid staff have achieved. Where the paid staff are members of trade unions, such situations will probably bring the organisation into conflict with those unions. Dealing with a trade union might involve senior management rather than a manager of volunteers, but emotions run high and any union action may spread through the organisation and affect everyone's work.

This issue was particularly of concern when the austerity agenda and cuts in public finance became formative for public and community services after 2008. In the UK, the public library service and the police were particularly affected. The library service which emerged was in many areas quite different, either because volunteers had become much more numerous and engaged in specialist work than previously, or because community groups had taken over libraries from local authorities.

Volunteers had been involved among police forces for many years, but austerity increased their participation. Many more volunteers were brought in to fill roles in back office and support functions, as well as in community and technical functions such as traffic safety and video surveillance, where volunteers helped to build relationships with the local community and brought additional skills.

Following the resolution of such changes in some public services and resistance against them in others, the problem perhaps seems less cataclysmic than it did a few years ago. We believe – though subsequent developments may prove us wrong – that there may now be more acceptance of the inexorability of budgetary restraint and more experience in resolving the job replacement issue, though undoubtedly some misunderstandings persist about what volunteers offer.

In charities, especially small and medium-sized community organisations, there was generally less conflict. Given their loss of income and consequently of paid staff posts, organisations were faced with a choice between cutting services or relying on volunteers; commonly, a commitment to the beneficiaries took precedence over taking a stand on resources for paid staff.

The normal guidance offered to organisations facing this problem was to ensure that volunteers were not expected to do the work in the same way as paid staff. In summary, that volunteers:

- did not bring the same professional or technical skills as paid staff;
- typically worked part time; but
- could offer relevant experience and understanding of beneficiaries, as well as time.

This guidance was founded in the view that volunteers should be regarded as complementing and supplementing the work of paid staff. The necessary core work would be undertaken by paid staff, and the complementary or supplementary activities, often crucial in the overall quality of the service provided, would be done by volunteers. The manager of volunteers – or the team leader now with volunteers in place of some paid staff – would then need to adjust the scheduling of tasks and their expectations of what different members of the team would contribute.

It should be noted, however, that this language of volunteers complementing and supplementing the work of paid staff has two drawbacks. First, it relegates volunteers to a second-class status behind that of paid staff. Second, it fails to acknowledge that sometimes volunteers can do things or bring qualities into an organisation that paid staff cannot – for example, enhanced credibility with beneficiaries because the volunteer is perceived to be wanting to be there, not being paid to be there.

Replacing volunteers

This brings us to the converse problem: the replacement of volunteers by paid staff. A well-worn path of development for voluntary and community organisations has been to expand their services through new sources of funds and thereby become able to resource new staff posts, sometimes in fresh fields but often in areas where volunteers previously did the work. Thus, especially in the initial stages of an organisation's development, a traditional process of evolution has been that volunteers got things going in the expectation that funds would be raised and paid staff would take over from them (see section 14.1).

This, of course, is problematic too, though it hasn't raised the same level of public concern or contention. Problems have been identified where voluntary management committee members have been anxious about management responsibilities for paid staff, and where there were fears that paid workers recruited from outside a community would not understand the people and issues as well as local volunteers had.

On a bigger scale, the ready acceptance of paid staff replacing volunteers neglects some key truths about volunteering. As Susan Ellis has commented, 'No one gets paid to rebel.'[1] Volunteering has commonly been the way in which experimental and imaginative activities have been created and run. And sometimes volunteers go on doing the main functions while paid staff are brought in to support them with administration.

Complementing and supplementing the work of paid staff may be a pragmatic solution to problems relating to working together in some areas, but in many areas volunteers can and do undertake the whole task. The areas where volunteering provides the main workforce depend on a mix of cultural, traditional and economic factors, and different societies have different patterns in how people join in to help each other in everyday or seasonal tasks. Moreover, voluntary and community organisations have to rethink how public and community services can be extended in an age when new finance is unlikely to be accessible, so the traditional path of moving towards paid staff posts may no longer apply – volunteering offers a different strategy.

14.5 PRACTICAL POINTERS

- It is to be expected that at times staff will be negative about volunteers. Think through how their concerns or anxieties are reasonable given the tensions in the working environment and the pressures they feel. Even when working for the same cause, staff and volunteers have different perspectives and different responses to the situations in which they are involved.

- The foundations for volunteer engagement set out in this book should provide a framework within which staff will be constructive about volunteers: your organisation should have a vision for volunteering and its place in strategic planning (see chapter 2), clarity about organisational policies and values (see chapter 3), staff involvement in developing volunteering roles (see chapters 4–5), and appropriate systems and managerial support (see chapters 8–13). And when, despite this, staff become negative about volunteers, you should have here the building blocks for recovering constructive attitudes.

- Managers need to work as a team, adopting consultancy approaches to help staff articulate problems and solutions. A manager who leads on volunteering across the organisation (sometimes in a big organisation called the 'director of volunteering') needs to act as a resource for colleagues who have less experience or fewer skills in managing volunteers.

- Wider challenges will be confronted when there is planning – or just talk – of replacing staff jobs with volunteers or of replacing volunteers with paid employees. The former will probably raise deeper worries and resistance, but moves in either direction will relate to political and ideological disputes and will require careful and tolerant debate to work out what changes can be accepted. The senior management and board (trustees or equivalent) will need to take the lead in deciding on the organisation's future in relation to the funding and policy environment and to the organisation's own changing nature.

15 Measuring effectiveness

Having developed and delivered volunteer involvement for your organisation, you will want to ensure that it has been effective. You will want to ensure that what your volunteers are doing is helping your organisation to deliver on its mission and that your management of volunteering is effective.

In this chapter, we explore how to develop processes of monitoring and evaluation that are appropriate to what you are aiming to achieve. We note the different usages of monitoring and evaluation and the differences between outputs, outcomes and impact. We offer guidance on selecting methods of measuring volunteering, combining quantitative (numbers and statistics) and qualitative (verbal accounts and descriptions) methods, and assessing the gains of volunteering against its costs. Consumer surveys may help you to assess the benefits of volunteering, while some professional bodies set standards against which volunteering may be assessed.

15.1 MONITORING AND EVALUATION

Monitoring and evaluating your involvement of volunteers is important so that you know what you're doing is actually helping to achieve your organisation's mission and offering the best service for your beneficiaries and your volunteers, as intended. There are four main reasons to do this. Although they overlap and the details of their implementation will vary from organisation to organisation, you should start by thinking about:

- monitoring or checking that your work is on track so you can adapt or adjust as you go;
- looking back and evaluating the successes and failures of your work so you can learn for the future, whether that involves reinvesting in the existing project or developing new services;
- producing a report for external stakeholders and funders to demonstrate how well your organisation or project has done, and maybe recognising how you could do better in future;
- sharing the lessons from your work with other organisations and managers of volunteers.

Measuring the involvement of volunteers may seem tricky as the contributions of volunteers are often intangible. Volunteers may appear to be a good thing, but working out what evidence you need to prove this and how you can collect it can be difficult. So, consider:

- Do you want to report on the achievements and shortfalls of volunteering as volunteering? For example, how well is the recruitment, retention (or moving on) and management of volunteers going? What are the volunteers getting out of it, and how satisfied are they?
- Do you want to report on the achievements and shortfalls of the services or activities to which the volunteers are contributing? For example, how productive are the roles done by the volunteers in delivering your mission and objectives, and how satisfied or happy are your beneficiaries?

The remainder of this chapter explores straightforward ways of planning and undertaking monitoring and evaluation for both purposes. We offer guidance through examples of key issues and suggest what can be measured.

Before we do that, we need to clarify some key terms:

- **Outputs:** the direct and early results of what you do, such as the number of meals served or events organised, or the number of volunteers recruited and the amount of time they give. Outputs help you tell whether you have provided the scale of activities or services you intended.
- **Outcomes:** the observable and measurable changes your work has achieved. Outcomes might demonstrate that the meals have had the desired dietary effects, or that your volunteers have got your beneficiaries more involved in their communities, or that your involvement of volunteers has helped them to gain confidence and got them into paid work.
- **Impact:** the difference made and broader benefits gained through achieving your outputs and outcomes. Impact enables you to show how your organisation has, following through the examples above, achieved improved health among your beneficiaries or strengthened communities.

15.2 THINKING IT THROUGH

The typical place to begin in thinking out monitoring or evaluation is to consider what your organisation or your project is intending to do, as discussed in chapter 2. What is your mission? Your strategic objectives? Your policy aims? The goals set out in your funding application for a specific project? What are you trying to achieve? The more you have written your objectives in the SMART form (see section 2.4), the less complex these questions will be to answer.

In engaging volunteers, you may have various aims. For example, you may be aiming to improve the quality of your services or programme through:

- volunteers' understanding of and responsiveness to the needs of your beneficiaries;

- expertise or specialist knowledge accessed through volunteers;
- making more time and attention available to beneficiaries through the presence of volunteers;
- artistic and recreational activities which public funding does not support;
- advocacy and campaigning, perhaps in greater or different forms than paid staff could undertake;
- trying new ways of working.

To take another example, you may be seeking increased engagement of the public, including engaging people from local, identity or interest communities.

Once you have determined your aims, ask:

- What would be observable if those intentions were achieved? What would you observe if everything was working well?
- What would be observable – or not – if it wasn't working? If the service or activities were falling short? Or leading to unintended consequences?

In considering these questions, remember the reporting purposes listed near the start of section 15.1. For example, your purpose might be to:

- monitor ongoing work;
- look back at the midpoint of a project to shape its future phases; or
- assess and report on the completion of a project.

So ask, what evidence do you need to enable you to make assessments for these purposes? Your answers to these questions will partly depend on what audience you are reporting to and what kind of action you want them to take (see 'Audiences' later in this section).

It is logical (although it is not essential) to think through at the beginning of a project how the various stages of reporting could form part of one system of monitoring and evaluation so the various processes and pieces of evidence fit together.

Numbers and stories

Very often, volunteering looks hard to measure in quantifiable terms. For example, while you may be able to count the time volunteers spend with beneficiaries, how do you measure the difference their time with the beneficiaries makes?

Issues to bear in mind include the following:

- Some of the things we want to measure are fuzzy – the objectives and the actions required to implement them are not precise and blend into other measures. For example, how do you isolate and measure the effect of a volunteer's shared experience with a beneficiary?

- Some of the things we want to measure are complex and only become evident over time; examples include changes in attitudes, behaviour and confidence. Collecting evidence to be used years ahead is often unrealistic, and it can be hard to be certain enough about the direct effect of your organisation's volunteers and services.

- Some of the things we want to measure might be measurable in numbers but only if we have the resources and expertise to develop or buy complex surveys. And, even then, we have to consider whether we have a large enough number of beneficiaries to produce statistical validity.

Section 15.3 sets out volunteering measures that can be quantified. These are measures of outputs and, in themselves, do not show that outcomes and impact are being achieved. The skill of designing processes for monitoring and evaluating lies in combining such quantitative measures of output with other qualitative evidence, such as stories, verbal reports of observations, case histories, and open or semi-structured interviews about people's views and experiences.

For example, suppose you need to evaluate a programme which aims for beneficiaries to gain the skills and confidence to use public transport. Quantitatively, you can count the number of bus journeys they make at the end of the programme. But, to demonstrate and understand what difference the programme has made to an individual, you might seek more qualitative information, such as a case history of a period in a beneficiary's life. This could explore their situation at the start of the programme, their participation in the programme and reflections on their experience, including what a volunteer did to assist.

In this example, the quantification of bus journeys does pin down a change, but it is the qualitative evidence in the case history which describes the process and the change and so demonstrates the achievement and what made the difference for the beneficiary. The quantitative and the qualitative are complementary and convincing in giving fuller evidence, more so than one method would be on its own.

You may be reluctant to use stories like this because you may fear falling into the trap of simply telling the story you (and your stakeholders) want to hear – there is a natural wish to want to confirm the success of the programme. It may, therefore, be helpful to work out in advance what evidence would tell you the programme had failed so as to sharpen your decisions about what evidence would be robust or rigorous.

In some areas, you may decide to focus on what would count as indicators of achievement or a proxy. How, for instance, can you assess a beneficiary's well-being as an outcome of your project? In some cases, you may be able to use an in-depth psychosocial survey, which would require a researcher who has the necessary academic qualifications to apply and interpret it. More feasibly, though, you could accept evidence of a beneficiary's network of friends, support and social involvement as an indicator of well-being.

It is always a good idea to remember that your evidence needs to be checkable and reproducible. Could someone else get the same account or a different account which confirms it? Basically, will people believe you and see that your description and analysis make sense?

It is also useful to consider how exact or precise your evidence needs to be. A wheelbarrow and a plane aren't built to the same specs. Statistics don't necessarily provide better evidence than stories; it depends what you want the evidence for.

Audiences

Consider whom you are reporting to or seeking to influence: what evidence is going to be persuasive and helpful for them? A politician may ask for statistics but you may notice they are most persuaded by a vivid case study. A department manager may be most interested in what volunteers have given to their unit and want facts about volunteer hours and activities for their own reports. A senior manager involved in fundraising may want to know figures that can be used to produce grant proposals (including details such as the composition of the volunteer population) and, alongside that, may want an illustrative individual story. As the manager of volunteers, you may be most interested in internal statistics about volunteer retention and turnover, or you may find stories of outliers – individuals who don't fit the picture of your typical volunteer – most helpful in thinking about how to introduce change.

If your organisation relies on any funding or commissioning bodies, they are bound to be a major audience. In some cases, they will have prescribed the ways in which your organisation has to report to them. In some cases, you will have committed yourself to specific measures in your proposal, but there may be times when you find you are asking yourselves what you meant and why you weren't clearer about your intentions or promises from the start.

Investigators and researchers

There are arguments about when and whether monitoring and evaluation should be done in-house or by commissioning outside experts. Obviously, the main factor is whether you have the resources within your organisation to do the work or can afford to pay external consultants. You should also consider:

- Do you have the necessary skills within your organisation?
- Would it be useful to have the work done close at hand so you can learn from it?
- Do your own people understand the issues better than an outsider ever could?
- Do you need a fresh or objective perspective?
- Would the specialist expertise in research methods and subject matter that you could gain from commissioning external consultants (such as a university team) bring useful academic credibility in the eyes of your audience?

You should also consider whether the data you seek already exists within your organisation or needs to be defined and collected specifically. For instance, if you have time sheets for volunteers as part of your management processes, then you have data on volunteer hours and don't need a questionnaire to find this out. Your finance department may be able to extract data on the costs around volunteering without a separate exercise. Reviews of beneficiaries' progress and of volunteers' performance can offer data on what progress you are making towards achieving your aims and objectives.

One kind of internally recorded evidence not to forget is to simply have a file or folder where you make a note of things like what your beneficiaries say about your service. Staff and volunteers alike can be trained to see the importance of keeping notes like this.

15.3   MEASURING VOLUNTEERING AS VOLUNTEERING

In this section, we briefly note the kinds of data you might collect to measure volunteering. Some of these we have already mentioned, such as numbers of volunteers involved during the past year and total hours contributed by volunteers (you could also look at the average number of hours over a given period). These can be counted as inputs (e.g. a certain number of volunteers are needed to deliver an event) as well the outputs discussed earlier. Further analysis of volunteer involvement could be gained by examining the number of beneficiaries served and the number of paid staff or projects helped.

You might want to examine the time patterns of volunteers, determining how many are involved:

- only one time during the year;
- three or four times during the year;
- on a short-term basis (depending on how you think of 'short term');
- for the long term.

And you might want to consider:

- the average length of service per volunteer;
- the amount of volunteer turnover during the year.

To monitor changes over time, you would compare each year's figures with a year you fix as the baseline.

You could collect and analyse this data across the whole organisation as well as by department, role, location, project or team. This might help you to understand whether some areas manage volunteers better or whether volunteers prefer some kinds of jobs. This can be helpful in improving your organisation's engagement with volunteers.

As with all evaluations, you need to be clear about what you want to achieve and compare the data with those goals. For instance, are you aiming to recruit more volunteers? Do you want them to stay longer? What is your policy for short-term or episodic volunteers?

As well as looking at overall numbers, you will need additional evidence to monitor and evaluate the recruitment of volunteers. If, for instance, you want your volunteers to reflect your community or beneficiaries or to demonstrate diversity, you will need to measure:

- the demographic mix of your volunteers (age, gender, ethnicity, etc.);
- how that compares to the make-up of your beneficiaries and/or the community.

Similarly, to monitor and evaluate your volunteer management, you might want evidence of:

- volunteers' satisfaction;
- volunteers' views on how they are managed and supported;
- skills gained or deployed by volunteers;
- volunteers' moves into education, training and employment.

You might also want to collect evidence of the roles performed by volunteers, such as:

- one-to-one work with individual beneficiaries;
- direct work with groups of beneficiaries;
- work in group projects (such as construction or special events);
- one-time or once-a-year projects or events;
- assistance to staff (such as working as staff aides, with little beneficiary contact);
- technical assistance or work requiring professional skills;
- general community-wide service;

- board or committee work (i.e. involved with policymaking);
- all-round volunteering (doing a little of everything).

This data can be collected through surveys of volunteers' experiences, but you may seek to achieve more breadth by undertaking more time-consuming processes such as interviewing volunteers, analysing records from managers of volunteers, asking volunteers to keep diaries, or observing and making notes of activities.

The quantitative data outlined above could be used to measure outputs and to provide a fairly straightforward assessment against your aims and objectives. Alternatively, to assess evidence of outcomes, you would probably need to combine this data with qualitative measures, as discussed in section 15.2.

You might want to present the evidence as numbers, tables or verbal reports, and you may want to build it into case histories or analyses of processes and how they contribute to achievements or shortfalls.

15.4 COSTING VOLUNTEERING

Many organisations are keen to compare the financial value of what volunteers contribute with the costs of involving those volunteers. This produces a measure of the return on investment of volunteer involvement.

England's Institute for Volunteering Research created a system to do this called the Volunteer Investment and Value Audit (VIVA).[1] This measurement system depends on the collection of volunteer hours. This may be done accurately through the regular completion of time sheets by volunteers or through a computerised sign-in procedure. However, some organisations use more relaxed methods of calculating how many hours volunteers have worked.

Once you know how many hours volunteers have given, this figure is multiplied by a figure representing the financial value of their time, for which different calculations may be used (see 'Valuing volunteer time' on the next page).

The costs of setting up and running volunteering can be worked out by adding up elements such as direct and indirect costs of staff time spent recruiting and managing volunteers; costs of equipment, special clothing and other supplies; costs of advertising and marketing for volunteer recruitment; and central costs attributed to supporting volunteers, such as expenses.

You can then do a fairly simple sum, which will give you a ratio (such as 4:1 or 10:1) representing the financial value of volunteers' total contribution of time versus the cost of involving them.

For example, let's say your volunteers work a total of 2,000 hours in a year and you put a value on their time of £10 an hour, giving a financial value for their total contribution of £20,000. You calculate the costs invested in your volunteer programme as adding up to £4,000 in the year. You can therefore calculate that your return on investment in volunteer involvement is 5:1.

There are various reasons for comparing the costs and benefits of volunteering. For example:

- Describing a situation in monetary terms can raise the interest levels of some people (funders, senior managers, etc.) more effectively than other approaches.
- You may need to identify the overheads and other costs involved so as to determine the amount of investment needed in the future or to help with planning.
- It is important to understand that time and money are finite, and no one should expect a programme to be initiated, or continue, unless the benefits outweigh the costs.
- It will help you to identify how closely the work of your volunteers conforms to your community and organisational goals; a programme which costs little but fails to contribute to your organisation's mission cannot be said to be cost-effective.

Valuing volunteer time

There are three basic methods of producing a figure for what volunteers' time would be worth in relation to wage levels, each taking a slightly different approach.

The living wage system

This system involves an estimate of what a volunteer would earn at a minimum if they were being paid: take the living wage for your nation or region and multiply it by the number of volunteer hours. This will almost certainly produce a figure below what your volunteers would have earned in the time, but the advantage of this system is that it is difficult for anyone to argue that you are overvaluing your volunteers.

The notional imputed wage system

This system involves estimating what volunteers might reasonably be earning if they were being paid. To calculate this amount, assume that a volunteer is an average member of the community, and would therefore be capable of earning at least the average per capita income which people receive in your country, region or field of business. In the UK, this is sometimes calculated using the gross average hourly wage, which reflects not only a worker's salary but also the costs to the employer of employing that person (i.e. National Insurance contributions, pension, etc.). This method gives a more accurate reflection of what it would cost to pay someone for the work done by volunteers as it includes the associated costs that come with hiring an employee.

The equivalent wage system

This system attempts to establish what a volunteer would earn if they were paid to do an equivalent role. The intent of the equivalent wage system is to produce, as nearly as possible, an accurate estimate of the prevailing pay rate for the actual type of work being done by each volunteer. This system depends upon the ability of the manager of volunteers to correctly classify and track the type of work done by each volunteer. The equivalent wage system requires you to:

- classify the type of work being done by the volunteer;
- determine the wage level for each job type, as applicable in your region and industry and/or the volunteer's profession;
- record volunteer hours according to job type, maintaining separate hourly records for the time donated in each volunteer job category;
- multiply the total hours within each job category by the wage figures for that category.

You then slot this information into the method of valuing the sum of volunteering in your organisation or project (as above), and work out what this information tells you about the return on the resources or costs invested in volunteering in relation to your mission, policy, goals or objectives.

Additional considerations in valuing volunteer time

Regardless of the method used, it is important to note that costing volunteer time in this way can have significant drawbacks.

All three methods outlined above assume that the value of the volunteer's time equates to what it would cost to pay people to do what volunteers do. This is often called the 'notional wage value' of volunteers. In reality, few organisations would ever pay people to do what volunteers do. Notional wage measures therefore have limited worth and some organisations are starting to move away from them.

It is also important to be careful about how these calculations of volunteer time are communicated. Your volunteers might feel undermined if their contribution is framed in monetary terms, and measures of the value of volunteers should never be stated as savings.

A few years ago during Volunteers' Week in the UK, a press release was issued saying that volunteers save the NHS £500 million each year. They do not. There is not £500 million of spare money in the NHS because volunteers are involved. Instead, volunteers have contributed time worth £500 million, with this figure based on calculating what the NHS would pay people to do that work – which it never would!

Aside from anything else, discussion of volunteers saving organisations money often results in paid staff becoming resistant to volunteers, who they come to see as a way to save money and so potentially do them out of a job. So, while calculating the value of volunteering in your organisation using the methods outlined above can be attractive, the results should be used with considerable care and caution.

15.5 CUSTOMER-BASED EVALUATION

A different approach in evaluating your work and your engagement of volunteers would be to adopt methods from consumer research, engaging with your beneficiaries to understand their perspectives. This can measure what you do and the quality of that work, and it can help you gather suggestions as to how to improve your work.

For example, ask about:

- what beneficiaries think of your service;
- how it meets their needs;
- whether they find your volunteers helpful;
- whether they would recommend your organisation to friends and family;
- what they most value;
- what more (or different) activities they would like.

You could collect this evidence through surveys done face to face, by post, by phone or online, depending on your resources and the capacities of your beneficiaries. Be mindful, however, that it takes time and expertise to write questions that produce the kinds of response you can confidently draw conclusions from; it's not cheap. It can be a worthwhile investment, though – a good survey could be used in future years and produce data that could be compared from year to year.

Alternatively, you could seek the views of beneficiaries through focus groups, which would provide fuller but usually less quantifiable data. However, you would need to commission researchers to conduct focus groups as you can't do focus groups about your own work.

It may be difficult to identify and analyse how beneficiaries appreciate your volunteers as volunteers (rather than paid staff) who give their time and help out of their own volition, though it is a central question. A full investigation would require qualitative evidence through open questions and narrative accounts which draw out beneficiaries' understanding of the volunteers' position, and all this would take time and research expertise. But you may be able to gather quotes from beneficiaries which illustrate beneficiaries' views.

Everyday methods such as feedback forms and suggestion boxes may be useful and show your willingness to listen to beneficiaries, but they depend on people feeling the need to tell you about something – and they might not always be the people you want to hear from.

You may also build into your internal processes ways of recording what beneficiaries are asking for and how you have met their needs, so as to give you leads on how your services are used and valued.

While consumer research methods will not help you to demonstrate the full accomplishments of your volunteer engagement, they can be used to measure the perceptions of those you are working with and those you are working to help. These methods provide a direct mechanism for both you and others to see whether people feel that you are doing the job the way it needs to be done. Survey methods also provide quantifiable data and statistical information that can be compiled and measured over time to show changes in views about your services.

15.6 STANDARDS-BASED ASSESSMENT

An alternative method of measuring effectiveness lies in assessing your volunteer engagement against external standards, using these standards to determine whether the programme is operating appropriately.

Some national organisations provide standards of operation for their branches. These standards may either suggest or require certain methods of operation. Some are connected to the overall evaluation of the local programme and some concentrate on standards for volunteer involvement.

In the UK, the Investing in Volunteers programme provides a process for evaluating volunteer involvement and offers a kitemark for public recognition. Its indicators refer to areas of volunteer management: planning for volunteer involvement, recruiting volunteers, selecting and matching volunteers, and supporting and retaining volunteers.[2]

Depending on your field, standards may be set and assessments may be carried out by public agencies, membership bodies, or trade or professional associations.

These standards will focus on the quality and appropriateness of your services rather than prioritising volunteer engagement. However, to take one example, in the UK the standards of the Care Quality Commission for organisations running care services include the ways in which volunteers are involved.

15.7 PRACTICAL POINTERS

- To work out the monitoring and evaluation of services or activities in your organisation, ask:
  - What do you want to assess?
  - For what purpose?
  - For what audience?
- What is your purpose? Do you want to:
  - monitor your work, checking you're on track to achieve your objectives so you can adjust what you're doing?
  - evaluate successes and shortfalls of a complete project or a phase of your work so you can develop effective services in future?
  - produce reports for accountability to external stakeholders and funders, demonstrating your achievements?
  - share the learning from your work with other organisations and managers of volunteers?
- Do you want to assess:
  - volunteering as volunteering – for example, how well is the recruitment, retention (or moving on) and management of volunteers going? How satisfied are the volunteers?
  - services or activities to which the volunteers are contributing, such as the effectiveness of the work done by the volunteers in delivering your mission and objectives? How satisfied are the beneficiaries?
- You may face a problem in assessing exactly what your volunteers contribute in a complex situation. For instance, how can you measure what a volunteer has added to the well-being of a beneficiary in a residential home? It may not be possible to measure the beneficiary's happiness. However, you could collect evidence of their networks of friendships and involvement in activities, and this could provide an indicator of their well-being.
- To decide what evidence you need to assess how your volunteers' engagement is achieving (or not) your organisation's objectives, think hard about:
  - What would be observable if the objectives of your services or activities were being achieved?
  - In what ways could you report on that?
- To help decide on the evidence you need, a useful discipline is to ask yourself: what would you be able to observe if your project were failing or falling short? Or leading to consequences you didn't intend?

- Given your purpose, would quantitative or qualitative evidence better represent what's happening? And, given your audience, which would be more credible?
  - Quantitative evidence – numbers and statistics – provides clear facts about what has been achieved (or not) and data which can be compared year on year, with other programmes and against investment.
  - Qualitative evidence – verbal accounts, cases and narratives – can help you to report on events and relationships, and probe whether and how certain factors were effective.
  - A combination of quantitative and qualitative methods can give a clear overall measure of achievement and enable you to analyse how your volunteers assisted.
- Behind these questions about evidence, recognise the distinctions between:
  - outputs: the direct results;
  - outcomes: the observable or measurable changes your work has achieved;
  - impact: the broader benefits gained through achieving your outputs and outcomes.
- Consider how other methods of evaluation could help your organisation report to different audiences:
  - To assess the return on the investment in the project, you can take the total of volunteers' hours multiplied by a figure representing hourly wages and divide the sum by the total costs invested in running the volunteering effort, so as to get a ratio of value to costs.
  - To measure the satisfaction of beneficiaries, you can use methods from consumer or market research and find out, for instance, whether beneficiaries would recommend your organisation to friends and family.
  - To assess your standing in relation to other organisations, you can take part in programmes to gain a kitemark or assessment from a professional body.

16 **Final thoughts**

In this chapter, we present some final thoughts on working as a manager of volunteers. These are intended to help you reflect on your next steps as you put the advice in this book into practice. We also signpost you to some further resources which you may find useful.

16.1 **START SMALL**

When taking on the responsibility for volunteer involvement, do not expect to accomplish everything at once. Engaging and supporting volunteers is a delicate and complicated task, made so in part by the fact that the more successful you are at some things (such as recruitment), the more work you will create for yourself.

A better approach is to begin with small things and then grow a little at a time, to avoid becoming overextended. Deliver a bad volunteer experience and you create unhappy volunteers. Happy paid staff and happy volunteers will become the best salespeople for volunteering in your organisation, but you have to make sure everyone is happy.

If your organisation doesn't currently involve any volunteers, then perhaps begin by engaging volunteers to accomplish just one thing. This will allow you to identify the strengths and weaknesses that involving volunteers brings to your organisation.

16.2 **PICK YOUR PRIORITIES**

It is highly likely that there are more ways that volunteers might be involved in your organisation than you can manage effectively. It is important, therefore, to ensure volunteer involvement is developed in the best way to meet the needs of your organisation and the community.

This requires you to think about the best way in which volunteers might make a contribution. We recommend looking for the following kinds of activities or projects in which to involve volunteers:

- projects that are core to the mission of your organisation over the next year;
- activities that really assist and support staff in their work and make their work easier;

- projects that truly make a difference to beneficiaries and the community;
- at least one project that is simply cool or fun, to demonstrate the wider potential of volunteering.

This may also require looking at the kind of work in which you have traditionally involved volunteers and making some tough decisions about whether that should continue. Sometimes volunteers are involved in doing things simply because those are the kinds of things that volunteers have always done and the organisation is afraid to disturb them. If you are spending time managing volunteers who are not making a contribution to the organisation, or who are not making as effective a contribution as they could, you are wasting both their time and yours.

16.3 FIND A CORE GROUP OF VOLUNTEERS

As you work with volunteers, you will find that some of them will become invaluable assets not just to your organisation but also to you. We recommend looking for a core group of volunteers who will assist you in your own volunteer management work. Remember that your job is to manage the involvement of volunteers, not to do all the work. In fact, if you demonstrate that you effectively engage volunteers in your own work, you will set an example for other paid staff to follow, as well as being in a position to evidence that you practise what you preach.

16.4 RELY ON PERSUASION, NOT COERCION

Do not try to force volunteers onto your organisation or onto any staff member. Involving volunteers will help an organisation, but only if a positive approach is adopted. Rely on the persuasion that is created by competence and success – when staff realise that some departments are gaining benefits through the involvement of volunteers, they will eventually decide to seek the same advantages for themselves. Have confidence in the value of volunteers, and be willing to let staff come to you, rather than feeling compelled to beg them. Never be foolish enough to believe that you can coerce anyone into using volunteers. A well-operated small volunteer programme is much more valuable than an ineffective and unhappy large one.

Do not be afraid to make paid staff earn the right to have volunteers assigned to them. For example, require them to develop a plan for how they will effectively involve and supervise volunteers. This will help to convince them that volunteers are not a free resource and will demonstrate that your organisation considers volunteers too valuable to be distributed to those who are not willing to involve them effectively. You might also consider focusing your efforts on new staff who haven't already bought into 'old' ways of doing things.

16.5 **GET CONNECTED**

Build support from the wider community of volunteer-involving organisations, communicating with other managers of volunteers, sharing information and resources, and enabling mutual support.

Managers of volunteers who are not involved with a local, regional, national or online support network are missing out on the wisdom of others, making their jobs and their lives a lot harder. In 'Top tips on networks of managers of volunteers' (see below), we suggest some useful networks to consider joining.

Managers of volunteers also need to build connections within their own organisation. A key issue in volunteer involvement lies not in finding new volunteers but in enabling those who are already involved to accomplish productive work. As we have seen, the primary co-ordinator or supervisor of volunteers may not be the overall manager of volunteers across your organisation but the staff member with whom the volunteer works on a day-to-day basis (see section 9.1). At least at first, these staff often have little or no experience in working with volunteers.

As a manager of volunteers, you should consider the competence and confidence of paid staff as a priority. Even if you establish the best possible system for engaging volunteers, if people receive poor treatment from the paid staff they will not keep volunteering for long. As your programme grows, don't be afraid to put more time and energy into enabling staff to be better managers of volunteers as well.

Top tips on networks of managers of volunteers

The following networks vary in their coverage of the UK. Some extend across all four nations while others are more England-centric. Details have been supplied for the four national volunteering infrastructure organisations in the UK and they can provide further details of networks in their own territories.

- **Association of Volunteer Managers (https://volunteermanagers.org. uk):** This is the national membership association for anyone working in volunteer management, whatever sector or discipline. Established in 2007, it offers regular events, a national conference, newsletters and a helpful website. It also has other resources in development, such as mentoring for new managers of volunteers.
- **Association of Voluntary Service Managers (https://avsm.org.uk):** This is the association for managers of volunteers working in the hospice movement. It holds an annual conference and has an active regional network providing a range of resources to members.

- **National Association of Voluntary Services Managers (www.navsm. org):** This is the association for managers of volunteers working in the NHS. It hosts an annual conference, provides a range of resources on its website and has an active regional network.
- **Heritage Volunteering Group (www.heritagevolunteeringgroup.org. uk):** This is a network of people working in volunteer management in the arts, culture and heritage sector. It puts on an annual conference, runs the Heritage Volunteer Manager of the year awards and supports a network on regional groups.
- **UKVPMs (https://groups.yahoo.com/neo/groups/UKVPMs/ info?guccounter=1):** Operating since 1997, UKVPMs is an email network of over 1,600 managers of volunteers. Joining UKVPMs is free and connects you with a wealth of knowledge and experience in volunteer management.
- **LinkedIn Groups:** A number of groups have been established on LinkedIn to allow managers of volunteers to connect and share resources. UKVPMs and the Association of Volunteer Managers each have a LinkedIn Group, the latter hosting two, one for members and one for non-members. A quick search of LinkedIn will uncover other networks. If one doesn't exist for your particular area of interest then why not start one?
- **National volunteering infrastructure organisations in the UK:**
  - Volunteer Scotland: www.volunteerscotland.net
  - Wales Council for Voluntary Action: www.wcva.org.uk
  - Volunteer Now (Northern Ireland): www.volunteernow.co.uk
  - National Council for Voluntary Organisations (England): www.ncvo.org.uk

16.6 FURTHER READING

- *The Disruptive Volunteer Manager: A step by step guide to reframing, redefining, reshaping and re-imagining* by Meridian Swift (CreateSpace, 2019). An honest and inspiring look at what needs to change if volunteer management is to truly be taken seriously as a strategic priority by many non-profits.
- *From the Top Down* (UK edition) by Susan J. Ellis and Rob Jackson (Energize, 2015). A book aimed at senior managers of volunteer-involving organisations to help them create the right culture and systems for effective volunteer engagement.
- *Keeping Volunteers: A guide to retaining good people* by Steve McCurley and Rick Lynch (Directory of Social Change, 2007). A guide that shows you how to nurture your best volunteers, looks at reasons why they might become dissatisfied and disappear, and suggests how to address those problems so you don't lose volunteers.

- *The Last Virtual Volunteering Guidebook: Fully integrating online service into volunteer involvement* by Jayne Cravens and Susan J. Ellis (Energize, 2014). The definitive manual on fully integrating online services into volunteer involvement.
- *The New Breed: Understanding and equipping the 21st century volunteer* (2nd edition) by Jonathan McKee and Thomas W. McKee (Group Publishing, 2012). An excellent resource for engaging today's baby boomers and millennial volunteers.
- *Volunteers and the Law* (National Council for Voluntary Organisations, 2018, https://knowhownonprofit.org/tools-resources/volunteers-and-the-law). Fully revised and updated, this former print publication is now available online only and remains the go-to resource on legal issues relating to volunteer involvement.
- *What We Learned (the Hard Way) about Supervising Volunteers: An action guide to making your job easier* by Jarene Frances Lee with Julia M. Catagnus (Energize, 1998). Ideas, tools and insights from fellow leaders of volunteers.

References

Chapter 1

1 Eddy Hogg, 'Constant, Serial and Trigger Volunteers: Volunteering across the lifecourse and into older age', *Voluntary Sector Review*, vol. 7, no. 2, 2016, pp. 169–190 at p. 170.

2 Amy McGarvey, Veronique Jochum, John Davies, Joy Dobbs and Lisa Hornung, *Time Well Spent: A national survey on the volunteer experience*, London, National Council for Voluntary Organisations, 2019, p. 8.

3 'Community Life Survey 2018–19' [web page], Department for Digital, Culture, Media & Sport, 2019, www.gov.uk/government/statistics/community-life-survey-2018-19, accessed 25 July 2019.

4 *Ibid.*

5 'Community Life Survey 2016–17' [web page], Department for Digital, Culture, Media & Sport, 2017, www.gov.uk/government/statistics/community-life-survey-2016-17, accessed 23 February 2019.

6 Natalie Low, Sarah Butt, Angela Ellis Paine and Justin Davis Smith, *Helping Out: A national survey of volunteering and charitable giving*, London, National Centre for Social Research/Institute for Volunteering Research, 2007.

7 'Community Life Survey 2016–17' [web page], Department for Digital, Culture, Media & Sport, 2017, www.gov.uk/government/statistics/community-life-survey-2016-17, accessed 23 February 2019.

8 Amy McGarvey, Veronique Jochum, John Davies, Joy Dobbs and Lisa Hornung, Time Well Spent: A national survey on the volunteer experience, London, National Council for Voluntary Organisations, 2019, p. 26.

9 *Ibid.*

10 'CAF World Giving Index 2017' [web page], Charities Aid Foundation, 2019, www.cafonline.org/about-us/publications/2017-publications/caf-world-giving-index-2017, accessed 9 February 2019.

11 *Ibid.*

12 'Community Life Survey 2018–19' [web page], Department for Digital, Culture, Media & Sport, 2019, www.gov.uk/government/statistics/community-life-survey-2018-19, accessed 25 July 2019.

13 Natalie Low, Sarah Butt, Angela Ellis Paine and Justin Davis Smith, *Helping Out: A national survey of volunteering and charitable giving*, London, National Centre for Social Research/Institute for Volunteering Research, 2007.

14 General information and recent years' results can be accessed at 'Community Life Survey' [web page], Department for Digital, Culture, Media & Sport, 2019, www.gov.uk/government/collections/community-life-survey--2, accessed 9 February 2019.

15 E. Gil Clary and Mark Snyder, 'Motivations for Volunteering and Giving: A functional approach', *New Directions for Philanthropic Fundraising*, no. 8, 1995, pp. 111–123.

16 Marc A. Musick and John Wilson, *Volunteers: A social profile*, Indiana, Indiana University Press, 2007, p. 50.

17 Daiga Kamerade, *An Untapped Pool of Volunteers for the Big Society? Not Enough Social Capital? Depends on how you measure it . . .*, Sheffield Hallam University, 2011, http://usir.salford.ac.uk/18041/2/FINAL_for_distribution. pdf, accessed 9 February 2019.

18 Ellie Brodie, Tim Hughes, Véronique Jochum, Sarah Miller, Nick Ockenden and Diane Warburton, *Pathways Through Participation: What creates and sustains active citizenship* [PDF], National Council for Voluntary Organizations/Institute for Volunteering Research/Involve, 2011, www. sharedpractice.org.uk/Downloads/Pathways_summary_report.pdf, accessed 9 February 2019.

19 General information and recent years' results can be accessed at 'Community Life Survey' [web page], Department for Digital, Culture, Media & Sport, 2019, www.gov.uk/government/collections/community-life-survey--2, accessed 9 February 2019.

20 Natalie Low, Sarah Butt, Angela Ellis Paine and Justin Davis Smith, *Helping Out: A national survey of volunteering and charitable giving*, London, National Centre for Social Research/Institute for Volunteering Research, 2007.

21 *Ibid.*, p. 39

22 'National life tables: UK' [web page], Office for National Statistics, 2018, www.ons.gov.uk/peoplepopulationandcommunity/birthsdeathsandmarriages/ lifeexpectancies/datasets/nationallifetablesunitedkingdomreferencetables, accessed 9 February 2019.

23 'Decision time: Will the voluntary sector embrace the age of opportunity?' [web page], New Philanthropy Capital, 2015, www.thinknpc.org/resource- hub/decision-time-will-the-voluntary-sector-embrace-the-age-of-opportunity, accessed 9 February 2019.

24 'UK labour market: September 2018' [web page], Office for National Statistics, 2018, www.ons.gov.uk/employmentandlabourmarket/peopleinwork/ employmentandemployeetypes/bulletins/uklabourmarket/september2018, accessed 9 February 2019.

25 Marc A. Musick and John Wilson, *Volunteers: A social profile*, Bloomington, Indiana University Press, 2007.

26 National Council for Voluntary Organisations, *Time Well Spent: A National Survey on the Volunteer Experience*, London, National Council for Voluntary Organisations, 2019.

Chapter 2

1   Natalie Low, Sarah Butt, Angela Ellis Paine and Justin Davis Smith, *Helping Out: A national survey of volunteering and charitable giving*, London, National Centre for Social Research/Institute for Volunteering Research, 2007.

Chapter 3

1   Angela Ellis Paine and Justin Davis Smith, *Exhibiting Support: Developing volunteering in museums*, London, Institute for Volunteering Research, 2006, p. 4.

2   Susan J. Ellis and Rob Jackson, *From the Top Down*, Philadelphia, Energize, 2015.

Chapter 5

1   Colin Rochester, Angela Ellis Paine and Steve Howlett, *Volunteering and Society in the 21st Century*, London, Springer, 2011.

2   Natalie Low, Sarah Butt, Angela Ellis Paine and Justin Davis Smith, *Helping Out: A national survey of volunteering and charitable giving*, London, National Centre for Social Research/Institute for Volunteering Research, 2007, p. 68.

3   Institute for Volunteering Research, *Volunteering for All? Exploring the link between volunteering and social exclusion*, London, Institute for Volunteering Research, 2003.

Chapter 8

1   James Kouzes and Barry Posner, *The Leadership Challenge*, San Francisco, Jossey-Bass, 1995, p. 31.

Chapter 9

1   J. Cravens and Susan Ellis, *The Last Virtual Volunteering Guidebook: Fully integrating online service into volunteer involvement*, Philadelphia, Energize, 2014.

Chapter 10

1   'Community Life Survey 2018–19' [web page], Department for Digital, Culture, Media & Sport, 2019, www.gov.uk/government/statistics/community-life-survey-2018-19, accessed 25 July 2019.

2   Katharine Gaskin, *What Young People Want from Volunteering*, London, National Centre for Volunteering, 1998.

3 'Community Life Survey 2018–19' [web page], Department for Digital, Culture, Media & Sport, 2019, www.gov.uk/government/statistics/community-life-survey-2018-19, accessed 25 July 2019.

Chapter 12

1 *Volunteer Rights Inquiry: Recommendations and call to action* [PDF], Volunteering England, 2011, www.ncvo.org.uk/images/documents/policy_and_research/volunteering-policy/volunteer_rights_inquiry_final_report1.pdf, accessed 8 March 2019.

2 *Ibid.*

3 *Final report of the Call to Action Progress Group following the Volunteer Rights Inquiry* [PDF], National Council for Voluntary Organisations, 2014, https://blogs.ncvo.org.uk/wp-content/uploads/mike-locke/call-to-action-progress-group-volunteer-rights-inquiry-report.pdf, accessed 8 March 2019.

Chapter 13

1 Natalie Low, Sarah Butt, Angela Ellis Paine and Justin Davis Smith, *Helping Out: A national survey of volunteering and charitable giving*, London, National Centre for Social Research/Institute for Volunteering Research, 2007, p. 64.

2 *Managing Volunteers: A report from United Parcel Service*, United Parcel Service Foundation, 1998, https://studylib.net/doc/11704642/managing-volunteers-united-parcel-service-a-report-from–..., p. 15, accessed 9 February 2019.

3 Harris Clemes and Reynold Bean, *How to Raise Children's Self-Esteem*, New York, Price Stern Sloan, 1990.

4 Jeffrey L. Brudney and Lucas C. P. M. Meijs, 'It Ain't Natural: Toward a new (natural) resource conceptualization for volunteer management', *Nonprofit and Voluntary Sector Quarterly*, vol. 38, no. 4, 2009, pp. 564–581.

Chapter 14

1 Susan Ellis, 'Start early: Teaching students about volunteering, not simply doing it' [blog post], Energize, www.energizeinc.com/hot-topics/2006/august, August 2006.

Chapter 15

1 Katharine Gaskin, *VIVA: The Volunteer Investment and Value Audit: A self-help guide* [PDF], Institute for Volunteering Research, 2011, www.scribd.com/document/352352437/VIVA-The-volunteer-investment-and-value-audit-A-self-help-guide, accessed 9 February 2019.

2 'What is IiV?' [web page], Investing in Volunteers, 2019, https://iiv.investinginvolunteers.org.uk, accessed 9 February, 2019.

Index

Page numbers in *italics* refer specifically to Figures.

What else can DSC do for you?

Let us help you to be the best you possibly can be. DSC equips individuals and organisations with expert skills and information to help them provide better services and outcomes for their beneficiaries. With the latest techniques, best practice and funding resources all brought to you by our team of experts, you will not only boost your income but also exceed your expectations.

Publications

We produce fundraising directories and research reports, as well as accessible 'how to' guides and best practice handbooks, all to help you help others.

Training

The voluntary sector's best-selling training, with courses covering every type of voluntary sector training.

In-house training

All DSC courses are available on your premises, delivered by expert trainers and facilitators. We also offer coaching, consultancy, mentoring and support.

Conferences and fairs

DSC conferences are a fantastic way to network with voluntary sector professionals while taking part in intensive, practical training workshops.

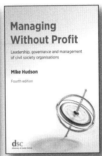

Funds Online

Funds Online contains information on over 8,000 funders giving a combined total of £8 billion. Find out more and subscribe now at:

www.**fundsonline**.org.uk

@DSC_Charity
For top tips and special offers

Visit our website today and see what we can do for you:

www.dsc.org.uk

Or contact us directly:
publications@dsc.org.uk